THE COMPLETE IDIOT'S GUIDE® TO

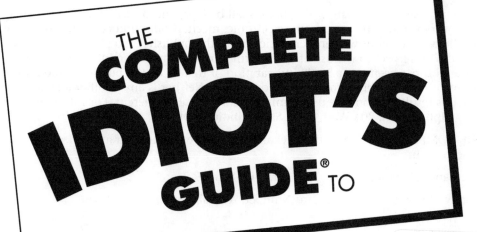

Getting Published

Second Edition

by Sheree Bykofsky
and Jennifer Basye Sander

alpha books

A Pearson Education Company

Publisher
Marie Butler-Knight

Product Manager
Phil Kitchel

Managing Editor
Cari Luna

Senior Acquisitions Editor
Renee Wilmeth

Development Editor
Amy Gordon

Production Editor
JoAnna Kremer

Copy Editor
Krista Hansing

Illustrator
Jody P. Schaeffer

Cover Designers
Mike Freeland
Kevin Spear

Book Designers
Scott Cook and Amy Adams of DesignLab

Indexer
Amy Lawrence

Layout/Proofreading
Angela Calvert
Svetlana Dominguez

Contents at a Glance

Contents

Foreword

From Ann Rule and Leslie Rule:

Someday I'm going to write a book.

All writers begin with that thought. Unfortunately, few get any further than that because they don't know where to start. Those who *do* manage to complete a book manuscript are still faced with the daunting task of getting it published.

Between us, we have logged 46 years of publishing everything from articles to books. (Ann writes about victims and killers, and detectives and trials; Leslie, Ann's daughter, writes about the paranormal—reincarnation, psychics, and ghosts.) Every day we hear from aspiring writers seeking advice. We understand their confusion and frustration because we have been there.

Although we publish regularly now, we have not forgotten our early days—and we have the rejection letters to prove it!

We both remember crying at the mailbox when yet another rejection arrived in the middle of a stack of bills.

Ann: *I had five straight years of rejection letters, most of them only printed forms with no personal response at all, before I ever sold anything I'd written. There was no one to ask what I was doing wrong. I had to find information about publishing wherever I could. I found a little bit here and a little bit there, but it was so long before I broke the "code."*

My main sources came from my local library, where I combed the shelves for the few books they had on how to write and sell. Many of those books were outdated. Through my hit-or-miss approach, I finally learned about writers' conferences and magazines published just for writers.

After those five years of getting manuscripts back in the mail, I finally sold a short article to a local newspaper. They paid me $35! The next year, I made $100; the next, $1,000; and finally, wonderfully, I was able to support my family with my writing. But it was a long, disappointing process to get there. If I'd had a resource like The Complete Idiot's Guide to Getting Published, *I would have jumped for joy!*

There are answers in this book to questions you haven't even thought of yet. Now when I get e-mails, letters, and phone calls from writers who are just starting out—or even venturing into a new genre—I heartily recommend it. No, you aren't really an "idiot"—no more than I was three decades ago. What you need is information on the business side of writing, and this is it. You'll find it akin to having your own private literary agent sitting beside you as you venture into the exciting—and sometimes frightening—world of publishing.

Ann Rule has published 17 books (15 of which have been *New York Times* bestsellers) and 1,400 articles. Her current books are *A Rage to Kill, … And Never Let Her Go,* and *Empty Promises.*

Leslie: *Contrary to what many people think, I did not have an automatic "in" because my mother is a famous writer—although I* did *understand a little more about the publishing business than the average beginner. What I picked up by osmosis was not enough to get me published. I began my first book 20 years ago nearly as much a novice as my mother was when she began hers. In fact, I had no idea what an SASE was. (If you don't, either, that's all the more reason to read this book!)*

Through trial and (lots of) error, the rejections in my mailbox eventually turned to acceptance slips as I began publishing articles. My earlier checks paying 3 cents per word jumped to 50 cents a word, and then to a dollar a word. And finally, *I saw my first book in print.*

Looking back, the hardest thing for me was approaching editors. I was terrified of writing query letters. When I complained about this to my mother, she replied, "Editors are just people." That may be, I thought, but those "people" have the power to squelch my idea or give me a ticket to my dream!

How I fretted over those query letters! What in the world would I say? How could I convince an editor to publish me? If only there were a magic formula.

Aspiring writers no longer need to fret, for now there is *a magic formula. You are holding it in your hands. Between the orange-and-white covers of* The Complete Idiot's Guide to Getting Published, Second Edition *are the hundreds of secrets I wished I had 20 years ago. Written by the two people I once feared the most—a literary agent and an editor—The Complete Idiot's Guide to Getting Published, Second Edition *shares a no-nonsense approach to achieving the goal of seeing your book in print. Sheree Bykofsky and Jennifer Basye Sander show you how to appear like a pro from the start.*

Sheree and Jennifer, where were you when I needed you?

Leslie Rule writes both fiction and nonfiction. Her novels, *Kill Me Again* and *Whispers from the Grave*, have been published internationally. Her newest book is *Coast to Coast Ghosts*.

Introduction

Books, wonderful books. It seems like such a dream that you might someday see your very own name on the cover of a book that's sitting proudly on a bookstore shelf. Well, dream no longer. It's high time you turned that dream into reality—*your* reality!

Together, we've been in the book business for 30 years, and we've seen it all (or nearly all). We've been interns, editors, authors, agents, and packagers, and we've learned what works and what doesn't.

As interns, well ... we won't tell you what we did as interns, but as editors, we've evaluated dozens of projects. As authors, we've struggled to come up with ideas for books that would catch an editor's eye. As agents, we've sorted through thousands of query letters in search of potential authors, and as packagers, we've tried to craft marketable books. Now we'd like to share all our hard-won knowledge with you. We will explain the whole book publishing process and guide you through it as smoothly as possible. You'll find yourself going from first-time writer straight through to publishing know-it-all in the time it takes to read this book.

Every writer has a reason for wanting to be published. Some of us want a forum for our ideas; some want fame, and some just flat-out want fortune. No matter what your reason, to get published you'll need to convince many other folks along the way to believe in you and your writing. There's an art to doing that, and we'll explain it to you step by step.

The book publishing business can be tough, and it can be crazy at times, but it's an exciting industry that's pretty darn fun just to be around. Although you may well experience some frustration and a disappointment or two on your way to becoming a published author, you can look forward to the satisfaction you'll feel: the pure pleasure of knowing that your ideas and your vision are being shared with the world.

How to Use This Book

The book publishing process is really a rather easy one to understand when you break it down into its five major steps:

Part 1, "Great Expectations: In Which You Begin to Write," explores the many reasons that writers write (what's yours?) and helps you determine what the market is like for the book you want to write. What are the hot and not-so-hot topics and genres today, and how you can stay in the know?

Part 2, "Gone with the Wind: Submitting to Publishers," is where you find the different, sometimes bewildering methods of submitting your proposal. Here you find everything from how to avoid looking like an amateur on the page to the reasons why so many manuscripts are rejected.

Part 3, "Romancing the Stone: How to Get a Book Contract," tackles the age-old problem that all prospective authors face: Just how do you get an editor and a publisher to fall in love with your proposal and offer you a contract? Do you need an agent, and if so, how do you get a good one? How do you find editors and win them over all by yourself, if that's the route you want to take? Here's where you find out what you need to know about how publishers decide to publish. Here's also where you find out what to ask for—and what to avoid like the plague—in book contracts.

Part 4, "War and Peace: Working with a Publisher," walks you through the actual process of being published. Now that you have a book publishing contract, a deadline, and an editor to work with, what's gonna happen? Here's where you'll see the entire production process.

Part 5, "My Brilliant Career: Continuing Your Career as an Author," helps you develop a life that extends beyond just one book. From building yourself a career as a speaker or consultant, to writing for magazines, this is where you'll find out about the many ways to make money from your writing skills.

And to make sure you don't get lost in publishing lingo, there's a glossary that contains all the words and terms you'll need to hold your own in conversations with agents, editors, publicists, and other book people. Want to see what a sample book contract looks like? Say no more! You'll find one near the back of the book, along with a sample author-agent agreement, a proposal for a bestselling book, a press release, and a collaboration agreement.

Extras

Look for the little asides and comments sprinkled throughout the chapters, extra bits of inside dope that we just can't resist whispering into your ear as you read:

Slush Pile

These are dire warnings, things to be avoided at all costs. They're the worst mistakes, the biggest pitfalls, and the most dangerous missteps to which writers can fall prey.

Bookmarks

Publishing terms are clearly defined here. Never again will you feel out to sea when the book talk turns technical.

Experts Say

Here's where our friends and colleagues share their expertise, too. This is real advice from those involved in the book world.

Hot Off the Press

We've got many tales to tell about the publishing world. Some will make you wiser, and some are just for chuckles.

Acknowledgments

Jennifer would like to thank the person from whom she has learned the most about the book business: Ben Dominitz of Prima Publishing. He was always willing to take a chance on my ideas. And how can I write a book without thanking my family? My husband, Peter, and my sons, Julian and Jonathan, were all amazingly cheerful about the amount of time I was unavailable; thanks, guys. And to the fabulous Paula Munier Lee—without her assistance, the chapters on fiction would be blank.

Sheree thanks the people who have been so very helpful with her agency: Janet Rosen and Vincent Scialla. Thanks to all the authors whom I represent—you are the reason I love my work. I'm grateful to all my agent and editor friends and colleagues for all their guidance, support, knowledge, and all the laughs. And, Dave, you're the best.

We'd both like to thank all the knowledgeable publishing folks who took our repeated phone calls and shared their expertise as we researched and wrote this book—and, indeed, throughout our careers. We'd also like to thank the folks at Shaw Guides for sharing their list of writers' conferences with us. Thanks also to Amy Gordon for helping us shape and refine the manuscript, and to JoAnna Kremer for superhuman production editing. Finally, thanks to Renee Wilmeth and her colleagues at Alpha Books for giving us this opportunity to share our knowledge with you.

Special Thanks to the Technical Reviewer

The Complete Idiot's Guide to Getting Published, Second Edition was reviewed by an expert who checked the accuracy of what you'll be reading and provided valuable insights and suggestions to ensure that this book gives you as complete a picture of the publishing process as any book can. Our special thanks to Kristine Puopolo.

Ms. Puopolo was an editor at Viking Penguin for six years and is currently senior editor in the Simon & Schuster Trade Paperback department. Her acquisitions have included paperback rights to the bestselling *Longitude* and *Galileo's Daughter,* by Dava Sobel; National Jewish Book Award-winning *The Prince of West End Avenue,* by Alan Isler; James Beard Award-winning *Cod,* by Mark Kurlansky; and National Book Award finalist *Who Do You Love,* by Jean Thompson. She also published Antony Beevor's award-winning *Stalingrad* and acquired *In the Heart of the Sea,* by Nathaniel Philbrick.

Trademarks

All terms mentioned in this book that are known to be or are suspected of being trademarks or service marks have been appropriately capitalized. Alpha Books and Pearson Education, Inc., cannot attest to the accuracy of this information. Use of a term in this book should not be regarded as affecting the validity of any trademark or service mark.

Part 1
Great Expectations: In Which You Begin to Write

You think you'd like to write—actually, you know you want to write. So just how do you get started? In this part of the book, we'll take a look at the major reasons why people write. The more you know about why you want to write, the greater your chances for doing it successfully.

We'll also give you an inside look at how book professionals come up with ideas for books that sell and sell. When you've mastered this end of the business, you'll get a close-up look at the markets for different types of books. From fiction to how-to, from health to travel, you'll learn what's hot and what's not.

Chapter 1

So, Why Write?

In This Chapter

➤ The best reasons to write

➤ The future of books

➤ The big business of book business

➤ Getting published can be like getting on a game show

➤ 50,000 chances to win

Well, now you've gone and done it. You've gone out and bought yourself a book on getting published. And that is exactly what you will learn in the following pages: how to get published.

Just imagine the glory and hosannas that await you as a published author: fat royalty checks, impressive literary awards, newspaper articles, speaking engagements, applause, and public recognition. Life will be grand!

Well, life might be grand—or maybe it won't change at all. In many ways this book hopes to serve as both a cheerleader (you *can* do it!) and a reality check (that's *reality*, not *royalty* check). Writing is hard work. Getting published is hard work. Selling books is hard work.

But before we usher you onto the path toward a career as an author, let's step back to ask a critical question: Just why do you want to write a book? Take it from us, writing an entire book is a whole lot of work and effort. What's in it for you?

What's Your Reason?

There are as many reasons to write as there are books on a library shelf. Is yours on the list?

➤ I'm compelled to write.

➤ I want the personal satisfaction of being published.

➤ I hope to advance my cause.

➤ I want to share my knowledge.

➤ I'd like to advance my career.

➤ I'd like to achieve fame.

➤ I'd like to earn a fortune.

➤ All of the above.

Bookmarks

An **author** is one who writes a book or books. The word usually implies a published writer.

Bookmarks

The **royalty** is the percentage of book sales that the publisher pays the author for each copy of a book sold.

I'm Compelled to Write

Some folks sit down and write because they are consumed with an inner need to write. These people must write—they can't not write. They wake up in the middle of the night with the urge to jot down a few lines or even write entire pages. For these folks, writing comes naturally; it just feels right.

Have you ever heard a novelist say that "the characters are writing the book, and I'm just holding the pen"? Or, "I've got to get these ideas on paper!" If either sounds like you, then you're someone who's compelled to write. Getting published may very well be your primary goal; making money would be nice, but it could be of secondary importance.

I Want the Personal Satisfaction of Being Published

Putting pen to paper (or to keyboard) can be very fulfilling. And once your writing project is finished, you will have accomplished something very real. Instead of talking endlessly about how you plan to write a book someday, you will have done it!

Not only is the process of writing satisfying, but there are also psychic rewards to be gained from being published. The pride and satisfaction that can come from writing a book are unsurpassed. Imagine the day when you can stand in a bookstore aisle and see your name on a book. Or better yet, imagine the first time someone asks for your autograph!

I'd Like to Advance My Cause

Have you got a message you want to share with the world (or at least with anyone smart enough to buy your book)? You want to share your beliefs—political, philosophical, religious, or whatever—to advance a cause. A great example of this is Rachel Carson. She wrote a book called *Silent Spring* that alerted an entire generation to the dangers of pesticides.

I Want to Share My Knowledge

You might know how to build a better mousetrap, and you think the world needs to know, too. This is not quite the same thing as writing to advance a cause, but it's a mission to help people do something—or do something better. Perhaps you've spent 20 years lying underneath cars and believe you can tell car owners a better way to care for and maintain their automobiles.

The market for how-to information seems endless, and writers with useful knowledge to share can sometimes hit the big time. "Find a need and fill it" is an old business axiom that still holds true in today's book market.

I Hope to Advance My Career

Publishing a book in your field can be a very powerful way to supercharge your career. Why languish in obscurity when you can gain recognition as an expert in your field? Who knows, you could build a second career as a consultant or a speaker.

While still in his mid-20s, David Chilton rocketed past his colleagues in the field of financial planning by writing the first-ever financial planning novel, *The Wealthy Barber*. "I was just another young guy starting out," he says, "but by writing a book about money, I was able to launch myself as a speaker." Now an international best-seller and the basis for a PBS series, this book has built Chilton's career.

Harvey Mackay was the owner of an obscure envelope company, but after his first book, *Swim With the Sharks Without Being Eaten Alive*, was published, he built a high-profile career as a speaker and a business consultant. He also wrote two more best-selling books after that one.

Don't get the idea that only business people can advance their careers with a book. Doctors see a huge boost in patients when the medical books they've written become popular. It worked for Drs. Andrew Weil, Arnold Fox, and Christiane Northrup. Almost any other type of career can be built up this way, including careers as motivational speakers, beauticians, massage therapists, and childcare providers. Could writing a book be your ticket to the top?

I'd Like to Achieve Fame

Similar to writers who hope to advance their careers, some writers hope that getting published will make them famous, if only in their own neighborhoods, towns, states, or among their colleagues. The world is a celebrity-conscious place, and who wouldn't want the things that come with fame: the best table in a restaurant, a complimentary bottle of wine, your picture in *People* magazine, admiring fans, and maybe a spot on the couch with Katie Couric on the *Today* show some morning.

Hot Off the Press

Perfectly ordinary folks with perfectly ordinary lives sometimes become famous authors. Danielle Steel was a high school teacher, John Grisham was a lawyer, Ernest Hemingway was a newspaper reporter, and Wallace Stevens sold insurance. Richard Paul Evans of *The Christmas Box* fame was in the advertising business until he hit it big with his self-published book. He later sold it to Simon and Schuster for $4.2 million dollars. So, why not you?

Slush Pile

Although many writers dream of earning a fortune, few actually do. The authors of most books published are employed full-time elsewhere. The money that they earn from royalties can be nice extra income, but it seldom pays the rent. Our advice? Don't quit your day job.

Do you long to be recognized as you walk down the street? A published book might get you that. Fame is not always linked directly to fortune, however. And getting your book published may make its title, but not your face (and sometimes not even your name) familiar to many. Quick, who wrote *Robert's Rules of Order?* (See * at the bottom of this page.)

I'd Like to Earn a Fortune

It's by no means guaranteed, but writing a book (or writing several books) is a possible route to fortune. Just ask Mark Victor Hansen and Jack Canfield, the creators of the bestselling *Chicken Soup for the Soul* series. When giving inspirational talks to writers, these two authors delight in showing overhead slides of their seven-figure royalty checks. "And we get these a couple of times a year!" they chuckle.

*Major Henry M. Robert compiled the Rules in 1876.

Making big bucks by writing books is a big goal that, quite frankly, isn't achieved by many. But if this is what drives you, then give it all you've got. Begin by making sure that your book idea has mass appeal. The smaller and more specialized the potential audience for your book, the dimmer the chances that you will make lots of money from it.

Just as fame does not always follow fortune, fortune is not always linked to fame. You might have recognized Mark Hansen and Jack Canfield's names, but there are many authors whose names you'd never recognize who have nevertheless earned lots of money writing books. The unsung authors of popular textbooks and other homely books that sell year after year without ever showing up on *bestseller* lists might be unrecognized on the street, but they are known at the bank.

All of the Above

Few writers have one single reason for writing. Most of us combine an emotional need to write with a secret desire for fame and a not-so-secret desire for fortune.

Why should you stop to examine the reasons that you write? Because if you understand why you want to write, you can do a much better job of planning how to get published.

Is a need for inner satisfaction the only thing driving you? Then you might be happy seeing your work published in a small literary journal. Do you have grand plans to advance your career and raise your professional profile? That calls for a specific plan of attack. Is making a fortune your primary goal? Then you'd better skip ahead to Chapter 3, "If You Need an Idea, Stalk the Bestseller List." To avoid disappointment, make sure that your ultimate goal and your book's sales potential match.

Do People Still Buy Books?

"Gosh, writing a book will take so much of my time. Are books still selling?" you ask. It seems like every newspaper and magazine has carried a story

Bookmarks

The term **bestseller** is used loosely in the publishing business. Strictly speaking, it refers to a book that has appeared on a bestseller list somewhere. In reality, publishers and their publicity staffs attach the word to almost any book that they haven't lost their shirts on!

Experts Say

Nothing beats the experience of hanging out in a bookstore. Even Jeff Bezos, the owner of Amazon.com, admits that he shops for many of his books in bookstores because he likes the ambiance there. For millions of Americans, the bookstore is a second home.

with dire predictions: Americans don't read anymore; the book publishing industry is dead; books as we know them will soon cease to exist. So why bother writing a book?

Well, here's our well-informed and professionally stated response to those naysayers: "Not!"

Mergers and Chains

While attending a publishing party, co-author Sheree was asked by a television reporter from PBS whether she thought the book publishing industry was in a crisis. With a microphone thrust under her nose and a plate of cheese and crackers balanced in her hand (standard fare at publishing parties), she smiled and managed a reply. Not a crisis, really, but a big change in the way business is done.

Large publishing companies are seldom run by book lovers these days but rather are headed by business folks with a strong sense of the bottom line. Even the number of large publishing houses is shrinking—these companies are being bought up and combined into "super houses" with 10 or 20 different imprints. One editor at a major New York house likes to joke that although she's had only two different jobs, as a result of mergers she's actually worked for seven different companies. But small and medium-sized publishers all over the country are willing to take risks with topics and authors that other houses might avoid.

Experts Say

According to *The Wall Street Journal*, there were 357 publishers in 1947. Staff reporter Cynthia Crossen writes, "Today, partly because technology has lowered the barrier to entry, there are more than 49,000 publishing houses in the U.S." Most of those are one-person self-publishers, but more than a handful are savvy publishers willing to take a shot at the marketplace.

Hot Off the Press

Publishing businesses are still anachronistically known as "publishing houses" after the days when most companies operated out of brownstones or townhouses that were formerly single-family dwellings.

And while publishing companies are merging, more bookstores are opening across the country. The decision-making power has quickly become concentrated in the hands of two or three large retail chains, and this, too, has affected the publishing business—as has the rise in book sales in nontraditional nonbook outlets such as Target and Wal-Mart. The brunt of this change has been borne by locally owned bookstores; sadly, many small, *independent booksellers* are disappearing. But the good news for writers is, no matter where they buy, Americans are still buying books, and that is what keeps the industry going.

Online Book Sales

As further proof of the health and vibrancy of the ancient art of publishing, we need only point to the newest development of all: the Internet and the arrival of e-commerce. One of the most remarkable things about this new high-tech business method is that one of the most frequently purchased items online is also one of the most old-fashioned—books. Amazon.com is far and above one of the highest-profile e-commerce companies, possibly the one that is the closest to breaking even. And beyond book sales, look at the extraordinary interest in electronic publishing, known as e-books. We'll delve into this later, but right now let's just add it to the plus column for the future of books.

Bookmarks

An **independent bookseller** is a locally owned bookstore. Before the rise of national chains such as Borders and Barnes & Noble, most towns were served by independents. Sadly, many of these stores have been unable to compete and have closed their doors. Fans of independent booksellers believe that the staffs there were more knowledgeable and better able to promote little-known and local authors.

Hot Off the Press

Unlike other retail businesses, books are 100 percent returnable in the bookselling business. If a dress shop has trouble selling a dress, it marks the price down until the dress gets bought. But if a bookseller can't sell a book, she puts it in a box and returns it to the publisher for full credit. According to industry figures from Open Book Publishing, the average bookstore sends back to the publisher 20 percent of its books. Publishers have tried unsuccessfully in the past to wean bookstores off the returnable model, with no success. (After all, they've got a good thing going; why should they change it?)

Leaner and Meaner

The days when publishing was a genteel pursuit for the wealthy are gone. The book business is catching up to the rest of the world and is streamlining its processes. After a few rocky years of high book returns, book publishing as an industry has emerged stronger and healthier, and is ready to compete in the fast-paced entertainment-driven world we now occupy.

So, should you put a part of your life on hold and devote yourself to writing that book you dream of? We say, "Go for it!"

Open for Business

Now that we have convinced you that the book business is a healthy one, here's your first insider's tip for success. If you learn only one thing from this book, let it be the following: The book business is a business.

Seems simple, doesn't it? But so few authors who want to be published approach it as a business.

Product Is King

Let's forget about writing books for a moment and pretend that you have an idea for a new running shoe that you think will take the world by storm. What's your first step? You go out and learn as much as you can about the shoe business. You learn who the top shoe makers are, the size of the market for running shoes, where shoes are manufactured, and how much it costs to make them. You read the business papers and magazines carefully to learn everything about the top industry players. And when you've learned everything possible, then and only then you approach a shoe company about your idea. Now, if you decide to write a book, do you take all those same steps to achieve success? Sadly, far too few authors do. But they should!

The book publishing industry is a business just like the shoe industry, the breakfast cereal business, or the auto industry. Product is king, and you need to learn how to approach the industry with your product. The more businesslike you are, the greater your chances for success.

Experts Say

"I stay in touch with the publishing world by reading *Publishers Weekly* (*PW*). At around $150 a year, it is expensive but worth every darn penny," says Lynne Rominger, a full-time teacher and part-time author. To subscribe to *PW*, call 1-800-278-2991. You might also find *PW* in your local public library or on the magazine rack at a big bookstore.

Research, Research, Research!

Start right now to learn everything you can about the book business. Become a permanent fixture in your local bookstore. Take the manager out to lunch and ask about the business. Read the trade magazine *Publishers Weekly*. Find out what the proper etiquette is when trying to get published. Learn the lingo. (Far from an admission of idiocy, buying this book was a master stroke of genius; you're on your way to learning the ropes!) Your goal is getting published, so be serious about it.

Once again the Web can be a tremendous help here. Web sites geared toward writers abound. One of the best is run by the *Writer's Digest* folks—check out www. writersdigest.com. To keep abreast of publishing news, take a look at www. thewritenews.com, or visit www.asja.org, run by the American Society of Journalists and Authors, to learn more about contract issues and other important publishing tips.

But I Don't Live in New York!

Although it sometimes seems that way, not all writers live in New York City. One of the great things about becoming a writer is that you can live anywhere in the country—anywhere in the world, even—and still pursue a career writing books. As long as the UPS driver can find your house (or you've got a phone, fax, and modem), you can deal with agents, editors, and publishers.

Co-author Sheree does live in New York City and wouldn't dream of living anywhere else, but co-author Jennifer has managed to build a book publishing career without ever having moved away from her hometown of Sacramento, California—not exactly a well-known publishing metropolis. If you are determined and professional, and if you keep at it, you can get published no matter where you live. Who knows, you might end up winning the author's equivalent of *Who Wants to Be a Millionaire?*

Think of Yourself as a Contestant

Sheree likes to encourage unpublished writers by telling them the story of how she got on the television game show *Wheel of Fortune*. She believes that for many types of books, both publishing and game shows require similar paths to success.

"I decided that I wanted to be on *Wheel of Fortune,* and so I studied everything about the show," explains Sheree. "I learned how to dress like the contestants I'd seen every night on the show, how to talk the way the contestants talked ('Hi, my name is Sheree and I'm a literary agent.'), and in general, how to act like a contestant. So when I walked into the room filled with hundreds of other folks who wanted to be on the show, I stood out as someone who looked, sounded, and acted like a contestant. And it worked! The producers chose me."

Literary agents, publishers, and editors (especially those involved in popular trade books) are like the producers of a game show. They know just what they are looking for to suit their needs. And it's up to you to show them that you are a contestant.

So you want to be a published author? Then learn how to walk, talk, and think like a published author. Go out of your way to meet other writers and learn what you can from them. Join writer's groups, go on writer's retreats, and buy books on writing and writers. Seek out other writers online. Ask published writers to tell you how they made it. And don't be surprised when they tell you! Everyone likes to talk about his or her own success (and maybe even about some of the disappointments). You just have to ask.

50,000 Chances to Win!

When newspapers and magazines aren't trumpeting the approaching downfall of the book publishing industry, they are warning readers against the avalanche of the 50,000 or so books published each year. As writers, it is all too easy to look at that figure and be discouraged. But we say, what a great business this is! With 50,000 books published every year, that's 50,000 chances to win! Why shouldn't yours be among the chosen? Although many (if not most) manuscripts meet with rejection, the odds that one of those books will be yours are much better than the likelihood of Ed McMahon and the Publishers Clearing House team showing up on your doorstep.

Writers Wanted!

Don't ever lose sight of the fact that the book business needs writers so that it can keep publishing books. Agents need authors, publishers need authors, and editors need authors—no matter what they tell you. Don't be intimidated or discouraged by your encounters with these folks because the real truth is that they need you to stay in business.

If your first efforts meet with rejection, use that as an opportunity to rework and refine your ideas. Perhaps a different approach might work. In our next few chapters, you'll learn more about how to successfully develop an idea for a book and put together a proposal that will help catch an agent (or editor's) eye.

So why write? Because you could get published!

The Least You Need to Know

➤ Writing can be a very rewarding experience emotionally or financially—or both!

➤ Perfectly ordinary folks have become published writers; there's no reason to be intimidated by the idea.

➤ Book publishing is a real business, and you need to approach it in a business-like manner.

➤ Americans are reading more and buying more books, and the market for books is strong and healthy.

➤ Far from discouraging them, the publishing business actually needs new writers to continue publishing.

Chapter 2

Write What?

> **In This Chapter**
>
> ➤ The importance of identifying your category
>
> ➤ Books the world doesn't need
>
> ➤ Major book categories defined
>
> ➤ Good-selling categories identified

Pick a Category, Any Category

So there you are at the holiday office party, regaling all who will listen to your plans to write a book in the New Year. "Writing a book?" your boss asks. "What kind of book are you writing?" Silence descends as you search for a way to describe your book. All eyes turn toward you as you stand there, dumbstruck by such a basic question.

What kind of a book are you writing? It is a simple question but one that too few first-time authors can answer with ease. What is your book about? If you can't clearly define it, you're headed for trouble every step of the way.

Start at the beginning. What book category does it fall into? Envision yourself for a moment in your local bookstore. Notice how carefully the categories are divided. There are shelves dedicated to cookbooks, health books, Westerns, new fiction, romance, and inspiration—there's row after row of books on all different topics. Where do you picture your book?

"What kind of a book am I writing?" you answer. "Well, it's kind of difficult to say, sort of a cross between a health book and an inspirational book, with a tiny bit of romance thrown in."

Sorry, but that won't cut it. If you can't clearly define your book, neither can an agent or a publisher—or, worse yet, a bookseller. So pick a category, the closest category that fits your book. Then stick with it.

What the World Doesn't Need

Books of all kinds exist, but some topics are overpublished, and some categories have too many books in them. We checked with booksellers to find out what topics are overpublished. Here are their top six picks:

➤ The Kennedy Family

➤ Web guides

➤ Simple living

➤ Get-rich books

➤ "Near-death" experiences

➤ Cats

Experts Say

"E-anything is egregious," says Terry Foley of Borders Books. "And dot com is even more over." Once we got him rolling on the topic of overpublished books, Foley also urged his fellow Americans, "Get back to work! Stop spending Tuesdays with Morrie!"

Bookmarks

A **memoir** is an account of the events in one's own life.

So are these the areas that we think you should steer clear of? Not necessarily. Stay clear of books on the Kennedys, unless you have some really new scoop. But there just might be another "near-death" book or an adorable cat book that could hit it big. Co-author Jennifer's publishing mentor, Ben Dominitz of Prima Publishing, believes there are two good reasons to publish a book: "One, because no one has published a book on that topic, and two, because everyone has published a book on that topic."

But Enough About You

What the world hardly ever needs, however, is a book about your life story. This is harsh news to deliver so early in a book on getting published, but we want you to have an honest idea of how personal *memoirs* are viewed in the world of book publishing. Somebody's got to tell you, and it might as well be us.

Personal memoirs are a tough sell. If the story of your life is rejected, don't take it personally. This is hardly a sign that your life's worthless. It only means that there aren't 10,000 or more people interested in buying a book about it! From a strict business standpoint, there is no market for the story. Remember your first big lesson in Chapter 1, "So, Why Write?"—the book business is a business.

When is there a market for your life story or personal memoir? When it is compelling and well-written. When there is a core message or theme that will appeal to large numbers of people. Frank McCourt won the Pulitzer Prize for his book *Angela's Ashes,* the gritty story of his youth in Ireland. Are large numbers of readers interested in McCourt's childhood? With hardcover book sales of over a million copies and the release of the movie, it sure looks like it.

Hot Off the Press

The Wall Street Journal's front-page story about a 98-year-old woman named Jessie Brown Foveaux sparked a frenzied bidding war among New York publishers. Warner paid Foveaux a cool $1 million for her book *Any Given Day,* and Hallmark created a made-for-television movie. Storytelling is the key to a successful memoir, and Foveaux knew how to tell the story of an ordinary American life in a lyrical way.

And the Categories Are ...

Before we tell you which are the biggies, we've got to ask you one question: Are you writing *fiction* or *nonfiction?*

Fiction

Long works of fiction are called novels. Short stories are just that—shorter pieces of fiction. If your writing is fiction, you're creating your own situations and characters. Or, you're taking real people, places, and/or events and weaving them into your own story—or substantially embellishing them with your own creations.

There are two major fiction classifications: literary fiction and commercial fiction. Literary fiction has a smaller, more intellectually inclined audience. This is the kind of book you had to read in English class: Virginia Woolf, William Faulkner, you know

Bookmarks

Works of **fiction** are the products of imagination, creativity, and invention. Fiction does not claim to be true. A **nonfiction** work is one that relates actual events, facts, and information. It includes books of all types other than fiction.

the type. Commercial fiction can be broken down into more classifications, such as hardcover mainstream, and then many subcategories, or genres. These include mystery, romance, science fiction, Western, and fantasy.

Nonfiction

Nonfiction is a very broad category that runs the gamut from personal finance to travel books to car manuals and everything in between.

Fiction Categories

Let's take a stroll through an imaginary bookstore and see what's on the shelf. First we'll take a look at the nine major categories of fiction:

➤ Mainstream fiction

➤ Westerns

➤ Romances

➤ Mysteries

➤ Science fiction

➤ Fantasies

➤ Thrillers

➤ Horror books

➤ Young adult books

Bookmarks

Genre fiction, usually published in paperback, refers to a particular type of fiction. This could be a Western, a romance, a sci-fi book, a horror book, a fantasy, or the like.

Mainstream Fiction

Mainstream fiction is pretty much everything that isn't defined in another category! Usually published first in hardcover, mainstream fiction is suited for a large, general audience. John Updike, Toni Morrison, and Philip Roth all write in this category.

Westerns

Usually published in paperback, Westerns range from Zane Grey's novels to Pete Dexter's witty book, *Deadwood*. Westerns are set in the old West and are filled with tough guys on horses, bumbling sheriffs, and saloon girls with hearts of gold.

Romances

Girl meets guy, girl hates guy, guy slowly wins girl over. The romance category is a large one, ranging from historical romances to very contemporary stories that deal with modern themes. These, too, are usually published in paperback—and more often than not (or so it seems!), that big hunk Fabio is on the cover, shirtless!

Mysteries

Who dunnit, and how? Mystery novels center around a murder (or murders) and sift slowly through all the possible suspects and motives. The reigning queen of mystery novels is English writer P.D. James. The kings include Elmore Leonard and Tony Hillerman. Mysteries can be published in either hardcover or paperback. Paperback mysteries are often published as a series, with at least one recurring character with unusual sleuthing ability.

Science Fiction

Sci-fi novels take place far in the future, in imaginary worlds and on imaginary planets. The *Star Trek* series rules the bestseller lists here, but many sci-fi authors have devoted fans. Once again, this is primarily a paperback category.

Fantasies

Also set in imaginary realms, fantasy novels are populated with elves, maidens, and animals that talk. The original fantasy novel was J.R.R. Tolkien's *The Hobbit*. It's usually published in paperback (unless it's a gift edition of *The Hobbit*).

Thrillers

Thrillers are several steps above mystery novels in terms of gore and violence. There might be serial killers with twisted motives and determined FBI specialists on their tail. *The Silence of the Lambs* is a good example of a thriller.

Horror Books

Stephen King. Dean Koontz. Any more questions? Horror books are an extremely popular genre. The pages drip with blood, ghouls, and other unworldly creatures that will keep you lying awake at night.

Young Adult Books

Novels that are written for young teens are called young adult novels, or YA, for short. YA novels can fit into almost every category, including horror, romance, mystery, and others.

Nonfiction Categories

That's it in a nutshell for fiction. Just about everything else in the bookstore is a further breakdown of the huge nonfiction category. The major types of nonfiction books fall into these categories:

➤ Biographies

➤ Travel books

➤ Self-help books

➤ Cookbooks

➤ Health books

➤ Business books

➤ Humor books

➤ Children's books

➤ New age and inspirational books

➤ True crime books

➤ Poetry and belles-lettres

Biographies

A biography is a nonfiction study of a real person, living or dead. The most successful biographies are well-researched and lively accounts of someone with a bonafide place in history. When a real person writes his own story, it's an autobiography. *Whittaker Chambers,* by Sam Tanenhaus, is a biography. *Witness,* by Whittaker Chambers himself, is an autobiography.

Travel Books

Travel books can be broken down into destination guides, travel accounts, and travel guides. Destination guides are meant to provide information about traveling in a specific geographic location. They offer details on hotels, restaurants, and interesting sights in a particular place. Destination guides have lots of phone numbers, addresses, and maps. The Frommer's and Fodor's series are destination guides.

Travel accounts, on the other hand, are more lyrical descriptions of a place. A travel account may contain hotels, restaurants, and interesting sights, as does a travel guide, but instead of providing short descriptive listings of such places, a travel account might devote an entire chapter to describing a good meal the author ate and the breathtaking ramble she took in the nearby countryside afterward. *Under the Tuscan Sun* is a travel account that has appeared on many bestseller lists.

Travel guides are nondestination travel books about how to travel. A good example is *All Aboard,* a book about how to travel by train in North America.

Self-Help Books

The self-help category is another extremely large nonfiction category. Self-help includes books about improving relationships, being a good parent, managing stress, and almost anything in what's called the field of pop psychology. Self-help books are designed to help readers try to solve problems in their personal lives. An example of a well-known self-help book is *Women Who Love Too Much.*

Cookbooks

Everybody knows what these are—books filled with recipes. Bookstore shelves abound with cookbooks, from those that contain regional foods (such as *The Regional Foods of Northern Italy*) to those devoted to a particular type of ingredient (such as *Lemons! Lemons! Lemons!*) to cookbooks about only one type of cooking (such as *Cooking Under Pressure*). Like travel guides and travel accounts, some cookbooks contain stories about food in addition to recipes.

Health Books

Health books provide helpful information about our bodies. From books by medical doctors about specific ailments (such as *The Breast Cancer Survival Manual*) to alternative health titles (such as the *Encyclopedia of Natural Medicine*), the health book category has grown significantly in the past 10 years. To learn why, check out the section "Life in the Fast Lane," later in this chapter, and read Chapter 5, "What's Hot, What's Not," for information on the hot markets.

Business Books

The category of business books lumps together everything from books on management techniques to books on telephone sales, from high finance to personal finance. Two very different bestselling books, *The Millionaire Next Door* and *The One-Minute Manager,* are both—strictly speaking—business books.

Humor Books

Cartoon books, joke books, parodies, and books with humorous observations are all classified as humor. This category ranges from Dilbert and Garfield to Paul Reiser and Drew Carey.

Children's Books

Nonfiction books for children abound. Some books explain science, some are biographies of important figures, and some are activity books for rainy days. An extremely popular area is that of bodily functions. A book called *Grossology* started the trend. You can imagine how delighted young children are to read all about snot!

New Age and Inspirational Books

A relative newcomer to the publishing scene, these books first appeared in the 1960s. New Age and inspirational books run the gamut from books on near-death experiences (such as *Embraced by the Light*) to books about astrology, feng shui, meditation, and other spiritual pursuits. "Feel-good" books (such as the *Handbook for the Soul* and co-author Jennifer's own book, *Christmas Miracles*) also fall into this category.

True Crime

Ever heard of Ann Rule? This author of the Ted Bundy book *The Stranger Beside Me* is the queen of true crime books. True crime books deliver the heart-pounding story behind the dry newspaper headlines. Murders, terrorists, gangs of bank robbers—all real-life events are fodder for a true crime book.

Poetry and Belles-Lettres

Poetry is getting harder and harder to define. Long gone are the days when poetry was prose that rhymed. (If you are a poet, you just know it.) And *belles-lettres?* That's a very fancy term that refers to literary studies and writing. Extremely high-end literary works fall under this category.

Hot Off the Press

What's a poet to do? Most large publishers do publish some poetry. But there's a plethora of other options, including small presses, online magazines, and literary journals. Many poets bypass publishers altogether and publish their poetry themselves. Known as chapbooks, these slim collections are a viable and honorable means of publishing for poets.

So what did we leave out? Gardening books, sports books, computer books, reference books—there are far more than just 11 different nonfiction book categories in the world. But we are not writing *The Complete Idiot's Guide to Book Categories* (which, FYI, would be categorized as a reference book). Instead of writing another 20 pages on this, we've got a better idea for you.

Walk out the door of your imaginary bookstore and through the door of a real one. Spend as much time as you can there. Wander the aisles. Familiarize yourself with the ways that bookstores divide their sections and subsections.

Here's another great way to learn more: Pick a book off the shelf and turn it over. On the back cover of most paperback books—and some hardcovers, too—on the very top line, you will see a category printed. In the book trade, this is often called the shelf reference. This is how the publisher defines the book (and this is where the publisher hopes the bookseller will shelve it). Become familiar with these categories.

Choose which category best defines your book.

Life in the Fast Lane

Although book sales are strong overall right now, it is possible to identify some categories that are moving faster than others. Here's a quick look at two of them: health books and inspirational books.

Health Books

Baby Boomers and their bodies are aging, and they're reading lots of books about staying healthy and fit, particularly alternative health books that deal with such subjects as acupuncture, herbal healing, vitamin therapy, and the like. Changes in the national healthcare system, particularly the growth of HMOs, have also helped turn many Americans to health books for medical help. This is a category that is expected to sell strongly in the years to come.

Inspirational Books

"I think we are returning to our storytelling roots," a radio talk show host told Jennifer recently. He was explaining his take on why books such as *Small Miracles,* the *Chicken Soup for the Soul* titles, and other inspirational storytelling books are on the rise. Modern life is a fast-paced and scary place, and to sit down with a reassuring book such as *Simple Abundance* and drink tea for an hour is a welcome respite. The market for these books will be strong in the years to come.

You can read more about the individual markets in Chapter 5.

Slush Pile

Don't describe your book as "a little bit of this and a little bit of that." To succeed in today's book market, you need to be very clear about the category that best describes your book.

From Category to Specific Topic

Now that you have a better understanding of where the book category lines are drawn, is there a market for what you want to write? In the next few chapters, you'll discover professional tips on how to create a bestselling book idea, if you don't already have one. We'll also give you a solid sense of the kinds of books that publishers, both big and small, are seeking—and how to find the right publishing house for your book.

The Least You Need to Know

➤ You are either writing fiction or nonfiction, not both.

➤ Countless categories and subcategories of fiction exist, from mainstream novels to mystery, from romance to science fiction, and many in between.

➤ Nonfiction is an even larger category, with cookbooks, travel books, self-help books, how-to books, and so on. This category covers any book that contains true information.

➤ The best way to learn all the different categories and distinctions is to spend time in bookstores, looking, looking, looking ....

➤ Do careful research to make sure you are not trying to enter an already over-published area or write a book about a trend that has already passed.

Chapter 3

If You Need an Idea, Stalk the Bestseller List

<table>
<tr><td colspan="2">In This Chapter</td></tr>
<tr><td>➤</td><td>The high-concept approach</td></tr>
<tr><td>➤</td><td>Find a subject need, and fill it</td></tr>
<tr><td>➤</td><td>To write well, read</td></tr>
<tr><td>➤</td><td>Eavesdrop your way to the top</td></tr>
<tr><td>➤</td><td>Hanging out in bookstores</td></tr>
</table>

Chances are, you bought this book because you already have an idea, and you think it's a good one. So why do you have to wade through all the information in this chapter about how to come up with a good book idea? You've already got one of those.

That's great, but we want you to know how the professionals do it. We want you to have a solid understanding of how the book business works and how to succeed in that world, no matter what your main reason is for wanting to get published. Even if you don't expect to make lots of money from your book, you do want people to buy it and read it, don't you? In order to share your knowledge and to advance your cause, the bottom line is that you need readers.

Despite the relative health of the book business today, publishers are taking fewer chances on books than before. If getting published is your goal, it is more important than ever that the book you're writing is one that will work in the marketplace. The methods you'll learn about in this chapter have been used by professional writers to develop marketable ideas that sold—and sold well.

The High-Concept Approach

Have you heard the term "high concept" before? It's a movie business expression. The screenwriter pitches his idea to the producer like this: "Baby, you'll love this one! It's a cross between *Top Gun* and *The Sting*. A group of Air Force pilots pull a fast one on some Libyan terrorists." In two sentences, the screenwriter paints a picture that the producer can quickly understand and get a sense of its market potential. That's high concept.

To the chagrin of many traditionalists, the book business has gradually become more like the movie business. That means that if you want your book to sell well, you've got to start thinking like the movie guys. Because sometimes the movie guys end up in the book business.

A Link in the Media Food Chain

Penguin Books, with its familiar orange-and-black logo, is one of the most recognizable publishing brands in the world. Many legendary literary figures have passed through its portals. A few years ago the Penguin Group named as its new chairman and CEO a youngish (39-year-old) fellow named Michael Lynton. Had Mr. Lynton toiled in publishing for years before rising to this spot? No. The job he had before Penguin was president of Disney's Hollywood Pictures.

According to *The New Yorker* magazine, Lynton's appointment was further evidence that in much of the publishing world today, "books are increasingly being regarded less as discrete properties than as one vital link in a media food chain that begins with an idea, takes early shape as a magazine article, gets fleshed out between book covers, gains bigger life on a movie or TV screen, and enters the hereafter as a videocassette or the inspiration for a toy." So, did the movie guy stay in the book business very long? Ah, you guessed it. After three years, he bailed on books to take over a division of America Online.

Experts Say

Who really is a creative genius, anyway? Thomas Edison has been widely quoted for his definition of genius: 99 percent perspiration and 1 percent inspiration. In a similar vein, writer Gertrude Stein believed that "genius is nothing more than energy." So go ahead—keep energetically thinking up those book ideas!

Find a Need and Fill It

Granted, not all books and all reasons for publishing are conceived to appeal to a mass market—is it possible to sit down and consciously create a bestselling book? It has happened before, as this little publishing tale illustrates.

Back in the 1980s, an ambitious young woman wanted to start her own business and decided to fund it by writing a bestselling book. She hired a market research firm to find out who buys books.

After spending a few days interviewing shoppers in a mall, the market research reported its findings to her: Women buy books. "Great," she said. "What are women the most concerned about?" The research came back: their bodies. "Hmmm ... what part of their bodies?" she asked. Answer: their thighs. So, this smart woman sat down and wrote a book called *Thin Thighs in Thirty Days*. Calculating? Yes. Bestseller? You betcha!

Whether that is the true story behind the thin thighs book, we don't know. But the message of the tale is true. You can set out to uncover a large potential audience and deliver a book that they will buy.

Finding the Success Factor

So many of us are attracted to the romantic idea of the life of the writer: long mornings spent with a steaming cup of tea and a blank pad of paper, setting the scene for the muse to come gliding in to inspire and guide us. That may be one way to write. But if you want to write and publish successful books, here is a better way: Sit down with your cup of tea and a copy of *The New York Times* bestseller list. Try to analyze why each book is on that list. Was it the Oprah factor? That worked in a big way for *Simple Abundance*, *Die Broke*, and *Men Are from Mars, Women Are from Venus*. These books took off after their authors appeared on her show. Does the author work for Oprah, like her personal trainer who wrote the big bestseller *Make the Connection*? Were any of the bestsellers a selection of the Oprah Book Club?

Is it because the author has widespread name recognition or a huge following, like Rush Limbaugh or Dr. Laura Schlessinger? Millions of people tune in or turn on some of the people whose names are regularly found on the bestseller list.

Or is it because a huge potential audience is interested in this kind of information? Is it a novel with a theme that will appeal to large numbers of readers? Who hasn't at some time pined for a long-lost love? Hello, *Bridges of Madison County*.

Hot Off the Press

Sometimes publishing success is as random as choosing a seat on the subway—literally. That's what happened to author/illustrator Daniel Peddle. He saw a woman reading a young adult novel on the subway and chose the seat next to her. Striking up a conversation, it turned out that—surprise!—she was a children's book editor. She gave him her card, he followed up, and the result was a two-book contract.

Wide Appeal = Good Sales

Unless you work for Oprah or already have your own radio or TV show, if you have your sights on selling in big numbers, you're most likely to score by choosing a subject with wide appeal.

Hot Off the Press

Here's what *Publishers Weekly* executive editor Daisy Maryles had to say on the topic of recent hardcover nonfiction bestsellers: "What hasn't changed is the fact that books by and about people in the news, and the very popular how-to category, dominate the list."

Audience Appeal

A big *audience?* How big? If fame and fortune are your primary goals, you need to write a book that will sell big, which means that it will sell to everyone. Richard Paul Evans did this when he wrote *The Christmas Box,* a book with a universal, sentimental message. *The Millionaire Next Door,* a financial planning title, was written to appeal to anyone who's dreamed of being rich. And a book called *Don't Sweat the Small Stuff* is designed for anyone stressed out by modern life. Those titles had big audiences—and very big sales.

Bookmarks

A book's **audience** is that portion of the population that will be interested enough in the book's topic to buy a copy.

You must be clear-eyed about how large the potential audience is for your book. Just because your mother raves about your idea doesn't guarantee it a mass audience. Even if your mother and your neighbor, too, like the idea, that still isn't enough. If you are hoping for big sales, you need to uncover big topics with big appeal.

Look Around You

How do you come up with an idea for a book with a big audience? The most important trait is observation. Always keep a keen eye trained on what is going on around you. What topics are in the news? On television? In magazine articles? What are your friends talking about? What kinds of concerns keep you awake at night?

To get published, you've got to work on your writing skills. But you've also got to develop your ability to create book ideas. Try the following exercise to get started.

What's Making the News?

Sit down every day with a copy of *USA Today*. It might not be the most sophisticated newspaper in the country, but it gives lots of coverage to topics of interest to middle America. Read the newspaper from cover to cover, and think of one book idea based on the articles you've read.

Perhaps there is a large article in the food section about how many men are using bread machines, or a chart that shows how many parents are home-schooling their young children.

Could you use any of these articles to come up with an idea for a nonfiction book or a novel that involves themes and characters that would appeal to the special interests of large audiences?

A recent example is a front-page story in *USA Today* with the headline "Boomer Brain Meltdown: Generation Faces More Frequent Memory Lapses." Big topic, big audience. Have there been books on memory before? Yes. Will there continue to be interest in this topic in the years to come? Yes.

Bookmarks

A **parody** is a comic imitation, usually of a well-known literary work. There's Ernest Hemingway's *The Torrents of Spring*, which is a parody of a Sherwood Anderson novel. A parody can also be a funny take on a famous person, such as *Rush Limbaugh Is a Big Fat Idiot* or *O.J.'s Legal Pad*. Under most circumstances, parody is a constitutionally protected form of speech.

Try, Try Again

Let's be realistic: Most of the ideas that you come up with using this method will be throwaways. But the more you do it, and the more you begin to think like this, the better the odds that you will eventually come up with a bestselling book idea.

What's That You Said?

Eavesdropping is also a critical skill for writers. Yep, we want you to listen in when other people talk. Let's call this skill "heightened observation." Not only can you get a great idea for a book, but you might also come up with a great idea for the title!

During a conversation at a party, Joel Saltzman told a friend, "If you can talk, you can write." "Hmmm ...", he thought, "what a great title and topic for a book!" Joel wrote it down on a cocktail napkin and carried it in his pocket for several months before finally sitting down to write a book called (what else?) *If You Can Talk, You Can Write*. And yes, it was published.

Experts Say

"If you want to write, read," says Gary Krebs, an editor at Rodale Books. What does he mean? All serious students of writing must also be serious readers. You can't expect to flourish in a field that you do not enjoy and also aren't very familiar with. Read everything you can get your hands on. Read books, magazines, newspapers, and online articles. Study what other writers are doing. The hours you invest in reading will pay you back when you sit down to write.

Co-author Jennifer's travel guide *The Air Courier's Handbook* is also a product of eavesdropping. She overheard two guys in a restaurant talking about cheap courier travel, something she herself was interested in. She leaned over and introduced herself, and got the phone number for a courier firm. She then went on to travel as a courier and later wrote a book about it. That's called listening for fun and profit.

Common phrases of speech sometimes spark an idea. They can also make great book titles. Some six years ago, Jennifer developed an idea for a cookbook called *Gooey Desserts*. She likes gooey desserts herself and realized that it's a phrase that makes people smile. Give a cookbook that title and it's sure to attract attention, she surmised. And anyone browsing in a bookstore will immediately understand what that cookbook's about.

Remember that *USA Today* article about memory loss a few paragraphs ago? The perfect title for a book on preventing memory loss was right there in the story. A memory expert said, "Use it or lose it!" Doesn't that give you a perfect image for a book? And you understand exactly what the book is about.

Let the Shows Show You

Another way to find ideas for books with large audiences is to attend major industry trade shows. There are trade shows of all stripes: food, gardening, health, fitness, computer, interior design, cars, gift shows, you name it. If you plan to write a nonfiction book on a particular topic, check to see if there is a trade show that's related to it. It's a great way to learn what's hot in the industry. Prowl the aisles, pick up literature, observe merchandise and trends, and, of course, eavesdrop on conversations to listen for news trends and possible titles!

I'm Not Hanging Out, I'm Working!

Spend lots of time hanging out in bookstores. Pay very close attention to the books in the front of the store and those marked "New Releases." Get to know what's new and hot in the area you're considering writing about. Become an expert on what's available.

The more you know about what's out there, the sooner you'll be able to spot what is not. When you find a hole, you've found yourself an opportunity! Good editors, agents, and writers spend countless hours wandering around bookstores without feeling the least bit guilty. They aren't goofing off—they're working.

How to Work the Bookstore Shelves

Here's another exercise that'll help you to develop your skills. Go to a bookstore and choose a book category. Are there two, maybe three shelves devoted to that category? Spend as much time as you need familiarizing yourself with the books on the shelf. You might need to write down the titles. Now, go back to the store every few days and check your section. Have new titles been added? Have many books sold? Which books? Why do you think they sold?

What Isn't Selling?

When browsing bookstores, don't skip over the bargain tables. If there is a big stack of sale books on bulb gardening, that might be an area to avoid. Have several titles on low-fat baking been marked down? Stay away. Learn from the mistakes of other writers about what doesn't sell.

I'm Not Surfing the Net, I'm Working

Just as you can legitimately spend hour after hour in a bookstore and call it work, you also can spend hour after hour online. Check out the news sites, the women's sites, and the money sites. What seems to be the topic of conversation on chat boards? You can use the same eavesdropping techniques in chat rooms to try to pick up phrases or figures of speech that might make good book titles. And no one can catch you watching!

Surfing the online bookstores for information also helps you learn more about what's selling and why. And just like the remainder tables outside the door of a bookstore, you can tell what isn't selling online by the big, big sales ranking next to it. Anything ranked beyond 75,000 or so on Amazon.com just isn't selling in very big numbers. (In other words, the lower the number, the better the sales.)

Bookmarks

A **series** is two or more books linked by a brand-name identity, such as *The Complete Idiot's Guides*, or *Goosebumps*, or *Nancy Drew*. Publishers are fond of series because they build awareness and momentum in the marketplace. Writers also like them because it can mean steady work. Sometimes a series begins with a single book that sells so well that the audience and the publisher come looking for more.

Sniffing Out Gaps and Niches

The more you can learn about what's available and how well it's doing, the better you'll be able to figure out what that category needs. Perhaps you'll notice that there's a need for a large reference volume, or maybe a small, inexpensive guidebook.

Not long after the phenomenal bestseller *Life's Little Instruction Book* started to appear on the shelves, co-author Sheree thought to herself, "Life's little instructions? Who needs that! What I need is life's big instructions." She realized that she had stumbled onto a book idea, got together a group of writers, and gave the world *The Big Book of Life's Instructions*.

Cookbook author and editor Fran McCullough saw something missing from the diet bookshelf. There were three bestselling books on the high-protein/low-carbohydrate diet, but none of the books offered much in the way of recipes. So, *The Low-Carb Cookbook* was born!

Here's another example of how this kind of observation can pay off. As a long-time player in the business book category, Jennifer has known that quote books were steady sellers. Anyone who has ever had to write a speech goes out in search of one. And "quotable women" books seem to have worked again and again. Women are making huge strides in the business world, but where was the quote book that combined women and business? Say hello to *The Quotable Businesswoman*, a Big City Books project that Andrews McMeel purchased.

Hot Off the Press

All books in a series are not necessarily written by the same author. Many travel destination series, such as *Best Places to Kiss* romantic travel guides, use the same format and structure but have different authors for different locations. Co-author Sheree met Paula Begoun, publisher of the guides, at a writer's conference; not long afterward, Sheree sent her several sample pages of a possible travel guide set in New York. Although the book was unsolicited, Sheree was careful to use the exact same style as the rest of the series. Surprise! Sheree got herself a contract to do *Best Places to Kiss in and Around New York City*. And now that she's a romantic travel writer, she has written the *52 Most Romantic Places in and Around New York City* for Adams Media.

Backlist Books: Sure and Steady

If you follow all our suggestions here—if you come up with an idea for a big topic with a big audience and then sell it to a publisher—will it become a bestseller? Perhaps.

Only 1 percent of all the books published in any given year actually make it on a national bestseller list. You might not be one of them, but there are many authors out there whose books are paying the rent, and you might find yourself in their company. These authors have books with strong *backlist* sales. A book that backlists, that sells for years, can rack up impressive sales totals over its lifetime.

Keep the word *backlist* in mind when choosing a topic for a book. Look for book ideas on subjects with staying power.

The More You Know

Now, we do realize that you might already have your heart set on a topic for your book. We also realize that everything we have covered here sounds a bit crass and calculating. Please do not dismiss it out of hand, though.

The more you know about what makes books work on a commercial level, the better you will be able to smooth and shape the book that you already have been working on. Read on to learn more about researching the market and gathering the information you'll need for your book proposal.

Bookmarks

Frontlist books are books that have been published recently. Many of these are piled on tables and placed in bookstore windows. **Midlist** books are those acquired for modest advances, that are given modest print runs, and that have a relatively short shelf life. **Backlist** books are those that have been in stores for more than 90 days—sometimes for years. Most of the thousands of books on the shelves are classified as backlist books.

The Least You Need to Know

➤ It is possible to create an idea for a book with bestseller potential.

➤ Good book ideas can come from anywhere; keep your eyes and ears open!

➤ Read as many newspapers and magazines as you can, always looking for big ideas for books and titles.

➤ Study bookstore shelves carefully to see what is missing.

➤ Spend as much time as you can in bookstores—they're gold mines of information.

➤ Look for ideas with long-term staying power.

Chapter 4

Super-Stealth Market Research Techniques

In This Chapter

➤ The bookstore: your no. 1 resource

➤ Researching catalogs

➤ Cracking the codes

➤ Surfing the Net

➤ *PW*, directories, and newspapers

Okay, now you've got an idea for a book. But how do you know if you've come up with an idea that will work? Be it nonfiction or fiction, there are good ways to test your market well in advance of even writing your proposal and sample chapter. Let's start with the strategies to use for nonfiction. (Fiction writers, do not despair; your turn comes later in the chapter.)

Is It a Book?

The first thing you need to ask yourself is: Does my idea have strong book potential? What sometimes seems like a big idea for a book turns out to be only a big idea for a magazine article. Make sure that you have chosen a topic with enough scope and substance to sustain a few hundred manuscript pages.

Put aside your subjectivity and take a good objective look at your idea, just like the book professionals do. The more work you put into this step, the better your chances of success months from now, when your proposal is sitting on an editor's desk. The investment will also pay you back when it comes time to write your proposal—you will have already done much of the required homework! Bonus.

Meet Your Customer

Now that you really have an idea for a book instead of a magazine article, try to picture your customer. That's right, close your eyes and try to imagine someone walking into a bookstore and asking a clerk for your book. If you can't envision that happening—if your idea is too weak, too abstract, or perhaps too specialized—then you need to re-evaluate it.

Before working as an editor, co-author Jennifer spent several years as a book buyer for a small chain of bookstores. She met with sales reps and looked at publishers' catalogs by the hundreds. Her buying decisions were always based on one simple question: Who will buy this book? She continued to ask herself that same question as an acquisitions editor at Prima Publishing. This is also a question that she asks herself today when evaluating book projects to develop. Memorize the question and ask yourself often: Who will buy this book?

Once your idea can pass these two basic litmus tests (Is it a book? Who will buy it?), you are ready to move on to the next important step.

Bookmarks

The **front matter** is the first few pages of the book. It typically contains (in this order) a half-title page, a title page, a copyright page, a dedication, the table of contents, sometimes a preface and/or foreword, and an acknowledgments page. Front matter pages are numbered i, ii, iii, iv, and so forth.

Sizing Up the Competition

Few books really are the first-ever ones published on their topic. You need to be clear-eyed about the books that have been done before in your area. Remember the technique in Chapter 3, "If You Need an Idea, Stalk the Bestseller List," about targeting a shelf in a bookstore and tracking the success of the books on that shelf? You now need to do this for the books that either compete with or complement your own book idea.

Just what do we mean by competition? Let's say that you're planning to write a book on arthritis. The first step is to go to the bookstore and look under "arthritis" on the health books shelf. Are there two books? Four? Twelve? Get out your pad and copy down the title, the author, the publisher, and the price of each book. Open up each book and look inside the front few pages to find a copyright date; it's usually on the flip side of the title page.

Now go home or have a seat in the bookstore café, and examine all this information carefully. You've got more than just some book information here—you've got clues to your own success.

Title

Do the titles and other language on the covers make the same kinds of promises that yours will? Are they clever and enticing? Or do they have a bland and general medical reference sound to them? We'll call your imaginary book *Accurate Arthritis Answers*. A browsing book buyer would see your book and think, "Hey, accurate answers. What I need are accurate answers about my arthritis problem," and reach for your book. The cleaner your proposed title is, the better.

What's missing from the shelf? Does the market need a beginner's guide, an A–Z reference, or a pocket guide to your topic? Maybe you could position yours to fill the gap.

Author

Who is this guy, anyway? What are his credentials? Does he have a big-name research school behind him? Does this author have a television or radio show?

Take a close look at your rival's credentials and see how yours measure up. Be honest with yourself. Are yours as strong as those of the authors whose books are on the shelf? If not, get to work now to improve them. Begin now to beef up your professional contacts, create workshops or public presentations on your topic, and write articles for industry magazines. By the time you are ready to shop your book to agents or publishers, you will be in a stronger position.

Publisher

Finding out who published these books can be very revealing. If all the books come from major New York houses, this tells you that arthritis is a hot topic and that major publishers thought it was hot. If a book sells well for its publisher, that publisher might just be looking for more!

But what if the topic is covered only by small publishers or by *self-publishers?* Both of those are fine and honorable ways to be published, but let's look strictly from a competitive point of view: Small publishers and self-publishers don't have nearly the distribution that the large houses do. If many of the books you've found on the shelves are from small publishers, then you might be able to use that information to your advantage when submitting to a larger publisher.

Speaking of small publishers, there is much good to say about them, if you're not aiming to write a bestseller. Your book is less likely to get lost in the

Bookmarks

A **self-published** book is one for which the author himself has paid the bills. Many successful authors started out as self-publishers before the big houses sat up and took notice. It's a fine and honorable thing to do, as self-publisher Benjamin Franklin no doubt would have agreed.

crowd, you may get more personal attention, and you may find your editor more accessible and open to your suggestions.

Bookmarks

Mass market paperbacks are those small, softcover 4-by-7-inch books you find in the racks at the grocery store and in the airport bookstores (they're also called rack-size paperbacks). Any other larger paperback is called a **trade paperback.** Mass market paperbacks are generally printed in bigger quantities and are priced lower than trade paperbacks.

Slush Pile

Never start a conversation with an agent or editor with the phrase "Never before has there been a book on this topic." Rather, say something like this: "To the best of my knowledge, this topic has never been covered quite in this way." You want to show that your idea is different and better than the competition, but not in a whole new category.

Price

Book publishing is a price-sensitive industry. If you see four books on the shelf that are expensive hardcover books, perhaps there is a need for a small trade paperback on the subject. Your publisher will determine the ultimate price of your book, of course, but you can always pitch the project in a particular way. When you write your proposal, you'll need to show that you've done your homework about the way the competing books are priced.

Publication Copyright Date

This information is critical when assessing the competition. Are all the books on the shelf a few years old? That means that the information is sure to be at least a little outdated. That might not matter for some books, such as fiction and cookbooks, but for all types of books it will mean that the book category could use a few new books. Better yet, you'll have little competition when you try to promote your book to publishers.

Bear in mind that the publishing process moves slowly. A book with a brand-new copyright date may well have been written as long as two years before its publication.

Are all the books brand new? This is also useful information. It lets you know that publishers think this is a viable category, one worth pursuing (unless there are so many books that the publishers consider it a saturated market).

Staying in the Know

All this information on current books is very useful, but keep in mind that it has its limitations. Maybe some books have been selling so well that the store can't keep them on the shelves. At the very moment you're scrutinizing the shelves, more new books are being shipped to bookstores. When those new books arrive, some of the books on your list may be boxed up and shipped back to their publishers!

To keep current, you've got to visit bookstores regularly. And you've got to do two more things. The first is to ask a bookstore employee to let you look at the directory *Forthcoming Books*. It's a big reference that lists page after page of upcoming books. Check in the subject guide under your category to see what is scheduled to come out in the next few months.

The second thing you've got to do is give your postal carrier more work.

Catalogs for the Asking

You've done good detective work so far. Now you need to hit the phones. To get a better sense of what publishers will be bringing out in upcoming months (particularly in your subject area), get their catalogs—no, not *L.L. Bean* and *Neiman Marcus*, but *Random House, Ten Speed, The University of Chicago Press,* and others. Identify the biggest publishers in your subject area. You already know at least some of them; you wrote down their names when doing your bookstore sleuthing. Call and request a catalog.

The big publishers generally put out catalogs three times a year: fall, winter, and spring. Medium and small houses usually do only two: fall and spring. Publishers plan their programs according to seasons, a concept you'll read more about in Chapter 20, "So, How Does My Book Get into the Stores?"

How to Reach 'Em

How do you find the address and phone number for a publishing company? There are a couple of good sources. *Writer's Market* is published annually by the folks at *Writer's Digest Books*. It includes an amazing array of information about publishing companies and is now available on CD-ROM. You can also access it online—just go to www.writersdigest.com.

There's also a book called *Writer's Guide to Book Editors, Publishers, and Literary Agents.* Written by Jeff Herman, this book is also filled with publishers' addresses and phone numbers. Of great help is the other information Herman provides: a lengthy description of each publishing company, including the kinds of books published recently.

Many large (and many small) publishers now maintain their own Web sites. Just take a stab in the dark by typing in their name after the old www. prefix and see what comes up. Or, check inside a book recently published by that house to see whether a Web address is listed.

Go Over Them with a Fine-Toothed Comb

Once the catalogs arrive, study them carefully. They'll give you a good idea of what the publishers plan to publish in the next six months or so. If you find a book that is in your category, study it carefully. Does it get a full page in the catalog? This means that the publisher thinks it's a big deal. Are big publicity and promotional

Slush Pile

When doing competitive research, don't pretend to be someone you're not. Don't be afraid to call and request a catalog. If they ask why, tell them you're an author. Publishers are happy to educate prospective authors by sending out catalogs. It cuts down on the number of inappropriate submissions they'll get (they hope!).

plans announced? What about an appearance on *Oprah?* Just as you did with the books you studied on the bookstore shelves, analyze these upcoming books by title, price, and author.

Free Stuff on the Counter, Too!

Most bookstore chains, and even some of the independents, have book catalogs for the taking, often right next to the cash register. These in-store catalogs, as they're called, contain lots of information about forthcoming titles from a variety of publishers. And every year at Christmas, gift catalogs are produced by associations of independent booksellers that are filled with advertisements of hot new books. Pick up these catalogs whenever you see them—they're chock full of news about the book market.

What Are the Clubs Selling?

As if we haven't talked about catalogs enough already, here is one more suggestion: Try to get your hands on as many catalogs from book club mailings as you can—you know, the little catalogs that the Writer's Digest Book Club, Book-of-the-Month Club, the Doubleday Book Club, and others send out to members every few weeks. No, we don't expect you to sign up for and get lots of those "six books for a dollar" deals. Just ask around and see if your friends or neighbors already belong. Why take the time to look at these book club catalogs? Because these people know what they're doing.

Except for the highly specialized ones, most book clubs base their success on their ability to sell large numbers of books to a mainstream audience. The more you study the catalogs, the more you will learn about what kinds of books sell in big quantities.

Cracking the Code

Important sales information on competing books is literally at your fingertips—but you have to know where to look.

The secret for finding out whether a book has sold well is to look at the number of printings it's gone through. When a book is first released, the number of books printed is referred to as the "first printing." Once most of those books have sold, the book goes back for a second printing, and hopefully a third and a fourth. You can tell just how many printings the book has gone through by checking the copyright page. You should see a series of numbers there that look something like this:

99 98   8 7 6 5 4 3 2

The numbers are a code that tells you when that particular copy of the book was printed. The rightmost number of the first series of numbers is the year of the book's printing; the rightmost number of the second series of numbers is the number of the book's printing. If you look at these numbers, you can see that the book is in its second printing since 1998. If the copyright date for that book is, say, 1994, that tells us the book is moving pretty slowly. It took four years for the first printing to sell out and for the book to be printed again.

Except for hot-selling titles, most books are reprinted in steady but modest quantities. Subsequent reprintings in the 3,000- to 5,000-copy range are common. Publishers do not find it to their benefit from a business standpoint to keep large quantities of unsold books stacked in a warehouse. The spiraling cost of paper has also had an effect on the size of most reprints.

On the other hand, if you see from the code that the book is in a sixth printing, that is impressive. This is a book that is selling.

How is this printing information useful? If you find a book that has sold in big numbers, you might wonder: Could this be a hot topic that has room for another book? If you find a book that has not gone into a second printing after having been out for some time, you might ask: Is this a dead category that I should stay away from?

To find the answers to these questions, you will have to keep asking booksellers questions, reading topical newspapers and magazines, and watching this part of the marketplace closely.

Pick a Bookseller's Brain

Booksellers are tremendously helpful and knowledgeable. If you ask, they will tell. Why not approach a friendly bookseller and say, "Hey, I'm thinking of writing a book on Topic X. What do you think? Is that a category that sells well for you? Which book in this category sells the best?" Most booksellers, the unsung heroes of the book business, will be happy to help if you catch them when they're not too busy.

Surfing for Info

The Internet holds wonderful information for writers. Not only is it a great place to do research, but you also can access lots of cool stuff to help you find out about the competition and the market for your book idea. Here are a few great sites.

The New York Times *Extended Bestseller List*

Sure, you know *The New York Times* Bestseller List. You check it every Sunday, don't you? But did you know that there are many more books on that list than are printed in the paper? To find the top 30 bestsellers, visit the paper's Web site at www.nyt.com, and go into the "books" section. You can also access it through www.barnesandnoble.com.

Amazon.com

Amazon.com, the grand-daddy of online bookstores, is also a good place to do research. Amazon can offer long lists of titles on any particular subject, giving you a quick look at what has been published. It, too, has bestseller lists, but keep in mind that these reflect the tastes of folks who are open to online shopping. Just a few years ago, the no. 1 bestselling title of all at Amazon was a book on how to design killer Web sites.

A fun way to waste an hour, though, is to go through all 100 of the Hot 100 and try to figure out why each book is selling well that particular hour. The Hot 100 is particularly sensitive to media; you can tell pretty quickly who was on the morning talk shows or in the major newspapers by a sudden jump in rank.

Barnes & Noble

Barnesandnoble.com is a relatively recent online entry. It links up with *The New York Times* Book Review site and allows you to read reviews and articles in addition to researching titles.

One thing we really like about BN.com is that you can type in a subject such as "natural health" (or whatever your topic is), and the site will give you the top 25 bestsellers in that category. This is very helpful when analyzing markets and putting together book proposals.

More Assigned Reading

As a serious student of the book publishing business, you need to keep up with news and trends. Read *Publishers Weekly* and study the articles about what's selling. *PW* does annual round-up articles about many of the major book categories. If you plan to write a health book, it's important that you read the health book round-up. If you plan to write a novel, be sure to read the fiction round-up. Don't stumble around in the dark; the information is there for the getting.

In addition to *Publishers Weekly*, *The New York Times* and *The Wall Street Journal* run frequent articles on books and the publishing world. Again, www.nyt.com often features articles about books and publishing in addition to its bestseller list and book reviews. Start keeping a file of important articles. You never know what you'll learn there.

But I Want to Write a Novel!

Do you really have to go through all this advance work for fiction, too?

Yes. Just as a health writer should know what's already on the health books shelf, a novelist needs to know what fiction is being published and read. Be a student of the art of writing, of course, but to succeed, you must study the marketplace, too. Learn what kinds of novels are selling well (ask a bookseller) and what kinds are not (ask a bookseller). For example, there's a big trend in "small novels" right now, short books such as *The Notebook*. Don't bury your head in the sand (or your computer); get into that bookstore and learn everything you can.

You know that you're an absolute original and that your style is unique. But if you absolutely had to name a writer or book that is most like yours, what would you say? You're not doing it to compare yourself with another writer, but to establish the fact that books like the one that you have written have sold well.

Minimize Your Rejection Rate

Why, you might ask, are we giving you all this inside information about how to come up with a good book idea? Or about how to research the market and the competing titles? Because, as longtime agents and editors, we're tired of saying "No." It's hard to turn down proposals and manuscripts from good-intentioned, hopeful writers. It is truly heartbreaking to know how much time and effort went into a book project that, from a business standpoint, was doomed from the start.

So, we figure that the more time and effort we put into teaching you how to come up with a book idea that will get a "Yes!" from an agent, an editor, and a publishing company, the easier our jobs will be.

Now that that's clear, let's move on to the next chapter and get back to that critical question: What do publishers want?

The Least You Need to Know

➤ Make sure that your topic is big enough for an entire book, not just a six-page magazine article.

➤ Never assume that your book is the first ever on the topic. There's at least one book already for every topic ever thought of, and your job is to learn from its/their strengths and weaknesses.

➤ Pore over publishers' catalogs, snoop around bookstores, and find out what the book clubs are hawking.

➤ Get with it—get online.

➤ The more time and effort you spend researching the market for your novel or nonfiction book, the better your book proposal will be.

Chapter 5

What's Hot, What's Not

In This Chapter

➤ Trend spotting

➤ Literary and mainstream fiction

➤ Love 'em, thrill 'em, kill 'em

➤ Niche writing

➤ Cookbook niches

➤ Books for kids

Just what do publishers want? That's a tough question. And what do publishers want right now? That's an even tougher question, and possibly an irrelevant one. The awful truth is, if you sat down at this very moment and wrote a book on a topic that this chapter says is hot today, odds are that by the time you had your finished book in your hands, the topic would have cooled down—maybe to subzero.

Let's say it takes you six months to write the book. That's not a very long time for anyone to write a good how-to book, much less the Great American Novel. Let's say you know somebody who knows somebody with an experienced and well-connected agent, and that agent just happens to be particularly hungry at the moment. Maybe he's going through an expensive divorce, or his biggest client just got hit by a bus.

You express-mail him your ready-to-publish manuscript. He reads it that very night and sees your book on Hot Topic X as his ticket out of mounting legal bills. The first thing the following morning, he couriers copies to the hotshot editors at his favorite publishing houses.

Bookmarks

An **instant book** is one that appears just weeks after big news. Instant books galore appeared after John Kennedy Jr.'s death. O.J. Simpson, Ross Perot, and even the World Cup–winning U.S. women's soccer team have been the subject of instant books. To write and produce an instant book, writers and production folks work almost around the clock for a week or two.

Experts Say

Are Westerns really dead? Although there's a hunger for American historical fiction, such as the successful *Lonesome Dove*, literary agent and author Donald Maass warns that the classic Western is dying. "The 'wagons west' stories have all been told," Maass says. "Find untold stories about the West."

Twenty-four hours later, he conducts an auction. Your book sells to the highest bidder for megabucks. (Why not? After all, this is a dream.) Smelling success (and desperate to recoup the investment), your publisher rushes the manuscript into production. Nine months later, your book hits the stores amid great fanfare—and is quickly placed on the remainder table. By the time your masterpiece is published, Hot Topic X is old news, and the public now wants to read about Hot Topic Y.

What's In, What's Out, by Category

What's a writer to do? Now there's a question worthy of Freud. Despite the transitory and, dare we say, fickle nature of the buying public, certain trends bear watching. The trick is to separate the wheat from the Paula Barbieri tell-alls. (O.J.'s ex-girlfriend's book was a $3-million bomb for her publisher.) So, with a grain of salt and an eye on Paula Barbieri, let's take a look at the trends affecting each of the various book categories.

Fiction

The odds for a first-time novelist are never good, but all sorts of first novels are published each year, some to great acclaim and greater profit.

The market for fiction is as good—and as bad—as it ever was. Fiction is a star-driven game; the John Grishams and Danielle Steels have become virtual brand names that publishers can count on to drive sales. An increasing dependency on this star system has created a classic chicken-and-egg scenario: Which comes first, the bestselling book or the bestselling author?

Every publisher worth its bottom line wants to publish Grishams and Steels. But there are only so many of these super authors to go around—and only so many publishers who can afford them. So, everyone is looking for the next Grisham, the next Steel. That's where you might just come in.

Hot Off the Press

Who is worth more than Stephen King? His long-time publisher, Viking, balked at a request for a mega-million-dollar advance and said, "No thanks." So Stephen King (and his agent) went shopping. He finally settled on Simon & Schuster for a much smaller advance and a greater share of the future profits. And with the stunning success of his e-book, his financial clout has risen even higher since then.

As you know from Chapter 2, "Write What?" the fiction market is divided into two general types: literary fiction and mainstream (or contemporary) fiction. The latter includes hardcover novels and genre fiction. Genre fiction includes mysteries, thrillers, science fiction, fantasies, romances, horror books, Westerns, and the like. What's selling in these categories?

Love Is a Many-Published Thing

The romance market is booming, and it's got the facts to prove it:

➤ Romances bring in roughly $900 million a year in sales.

➤ Nearly half (48.6 percent) of the paperbacks sold in the United States each year are romances.

➤ Some 1,800 romance novels are published each year.

➤ Faithful romance readers span the globe, including the new markets in China and Russia.

But, you might say, I couldn't write those bodice-rippers. Well, if you think that bodice-rippers are the only romances, think again. Today's romance genre is a versatile one. It encompasses many series, subgenres, and hybrids, as well as mainstream titles. Consider these subcategories, to name just a few: historical romance, time-travel romance, science fiction romance, romantic suspense, romantic mystery, inspirational romance, multicultural romance, and young-adult romance. Then there are the new, super-sexy romances.

And if you think that romance heroines are generously bosomed virgins looking for Mr. Right to carry them off into the sunset, think again. Today's romance heroines run the gamut from fresh-faced junior high school girls to divorced career women.

Experts Say

Aspiring romance writer Caroline Amneus says, "I never had to send for guidelines. Major romance publishers attend the romance conferences sponsored by Romance Writers of America and bring along copies of their guidelines. It's a great place to meet editors and agents and learn what they're looking for." For more information, call RWA headquarters at 281-440-6885.

Bookmarks

An **English cozy** is a type of mystery that typically takes place in England and follows a sweet old lady detective and a few of her doddering friends. They stumble onto a cold, dead body one afternoon, and the story unfolds from there. The term "cozy" comes either from the fact that you can settle in front of the fire for a cozy afternoon with one of these books, or from the tea cozy on the pot of Earl Grey you brew to drink while you read.

Get the Guidelines

If you'd like to cash in on this lucrative market, you'll have to do your homework. Don't write one single word without first consulting the guidelines from the publisher you plan to target, and without reading all the romance novels you can get your hands on.

Harlequin, Silhouette, Bantam, and other romance publishers happily provide writers with guidelines for their series. These guidelines are jammed with information on the exact word counts for their books, definitions of style, and level of sensuality permitted. They include lots of "absolute no-no's" and "absolute musts" as well as submission information. By following these rules, you'll save yourself lots of rewriting, and you'll greatly increase your chances of breaking into the romance field.

Love Writing About Love?

The one thing all romances have in common, from romantic suspense to mainstream historical, is that they are all stories about relationships. If you can write a love story that will move readers, this could be the field for you.

Thrill 'Em, Grill 'Em, and Kill 'Em

Mysteries, thrillers, and all their kin are more popular than ever, a fact that's readily confirmed by a quick glance at the bestseller list. At the time of this writing, four mysteries were on the *Publishers Weekly* hardcover bestseller list. The paperback list was even more impressive, with 8 of the top 15 slots going to these types of books. Such news reflects not only the immense popularity of these genres, but the versatility of them as well. From forensic thrillers to historical mysteries, with protagonists as different as Teddy Roosevelt (in *The Alienist*) to Navaho shaman/policeman Jim Chee (in Tony Hillerman's books), the mystery and thriller genres rival the romance category in both variety and readership.

Today's market is witnessing a boon in historical mysteries, medical thrillers, techno thrillers, and legal thrillers. But whether you're writing a hard-boiled detective story or an *English cozy,* it doesn't really matter. In these genres, there's plenty of room for your novel, regardless of which category it fits.

Hot Off the Press

What's hot in fiction, according to St. Martin's Press Senior Editor, Ruth Cavin, are great books. "There is no formula for a good book, so write what interests you and what you think is good," says Cavin, who has worked with most of the greatest names in mystery fiction. "Write characters you can believe in, plots that make you keep reading, settings and minor characters that are interesting." Cavin, who reviews "hundreds of submissions" every year, says, "There may be more competition in terms of numbers, but not in terms of quality. I'm looking for books that stand out because of the writing, plot, setting, or characters."

Nouveau Niche

The marketing types in publishing love nonfiction. Why? Because the nonfiction market is much more quantifiable—some would say more reliable—than the fiction market. Those marketers don't really know how many readers out there are going to want to read your coming-of-age novel, and they can't even begin to guess. But they can guess with slightly more accuracy how many of the nation's 38 million arthritis sufferers would be interested in *The Arthritis Cure,* or how the worldwide outpouring of grief for "the People's Princess" could translate into sales of *Diana: Her True Story: A Commemorative Edition.*

The same goes for all the trends—demographic and otherwise—that are reported in the media each day. Nonfiction publishers pay attention to what's hot, and (as we've told you before) if you want to succeed at nonfiction, you need to pay attention, too.

The Niche Is Riche

Identifying a niche in the marketplace and then publishing to that niche is called— you guessed it—niche publishing. Three of the most successful niche markets right now are alternative health, spirituality, and computers. All of these niches fill a need for readers.

As the world grows more technologically complex, all of us non-nerds need help keeping up. As people grow more disenchanted with conventional medicine, they're exploring alternative therapies.

And the Baby Boomer generation that once turned away from organized religion is now looking for spiritual guidance as they become more aware of their own mortality. A recent article in *The Wall Street Journal* noted that, in the same way Boomers changed giving birth (and sold vast numbers of *What to Expect When You're Expecting*), they are now changing death.

"Fine," you say, "but I don't know St. John's Wort from St. John the Baptist, and I don't know a thing about computers." No problem. There are myriad trends and niches to explore, from home-schooling to women's golf, from small business to eBay auctions. You don't even have to be an expert—you can always team up with one.

What's Cookin' with Cookbooks?

Long a staple of nonfiction publishing, the cookbook market has disappointed many publishers over the past couple years. "The cookbook field was overpublished," admits one long-time cookbook editor, who also reveals that many cookbook editors are looking for new jobs in new fields.

Despite this recent softening of the market, some cookbooks are finding favor with the public. "Editors say to me that superstar chefs are both overpublished and still selling," says cookbook agent Martha Casselman of Calistoga, California.

From her wine country office, Casselman is well-positioned to observe the industry trends. "Anything that ties into a product has a chance, like grilling, for instance." What does Casselman mean? Cookbooks with product or equipment ties might succeed because the publisher can persuade the manufacturer to purchase the book in bulk. Literary food writing is also still selling.

"It is hard for unknown cookbook writers to break in," Casselman admits. "But we still get excited when we see a good book."

The Publishing House at Pooh Corner

By definition, the children's market is a perennial one. Write for children, and you can build a body of work that will enchant the little ones generation after generation. But if you think that writing for children is easy, think again. To paraphrase beloved author of *A Wrinkle in Time,* Madeleine L'Engle, writing for children means writing stories too mature for adults.

L'Engle's point has been made quite clearly by the extraordinary success of the Harry Potter books. These charming books have made frequent appearances on both the children's *and* the adults' bestseller lists!

When you write for children, be it picture books or young adult novels, you can expect somewhat smaller advances. But with the potential of a lifetime of royalties as each generation of little folks discovers your writing, it's a much-anticipated legacy.

The children's market is as varied as the market for grown-ups. You have your pick of options, from picture books to young adult mysteries to middle-grade nonfiction.

Picture This

Picture books have been and remain this category's biggest sellers. The classic picture book is as popular as ever, but there is an increased interest in other types of picture books as well, most notably these types:

➤ Picture books made into baby board books (those little books whose pages are cardboard to make turning easier for little fingers)

➤ Picture books for slightly older toddlers

No Kidding About Kids' Fiction

Middle-grade and young adult books also offer writers a wealth of opportunity. Trends indicate a comeback for fantasy and historical fiction geared to this age group, even as the horror trend wanes. Sales of *Goosebumps* (the horror series that topped the children's bestseller lists for years) are down. But sales of *Animorphs,* the series featuring kids who morph into animals, are taking off.

Just the Facts, Ma'am

Nonfiction for children, particularly in the areas of science, technology, and biography, are staples of this market. If your writing can entertain as well as educate, this may be for you.

Slush Pile

Never send illustrations for your children's picture book with your manuscript unless you're a talented artist. Most publishers like to hire their own illustrators. Never mention the following in a query letter or proposal: "My niece (nephew, son, daughter, or next-door neighbor) is a wonderful artist whose work would really complete the book."

Experts Say

"I never intended to write a young adult novel," says Paula Munier Lee, author of *Emerald's Desire.* "But an editor who'd considered a mainstream novel that I wrote remembered me. When she took a new job as an editor for YA novels, she called me up and asked if I'd like to give it a try. As it turns out, I'm pretty good at it! I never did sell that other novel, but what the heck, it eventually got me a contract."

Market Savvy for Success

And how does knowing what's hot and what's not work in real life? Let's look more closely at the experience of two authors who found success by paying close attention to the marketplace.

Better Late Than Never

Nadine Crenshaw, author of 10 novels and 4 nonfiction books, wrote for more than a dozen years before she sold a book. During that period of time, she also wrote a column for her local newspaper, but she was bound and determined to become a novelist.

"I wrote eight novels before I wrote one I could sell," Crenshaw remembers. "It was a painful period." Eight novels is a lengthy apprenticeship. Looking back, Crenshaw believes that her publishing breakthrough need not have taken her so long. "I wrote those eight novels blind. As soon as I started writing with the market in mind, my apprenticeship was over."

What did she do? Exactly what we've advised in these last few chapters.

Crenshaw began to study the marketplace. She subscribed to *Publishers Weekly* and *Writer's Digest,* joined Romance Writers of America, and spent lots of time in bookstores familiarizing herself with the competition. Her efforts paid off: The next novel she wrote, *Mountain Mistress,* was published. That novel won the Romance Writers of America Golden Heart Award, and she went on to publish nine more historical romances.

The path to publishing has not always been smooth, however. After 10 years of writing historical romances, Crenshaw's market dried up. She turned back to her own market research. She wrote a few nonfiction books on trendy topics (Scully on *The X-Files* and *Xena, the Warrior Princess*) before turning back to fiction.

What has she chosen this time? A thriller. She plans to go on writing both fiction and nonfiction to ensure a steadier income. "Write what you want," says Crenshaw, "but write with the market in mind."

Homework

Author Mel Odom believes that writers make a big mistake by not paying attention to markets. "It doesn't matter whether you're writing fiction or nonfiction," says Odom, prolific author of some 60 fiction and nonfiction books in the past 10 years. "You need to do your homework. You have to study the type of book you want to write, as well as the market for that type of book. Take it apart and know it."

Odom attributes his prodigious output to his ability to analyze markets, genres, and trends—an ability that has given him the versatility to write in a number of categories, including action/adventure, science fiction, horror, young adult, children's books, computer books, how-to books, and even comic books!

Writers worried about slavishly following the market rather than their own hearts need not lose sleep at night. As Odom puts it: "Assimilate it and then do it your way."

The Early Bird ...

Keep your ear to the ground, and you can turn today's trends into tomorrow's best-sellers. But don't dawdle; when it comes to trends, the first writer to the marketplace usually wins.

The Least You Need to Know

➤ Publisher's predictions can be hit-or-miss, but certain trends bear watching.

➤ If you're writing romance, get publishers' guidelines first.

➤ Good-selling niches right now include alternative health, computer books, and spiritual books. But keep your antennae out for tomorrow's hot areas.

➤ Children's books can mean small advances but long-term sales.

➤ Put (almost) as much effort into your market research as into your writing.

Part 2

Gone with the Wind: Submitting to Publishers

So you've got an idea for a book—now what? Here's where you'll learn the actual process of putting together a book proposal. We'll clue you in on the common mistakes new writers make so that you can look like a pro on the page, right from the beginning!

From submitting professional query letters to compiling appealing proposals, these chapters explain what you need to get the attention of an agent or editor.

Both nonfiction and fiction proposals are covered in detail. You'll learn the ropes on how to do either (or both!).

Chapter 6

Submit What?

In This Chapter

➤ How the submission process works

➤ A day in the life of publishing

➤ Ten mistakes new writers make

➤ "Forward" and other foibles

➤ Looking like a pro on the page

Once you come up with an idea that you think is dynamite, what then? How do you move your book idea closer to becoming the finished thing? You must begin to submit.

Submit, you say? What's that? Simply stated, the submission process is the process by which you let the publishing world know that you have a great book available for publication.

Simply Submit

To get your book idea of a manuscript in front of the publishing decision-makers, you need to know how to make your way through the submissions process. This involves two important steps.

➤ **Important Step One:** The query letter

➤ **Important Step Two:** The book proposal

Bookmarks

The process by which a writer submits a book proposal or manuscript to a publisher is called **submission.** If the author is not using an agent, it is called an **unagented submission.** The initial contact between a writer and an agent comes in the form of a **query letter,** which is meant to spark interest in the project and prompt its recipient to ask for more material.

Bookmarks

The packet of information about the writer's manuscript or book idea is a **book proposal.** It contains a solid description of the book's purpose, the potential market for the book, its competition, and the author's credentials. The proposal also contains a complete table of contents, an extensive book outline, and at least one sample chapter.

Why is the submission process broken down into two steps? To see why this came to be, let's peek in on a typical day in the publishing world.

A Day in the Life of Book Publishing

It is early morning in Manhattan, and unbeknownst to each other, an assistant editor and a literary agent are sitting next to each other on the subway. The doors open, and the two hoist their heavy tote bags onto their shoulders and head for the same towering black skyscraper. The elevators deposit them on two different floors. After greeting colleagues, they settle into small offices with their first cups of weak office coffee. And for the next two hours, on two different floors, these two hard-working members of the New York publishing world lead oddly parallel lives. Both eye the fresh stack of mail perched on their desks, and both sigh when beginning the task of opening and reading the mail.

What comes in the mail every day? Query letters, book proposals, finished manuscripts, editorial correspondence, newspaper clippings, promotional information—there seems to be no end to the pieces of paper that must be read. Interrupting the ritual of reading the mail, the phone rings continuously.

This scene takes place simultaneously not only in the office of our unnamed assistant editor and faceless literary agent, but also in the offices of the senior editor, the editor-in-chief, the publisher, the associate editor, and even the new college intern. Let's face it—everybody wants to write a book, and everybody writes to people in publishing. So how do publishers, editors, and agents handle all this mail?

Query letters, that's how.

Quantum Query

A query letter is a simple, one-page letter. In the letter, the purpose of the book is described, and the author makes a short case for why the world needs this book.

If the contents of the query letter pique the interest of the recipient, that recipient requests a proposal. If the proposal is good and the book-to-be is deemed marketable, a publisher offers a contract.

But why can't you send your entire book? Because in most cases, the harried fold in publishing haven't met you and don't know about your project. You need to try to get their attention in the easiest and fastest way possible. A query letter is the correspondence equivalent of tapping a stranger on the shoulder and saying, "Excuse me, do you have a minute to talk?"

Sound intimidating? Don't worry. We'll show you how to write a top-notch query letter that will help your project stand out. We'll also tell you how to put together a bulletproof book proposal that will knock the socks off everyone who sees it.

Hot Off the Press

Dallas-based literary agent Jan Miller has been called the Queen of Self-Help. In 1996, her agency's revenues surpassed $12 million. Clients include Stephen Covey, author of *The Seven Habits of Highly Successful People,* and Susan Powter, author of *Stop the Insanity.* According to the *Dallas Business Journal,* Miller receives 800 unsolicited manuscripts a month. Is Jan Miller the agent for you? Here's what she looks for in clients: "A personality with celebrity potential; a marketing mechanism outside normal bookstore channels (such as infomercials, seminars, or consumer products); and a personal story of overcoming adversity and a life-transforming message that could be easily packaged for talk shows and advertising." Do you have what it takes to get her attention?

But Before We Begin ...

We've seen it all. We've read thousands of query letters and book proposals. Don't make the mistakes others have. Here you'll learn the things that you must avoid, the no-no's that will brand you as an amateur. Read them, and believe them. Commit them to memory before moving on to the next two chapters. The publishing world has rules, and you've got to follow them to get people to look at your stuff.

Co-author Jennifer recently received a large package from someone she met at a writers' conference. Thankfully, it did not arrive postage due, but his letter began, "Although all the books I've read tell me to send just a query letter first, I've decided to take a different approach and send a complete manuscript of the book." Arrgh!

Experts Say

"I can always spot an amateur," says longtime agent Martha Casselman. "Instead of trying to sell me on an idea, the letter brags about the fact that she has obtained a copyright for her work, and proudly gives me the copyright date and number. What does that mean to me? Nothing. Tell me about your book; don't tell me about your housekeeping details."

Not only did this fellow come off as arrogant, but he also signaled that he is not someone who follows the rules. What agent or editor wants to sign someone who clearly doesn't take direction? Not many.

And what happened to the package Jennifer received? She sent it right back, unread.

Top Ten Mistakes New Writers Make

If you take the following list to heart, you won't repeat that faux pas or others that raise red flags. Here are the few simple no-no's that can easily undermine all your hard work:

➤ Letters that contain a misspelled name

➤ Packages or letters with postage due

➤ Letters printed with outdated equipment

➤ Query letters that don't quickly come to the point

➤ Proposals that criticize other books

➤ Letters that are too flip or amusing in tone

➤ Queries that say, "All of my friends think this is a great idea"

➤ Proposals that smell like cigarette smoke

➤ Queries that mention the minimum advance the writer will accept

➤ Proposals that arrive in a package filled with shredded paper

Letters That Contain a Misspelled Name

How hard is it to call and check the spelling of someone's name? Why brand yourself a careless writer before the package is even open? A simple phone call helps you to show that you are serious about getting things right. Don't assume that what is prin-ted in a professional directory is right. For many years Jennifer's name was misspelled in a major writers' guide.

Package or Letter Arrives Postage Due

You look careless and irresponsible from the moment your material arrives if your package requires postage due. Another way to annoy your recipient is to send a package laden with little slips of paper that need to be signed to prove that it arrived. Remember, you are sending something that, under most circumstances, this person did not request.

Author Uses Outdated Equipment

Avoid using a typewriter, a dot matrix printer, or other out-dated equipment at all costs. Sounds harsh, doesn't it? But using outdated equipment signals that both you and your ideas are old-fashioned and behind the times. Can't afford the fancy stuff? Just go to one of the retail places that rents computer time and use a better computer system. You need to look as good as you can on the page. (And this means checking to make sure that your printer cartridge is fresh enough to print nice and dark.)

Letters That Don't Quickly Come to the Point

By "quickly," we mean in the first paragraph or two. Why is this so important? Remember our typical day in publishing? The one in which the agent and editor's desks were piled with mail? We didn't tell you about the blinking light on the phone message machines or all the other things that needed doing that day. Time and attention are short. You need to get to the point.

Proposals That Criticize Other Books

This is a major gripe of editors. You worked hard to put together a book proposal, and your agent spent a lot of time deciding which editors should be approached with it. So why annoy the very editor that you are hoping to impress?

"The author should never use the competitive analysis section to slam other books—chances are, publishers who published those books will be reading the author's proposal," says Laurie Abkemeir. As the former senior editor at Hyperion, she should know. "Also, many times the books that are being slammed are books that were huge successes. It doesn't make sense to slam something that was a big bestseller, but many authors do." Chapter 8, "Bulletproof Nonfiction Book Proposals," explains how to position your book in a positive light without making enemies.

Letters That Are Too Flip or Amusing

A query letter is not a letter to a friend, your mom, or a long-lost chum. This is no time to be silly. Even if friends think you're the next Seinfeld, it is safer to write a straightforward, businesslike letter. Humor can easily work against you. So can arrogance, boasting, or conceit. How can you impress an agent if you can't boast about your accomplishments? Be confident, not arrogant. Don't worry—in the next chapter, you'll learn how to do this.

Queries That Mention Your Fan Club

Don't ever write, "All of my friends and relatives think this is a good idea." Book publishing is a business. And professionals in the book business aren't interested in hearing about your friends and relatives (unless they are famous friends and relatives who will be endorsing your book). They want to know about markets and demographics and national publicity.

Proposals That Smell Like Cigarette Smoke

Hey, go ahead and smoke. But don't send off a query letter or proposal that will make your target's eyes swim from the tobacco fumes. If you smoke, you probably don't notice it, but take our word for it: Smokers send letters that smell like smoke. So just to be sure, take your disk over to Kinko's and print out your work in a smoke-free environment. Does this seem like petty advice to you? Yes. But remember, you want these publishing people to like you and your project. You need to use every little method you can to woo them.

Slush Pile

Still devoted to using the same old typewriter you had in grad school? Go ahead and type to your heart's content, but don't use it for queries or proposals. It sends the wrong signal to the folks who make the publishing decisions. In today's publishing environment, you'll look like a hobbyist—or at the very least, a bit of a nut. Borrow a friend's computer, or rent one.

Letters That Mention a Minimum Advance

Letters that mention the minimum advance the writer will accept or the phrase "resources needed to complete this project" expose you as a beginner. Like writers who are paranoid that someone might steal their ideas, this is the mark of an amateur. Never mention money in a query letter. Never mention money in a book proposal. When considering whether to pursue a book idea, agents and editors don't care what kind of "resources" are needed to complete your project. That's your problem, not theirs. Sooner or later the topic of money will come up, but let them mention it first, not you.

Proposals That Are Buried in Shredded Paper

You want these publishing folks to be in a pleasant mood when they're reading your material. But years of experience in opening packages has taught us that there is no way to open one of these types of packages without getting a lapful (or noseful) or shredded paper. Maddening! You want someone to love your project. Don't risk ticking them off before they can get to it.

Can't find a padded envelope that doesn't have that shredded paper stuff in it? If your proposal doesn't fit in a FedEx letter-sized envelope, it's probably too darn long. And a query letter that doesn't slip right into a regular envelope is definitely too long.

"Forward" and Other Foibles

The world of book publishing is a peculiar place with peculiar rules, and it's frequently filled with peculiar people.

Even if you have learned all that you can from the many books you've read, the courses and seminars you've attended, and the writers you know, there are still tiny mistakes that only persnickety publishing people will notice.

Here's the big one: forward vs. foreword.

Look up these two words in your dictionary. Here's what ours says:

> **forward** (adj.) directed or moving toward the front, situated in front

So if the President of the United States has agreed to write something nice for the front of your book, you think, it must be a forward. These are introductory remarks situated in front of your book, so it would seem perfectly logical.

But no! The president is writing a *foreword,* not a *forward,* for your book.

> **foreword** (n.) introductory remarks at the beginning of the book, usually by someone other than the author

Even longtime authors make this mistake sometimes, and persnickety publishing people feel very smug when they spot it.

As long as the dictionary is out, let's tackle two more confusing words.

> **which** (adj. & pronoun) what particular one or ones of a set of things or people

> **that** (adj. & pronoun) the person or thing referred to or pointed to or understood

Co-author Sheree spends a great deal of her time combing through her clients' proposals changing *which* to *that.* What's the rule? If *that* works, use it.

Look Like a Pro on the Page

If you've got a computer, no doubt it's loaded with the latest tricks. This is not the time to use them. Query letters and book proposals are not the right place to show off your fancy fonts and graphics capability. Use a basic font, such as Times New Roman or Courier. Skip the shaded boxes, the cartoons, and the artistic borders. Keep it plain.

Plain is also the order of the day for paper. Don't send off a query letter on scented paper, fancy marbled paper, or anything other than plain white, businesslike stock. And don't get fancy with the inks. Use plain black ink, please.

Now Where Should I Send It?

With all this talk of submitting, to whom shall you submit? It's a reasonable question. Sometimes writers submit their stuff to an agent, who decides to represent them.

The agent then submits the writer's material to an editor. Other times a writer just goes ahead and submits to an editor. So what do we think that you should do?

If you plan to write a book with broad national appeal, we think that you should first try to get an agent. (More about agents will come in the following chapters—particularly Chapter 10, "What's an Agent For, Anyway?") If that doesn't work, you should try to submit directly.

In the next two chapters, we discuss query letters and book proposals. It is our aim to help you prepare these materials in such a way to interest an agent. And if you can't? We'll cross that bridge when we come to it, in Chapter 13, "Submitting Without an Agent."

The Least You Need to Know

➤ There is a well-defined process for submitting your materials: Submit a query letter and then, if requested, a book proposal.

➤ Follow the rules, or you risk looking like an amateur—or, worse, a difficult author to work with.

➤ Careless errors in query letters or book proposals can undermine your other efforts.

➤ If you are writing a book with a large potential audience, try first to get an agent to represent you.

Chapter 7

Query Letters That Sell Nonfiction

In This Chapter

➤ Query? What's that you say?

➤ But I can't say it all in one page!

➤ Why does this have to be perfect?

➤ An agent's five pet peeves

➤ Hook 'em early

➤ Can't I just phone?

Now that we've frightened you into thinking that your entire publishing career rests on a single typed query letter, how can we calm you down? By telling you this: The formula for writing successful query letters can be learned, and your lessons begin now.

This chapter tackles query letters for nonfiction books. Novelists, your turn comes up soon, in Chapter 9, "Fun with Fiction." We do, however, urge you to keep reading this chapter, too.

Although you learned the basic idea behind a query letter in the last chapter, it bears repeating: The query letter is your first contact with either an agent or an editor. It is your calling card, your way of introducing yourself and your book idea to the publishing world at large.

Query? What's That You Say?

A successful query letter should contain the following items:

➤ A brief description of the book

➤ A brief description of the market for the book

➤ A brief description of the author

Brief? Just how brief are we talking here?

But I Can't Say It All in One Page!

One page, that's how brief. Your query letter should never, ever be longer than one page. You need to distill your brilliance, your wisdom, and your expertise into one potent page-long brew that will leave a reader reeling from its power.

Here is a quick exercise to help you distill that brew:

➤ Sit down with one blank page of paper.

➤ Write out a two-paragraph description of the book.

➤ Write out a two-paragraph description of the market for the book.

➤ Write out a two-paragraph description of yourself, the author of the book.

Okay, now pretend you are Ernest Hemingway. No, you don't have to run in front of a herd of bulls; all we want you to do is simplify your writing. Take a hard look at what you have written, and start cutting out extra words. Make two long sentences into one sentence of medium length. Get rid of adjectives. Turn two wordy paragraphs into one punchy paragraph.

Here is an example of a Hemingway-esque transformation.

About the Author, Take One

This is the first draft of the bio.

> Jennifer Basye Sander entered publishing as a way to escape a failed career in California politics. Her first book was published in 1983, *The Sacramento Women's Yellow Pages,* a directory of woman-owned businesses. She worked for several years as a book buyer for a small, independent northern California bookstore chain before becoming an acquisitions editor for a nonfiction publisher.
>
> As an editor, Jennifer worked with many bestselling authors, including Mary Kay Ash of Mary Kay Cosmetics, and award-winning writers such as the James Beard and IACP Award–winning food writer Elaine Corn. As an author,

Jennifer's own books range in topic from travel (*The Air Courier's Handbook*) to small business (*101 Best Extra Income Opportunities for Women*) to inspiration (*Christmas Miracles*). Her most recent book, *Christmas Miracles,* was a seasonal bestseller. Since the spring of 1997, Jennifer has operated her own book packaging company, Big City Books, in Granite Bay, California.

About the Author, Take Two

After a short consultation with Mr. Hemingway, we now give you the revised paragraph.

Jennifer Basye Sander first entered publishing in 1983 with the publication of her book *The Sacramento Women's Yellow Pages.* Her early success with that book led to a career in publishing that includes both a short stint as a book buyer and many years as an acquisitions editor. She worked with several bestselling authors and has herself authored six books, including the recent bestseller *Christmas Miracles.* Now a book packager, she lives in Granite Bay, California.

Get the idea? Write as much as you want, and then go back and delete most of it. (Don't really throw it away, though; you'll need the long stuff for your proposal.) Keep the good stuff that sells you and your book.

About the Book, Take One

Let's see how that works with a description of a book. Here is a two-paragraph description of our imaginary book *Accurate Arthritis Answers:*

Accurate Arthritis Answers is a unique idea. Instead of relying on the advice of just one arthritis doctor, I plan to seek out advice from top arthritis experts around the world. Research schools, government studies, magazine and newspaper articles, and medical journals will all be scoured to cull the latest information on arthritis. Arthritis sufferers will learn about cutting-edge medical treatments, the dramatic difference that exercise can have, and the effects of nutrition upon their affliction. Special attention will be paid to recent discoveries in alternative treatments, such as herbal therapy.

The book itself is divided into four different sections: Traditional Medicine, Nutrition, Exercise, and Alternative Therapies. Each section is written by a top expert in the field. Organized in an easy-to-understand style, *Accurate Arthritis Answers* will also contain colorful charts, illustrations, and a useful medical glossary. At 175 pages, the book will be a small and handy size for the lay reader.

About the Book, Take Two

Okay, how do we say that in one short, punchy paragraph? Like this:

> *Accurate Arthritis Answers* fills a real need in the marketplace. Unlike other large medical books, it is a short, easy-to-read book for the general reader. Instead of relying on the knowledge of just one doctor, it brings together the expertise of a wide range of international experts in the field. All types of treatments are examined, from the traditional medical approach to the latest research in herbal and other nontraditional remedies. Arthritis sufferers will now be able to turn to one single source for all the latest information.

Slush Pile

A query letter is not the place to mention your past bad experiences with agents, editors, or publishers. "I just got a query letter that began 'I've had it with agents!'" says literary agent Bill Adler Jr. "Why on earth would I want to take that person on as a client?" Even if you have had crummy experiences, keep them to yourself. You risk branding yourself as a troublemaker from the start.

Writer, Edit Thyself

Go ahead, give this exercise a try. Start writing long descriptions of your book, your market, and yourself. Then shrink them down to query size. You'll quickly learn to spot what needs to stay and what needs to go.

A one-page query letter does have more than three paragraphs sometimes. What is your strongest area? Your credentials, your book idea, or the potential market? Choose your strength and devote two entire paragraphs to it.

Why does your query letter have to be perfect? A well-written query letter is your best shot at seeing your book published. So work on it, over and over again, until it looks right to you. This is not the time to dash off a quick little something. This is the time to set aside a week to perfect your query letter.

What Not to Say

Agent Martha Casselman is not alone in her pet peeves. Here are five things she (and most other agents) don't want you to put in your query letter:

➤ The kind of computer program you write in (it doesn't really matter)

➤ That this is an exclusive submission if it really isn't (don't lie)

➤ Asking after her health and happiness (she wants to know more about you)

➤ How well you can write (show her how well you can write)

➤ Stating that if an editor doesn't want this particular project, you'd be happy to write anything he or she wants (you're writing to demonstrate your knowledge and your talent, not your flexibility)

Hook 'Em Early

The best query letters have a strong hook in the first two lines. What is a strong hook? Something that grabs the readers' attention and keeps them reading. Let's look at a good example, a query letter that co-author Sheree received:

> Dear Sheree,
>
> More than 2.2 million families in the United States are affected by death every year—6,027 each day.
>
> Studies reveal that more than 90 percent of the survivors of a death in the family are unprepared to handle the heavy responsibilities that arise when a death occurs.
>
> What do you do first? And then what? How do you cope with the hundreds of urgent decisions and details to be handled in the difficult days and weeks ahead?
>
> People don't know what to do, and—just as unsettling—they don't know how to behave in the face of death. When death comes, the survivors must not only cope with their grief, but at the same time organize an event of great significance emotionally, socially, and financially. They urgently need help.
>
> *Saying Goodbye with Love* is the only step-by-step workbook for survivors who are responsible for handling the practical, legal, and financial decisions after a death in the family. This book is not a dense, sociological treatise as are so many books on death. Instead, *Saying Goodbye with Love* is a warm and well-organized "tool kit" for use in a time of crisis.
>
> The first question people ask me when they learn of this book is: "Did this book come from your own experiences?" The answer is "Yes." Most of all, it comes from looking after the details following the deaths of my grandmother, Jenny; my friend, Paul; my cousin, Bob; and my sister, Toni. My experience as a technical writer taught me to organize information in a way that is easily accessible and useful to the reader.
>
> Readers have told me that *Saying Goodbye with Love* is like having a knowledgeable, organized friend at their side.
>
> Would you like to see a proposal? I've included an SASE. I look forward to your response by phone, fax, mail, or e-mail.
>
> Yours truly,
>
> Sheila (Simpson) Martin

Great letter. Sheree picked up the phone and called her right away. Why? Let's take a closer look at this query letter:

➤ In her first few paragraphs, the writer established a huge market for her book (more than 2.2 million families a year, 6,027 a day), and a big need for her book ("people don't know what to do …").

➤ She describes the book itself ("the only step-by-step workbook for survivors") in one short paragraph.

➤ When describing her own credentials, she takes what could have been a draw-back (no professional experience with medicine or grief counseling) and puts a very positive spin on it by first mentioning her own personal experiences with death and then tying in her background ("My experience as a technical writer taught me to …").

It all pulls together into a very effective query letter that grabbed an agent's attention. It also grabbed a publisher's attention; Sheree sold the project to The Crossroads Publishing Company.

Another Approach

Here is another good approach for a query letter to an agent:

Experts Say

"Here are the three things I look for in a query letter," says literary agent Bill Adler Jr., based in Washington, D.C. "One, that the writer can write. Two, that she understands her market. Three, that she is professional in her approach to me." Don't be overly familiar in your query letter. You are not writing to a long-lost college buddy. You are trying to interest a professional literary agent or editor in taking you on as a client. Use a businesslike tone in your writing.

Dear Bill,

Ummm, chocolate. The bad news is it can't make you thin. The good news is it could make you rich!

In several bestselling financial planning books, Peter Lynch has urged Americans to become better stock pickers by using what he calls "The Power of Common Knowledge" and simply paying attention to what goes on in their own neighborhood. As a long-time stockbroker and financial planner, I have taken Lynch's theory one step closer to home by advising chocolate lovers to simply walk around their kitchens, peek into their refrigerators, and look closely at vending machines for terrific investment ideas!

Chocolate Can Make You Rich: The Chocolate Lover's Guide to the Stock Market will give investors a whole new way of looking at the stock market. Forget "Blue Chip" stocks; think "Chocolate Chip" stocks instead! Chocolate cookies, cakes, candies, drinks, and more—Americans literally do eat chocolate by the ton. What stronger, more stable market can there be? When I give speeches, I like to tell my audience it's time they put their money where their mouth is!

Many investors—particularly women—are scared off by high-tech stocks in industries that they don't understand. With the knowledge gained in *Chocolate Can Make You Rich,* shy, first-time investors could invest in solid megacompanies such as Procter & Gamble (who make the Duncan Hines brand of cake and brownie mixes), Hershey Foods (Reese's Peanut Butter Cups, York Mint Patties, and their own Hershey's brand), or Archer Daniels Midland (corn syrup producers, without which candy bars would cease to exist). More adventurous investors will learn about Starbucks Coffee (now not only the kings of coffee, but leading ice cream makers as well) or Eskimo Pies (yes, a publicly traded company!).

I have been a stockbroker for the past 10 years, ever since graduating from UC Berkeley with a degree in business. I developed my theories about "comfort stocks" as a way to make women feel more comfortable with investing, and I would like to bring my message to greater numbers of readers.

A 30-page proposal is available for *Chocolate Can Make You Rich.* Chapters include "Frozen Assets," "Sugar-Coated Investments," "Eat and Grow Rich," and many more. I look forward to hearing from you soon.

Regards,

Julia Berenson

"Ummm, chocolate." Now there's a delicious hook! Kept you reading, didn't it?

Chocolate can make you rich? Sounds like a goofy idea, so the writer's second paragraph wisely links her idea to those of perennial bestselling author Peter Lynch—a smart way to look even smarter.

She quickly describes the book and the theory, and establishes herself as qualified (a stockbroker for 10 years and public speaker) to write on this topic. By describing the names of some of her chapters, she whets the readers' appetite for more. It's a good letter.

Experts Say

Robert Kosberg is known as Hollywood's "Mr. Pitch." He pitches 20 to 50 ideas a year to studio heads. What can you learn from him for your book pitch? "Ask yourself if your idea can be boiled down to two power-packed sentences that generate excitement." Look for more ideas on his Web site at www.moviepitch.com.

Write a Good One and Then Let It Be

Go ahead and write that query letter—as perfect a letter as you can make it. But once you drop it in the mail, leave it alone. Believe it or not, many authors out there can't leave it alone even after mailing it.

Agents and editors have all received them, the letters that begin, "Please disregard the query letter that I mailed to you on January 22, and replace it with this version, which I think more accurately captures the essence of my book." Or, "This information should be added to the proposal that I sent to you last week. Please remove pages 4 through 8 and replace them with these new pages." Crazy, but true.

Do not under any circumstances attempt to do this! Once your query letter disappears through the slot in the mailbox, move on to something else in your life. Don't lie awake at night wondering how you might have done it differently. It will just drive you nuts.

Online Etiquette

As in other parts of the world, publishing is going online. And although online queries would have been strange just a few years ago, they are becoming more acceptable. Agent Bill Adler Jr. enjoys receiving online queries from prospective authors. It gives him a good chance to answer back quickly and not make writers wait for weeks for him to open the mail. Sheree, on the other hand, doesn't care much for lengthy online queries.

Each agent has his own policy, of course. The major guides to agents, such as Jeff Herman's *Writer's Guide to Book Editors, Publishers, and Literary Agents,* have only a few e-mail addresses listed now, but as the years go by, expect to see more of them. It is worth typing an agent's name into your search engine—some even have home pages. Sheree's Web site, at shereebee.com, was designed to help writers.

Bookmarks

What is an **SASE?** It's short for a "self-addressed, stamped envelope." Never send a query letter or proposal without one. The publishing industry would go broke if editors had to pay to return all the unsolicited material they receive. If you haven't included an SASE and the agent or editor isn't interested, your stuff goes straight into the recycling bin. Harsh, but true.

The nice thing about an e-mail query is that you won't have to worry about choosing the wrong kind of envelope!

SASEs and Other Ways to Hear Back

Remember the definition of "unsolicited submission"? It's one that the agent did not ask you to send. Because you are sending something that was not requested, it is up to you to cover the cost of getting a reply. Always include an *SASE* with your correspondence. That way the agent can easily reply.

If you want to know whether your query arrived at its destination, include a small, self-addressed and stamped postcard that the agent can just pop into the mail. Write something like this:

Yes, the attached query letter was received in my office on _____ .

You can also send your query letter via FedEx or UPS. This is more expensive than the good old U.S. mail, but it also lets you track your letter and ease your mind about whether it ever arrived. (Two-day express mail is considerably less costly than next-day air.)

Do not call an agent's office to ask whether your query letter arrived. You will appear anxious and unprofessional.

But They Asked for It!

You met an agent at a writer's summer camp who encouraged you to send your proposal? Congratulations. But please don't assume that the agent remembers the invitation. Remind him in the first line of your query letter: "We met at the Mendocino Writer's Conference, and you asked that I send the following proposal." An agent might meet a hundred writers at conferences throughout the year (and talk to another hundred on the phone). So don't be hurt if he doesn't remember you or your book. And don't forget to include an SASE with your query.

Bookmarks

As in most businesses, assistants make the world go 'round. **Assistants** are the unsung young folks who open the mail, sort the mail, answer the phone, and otherwise keep an office running. Chances are, your query will be seen first by someone's assistant. Editorial assistants, literary agents' assistants, production assistants—be nice to them all. Today's assistant may be tomorrow's editor-in-chief.

The Rules

Now that we have given you the rules, please believe us when we say it is in your best interest to follow them. If you try to get around them, if you try things that you think are clever or devious, it can backfire. At the very least, an agent might think you are annoying. In the worst-case scenario, you could come off as a nut—and agents are not very eager to sign up nuts! Let them know that you have done your homework, that you know how the routine works, and that you will follow the rules.

Having said that, we must confess that sometimes people do break the rules and succeed because of it. And sometimes people win the lottery. But as a first-time writer, you improve your chances tremendously by playing it straight.

The Least You Need to Know

➤ Query letters should be one page long and should contain a brief description of the book, the market, and the author.

➤ Practice being brief by editing your writing down to one powerful paragraph.

➤ Don't use a query letter to air your grievances with anyone.

➤ Unless you include an SASE with your query letter, you might never hear an answer.

➤ A good query letter states its purpose up front in the first paragraph.

➤ Be businesslike. Don't try to be clever or witty; don't use scented paper or fancy typestyles.

Chapter 8

Bulletproof Nonfiction Book Proposals

In This Chapter

➤ What goes into a book proposal

➤ Building a book proposal, step by step

➤ Selling your idea

➤ Selling your market

➤ Selling yourself as an author

➤ Choosing the best sample chapter

Congratulations! You wrote a great query letter, and an agent or editor has asked to see your book proposal! Uh, now what do you do?

The Art of Proposal Writing

In a book proposal, you are proposing an idea for a book. You *propose* to do it because, in most cases, you haven't actually written the book yet!

You Mean I Don't Have to Write the Book First?

We'd like to let you in on an industry secret. Here is how most professional nonfiction writers work:

➤ First, they come up with an idea for a book.

➤ Next, they write a book proposal 20 or so pages long.

➤ Then they send it off to their agent and wait.

If a publisher decides to publish the book, the writer sits down in front of the computer and writes the book. But if there are no takers, the professional writer comes up with another idea and starts the process over again.

That's right. To sell a nonfiction book and get a contract from a publisher, you don't really have to write the book first. You can write it later. First, you have to write a good proposal.

But When Should I Start the Proposal?

Don't even think about querying agents or editors until you have written at least some portion of your book proposal. Not only will it give you a more solid sense of what you are doing (and help you distill it into a good query), but it also cuts down on the lag time between when an agent or editor says, "I'd love to see your stuff," and when you can actually send it. So get a jump on things and start now.

Hot Off the Press

It's hard to keep a secret in the publishing world. But that is exactly what happened when Trevor Rees-Jones, the lone survivor of the crash that killed Princess Di, began shopping his book proposal several years after her death. Publishing executives were invited to a London hotel and made to sign a confidentiality agreement. They also were not allowed to take the proposal out of the room. Once Little, Brown became the publisher, the topic of the book was even concealed from its own sales force until just before the book's release.

Building a Book Proposal

Here's a short list of what you should include in your book proposal. It'll give you a quick overview. Then read on for a longer description of each key element. If you have trouble understanding any elements, don't panic. In the back of the book, there's an entire sample book proposal for you to read.

Read through this list once, and then sit down and begin to write your own version. A book proposal should develop before your very eyes.

The parts of a book proposal are as follows:

➤ A cover page with the title, your name, your address, and your phone number

➤ A three- to five-part pitch

➤ A detailed table of contents

➤ A sample chapter of the book

➤ Attachments such as recent news articles about the topic, or recent news articles about the author

Your Cover Page

This is a great first step. It takes only about five minutes to do it, and once you have made a cover page, you can consider yourself on the road to building a book proposal. Flip to Appendix C, "Sample Proposals: *Christmas Miracles* and *The Quotable Businesswoman*," in the back of the book and take a look at the cover page for the *Christmas Miracles* book proposal. Follow that same basic design, and fill in your own title, name, and address.

If you are sending off the proposal to an agent who requested it, put your name and address on the cover page. Once you have an agent and she is shopping your book to editors, she'll put her own name and address on your proposal's cover page.

After you've made a cover page, print it out and hang it on the wall next to your computer. Whenever you are feeling discouraged, glance up and see your title and your name in large type!

The Pitch

Ever heard the sales term "pitch"? In a book proposal, you are trying to pitch a book idea. The pitch section of the proposal can be broken down into five smaller parts:

➤ The idea

➤ The market

➤ The competition

➤ The publicity and promotion potential

➤ The author

Slush Pile

Remember how businesslike your query letters should be? A book proposal should be equally businesslike in appearance—no fancy graphics, colored paper, or elaborate typestyles. Your writing skills are on display here, nothing else.

Bookmarks

Be prepared to answer the question, "What is the overview of your book?" An **overview** is another term for the synopsis. In the movie business, they call it a "take-away." What will your reader take away with him after reading the book? Write it out in one succinct sentence.

Remember all that work you did while writing your query? Those long paragraphs describing the book idea, the market, and the author? Pull them out now and see what you can use.

What a Great Idea!

First, describe the idea behind the book. What kind of a book is it? What kind of information will it contain? Describe your book in one tight sentence, and then elaborate on the idea for several paragraphs. Co-author Sheree tells her clients that this is their chance to describe the contents of their book "enticingly and thoroughly."

Off to Market

Now describe the market for your book. Who are the millions of potential readers? Why will they be interested in your book? The market section should contain as much hard data about demographics, trends, and other facts as you can get your hands on. Remember to avoid using the sentence "Everyone should read this book."

The market section of your proposal could also contain information about possible nonbookstore outlets for your book. Where will these millions of potential readers be found? In gardening stores, lingerie shops, or hospitals? Let the publisher know if there are specialized sources of distribution that target these folks.

Compete with the Best

This is an easy section to write. As a matter of fact, you've already done much of the work. You've spent hours wandering the aisles of your local bookstore. At last you get to display the knowledge you gained!

To create the competition section, list all the books already published with which your book will compete. The purpose of this section is to establish that you know what else has been done in your area and that you believe your book fills a need that exists. Describe these books at length, but also be fair and balanced in assessing what you perceive to be their weaknesses. Do not attack. Remember the advice of former

Bookmarks

Some folks out there are known as **proposal doctors,** also known as book doctors. You can hire one of them to help you write your proposal. Mostly former editors or longtime writers, you will see their advertisements in the back of writers' magazines. You might also ask an agent for a recommendation.

Bookmarks

Publishers love **demographics.** Publishing is an inexact science, and the more an author can cite demographics about population statistics, the size of an age group, or personal income levels when describing the potential audience for his book, the better the agent, editor, and publisher can sleep at night.

Hyperion senior editor Laurie Abkemeier from Chapter 6, "Submit What?" Never use the competition section to slam other books. You never know who will end up reading your book proposal!

A secondary purpose of the competition section is to highlight books that, instead of competing with your proposed book, complement it. Complementary books can help you establish that a book like yours will succeed. Flip to the sample proposal in the back of this book to see how this works. Check out the section that begins: "Books that are not directly targeted toward the Christmas market, but that display the public's strong interest in miracles and in spiritually uplifting stories are ...." This helps you to use the success of other books to build your case.

Bookmarks

What's the difference between **publicity** and **promotion?** The two words sometimes seem to be interchangeable. The bottom line is—the bottom line! Publicity is free. Promotion (which can mean advertising) usually costs money.

La Publicité

The publicity and promotion section is of critical importance in today's publishing market. All publishers want to know how hard the author plans to work, how many media contacts the author already has, and whether this topic lends itself to publicity and promotion. So, the more you can supply here, the better. How do you find this stuff out? By paying attention to how often the media writes about your topic or about the audience that your book targets.

Publicity Opportunities

Using *Accurate Arthritis Answers* as an example, quickly come up with some of the different places that this book could get publicity:

➤ National magazines targeted to older Americans (such as *Modern Maturity*), and the national network of small newspapers for seniors

➤ The morning news shows, such as *Today* and *Good Morning, America,* which frequently devote time to issues of health

➤ Nationally syndicated radio health shows, which are growing in popularity

➤ Health editors at all major newspapers and magazines

➤ Newsletters in retirement communities, such as the various Sun City communities around the country

Is It Especially Timely?

Are there special times of the year when your book could be promoted? Talk about the potential for gift or seasonal promotions. Is there any major event (such as an upcoming election, or a hot new movie) that your book ties into? Mention it.

Bulk Sales?

This is also a good place to mention any possibilities you see for large sales of the book to groups, businesses, and organizations. Publishers are very interested in pursuing large, nonreturnable sales. Using the arthritis book again, here's how you could say it in a proposal:

> The pharmaceutical manufacturer behind one of the major drugs used to treat arthritis has expressed a willingness to purchase 2,500 copies of *Accurate Arthritis Answers* to use as a premium. The author also intends to seek out other large group purchases for the book.

If you already have a solid commitment for a large buy for your book, be sure to mention it. If you plan to buy a large number of the books yourself (to give away to clients or sell at speeches), mention that also. Publishers are interested in protecting their investment, and this kind of information could help tip the balance in your favor.

A Stamp of Approval

Have you approached any big-name authors or professionals who are willing to give you endorsements for your book? Let the publishers know who you plan to approach, and if you have existing ties with these folks. Deepak Chopra is your brother-in-law? Colin Powell lives next door? Write it down! If you do have close personal or professional ties to big-name folks, approach them now. It is even better to have an endorsement in hand when you are in the proposal stage. This, too, could help tip the balance in your favor.

Let's Hear About You!

Finally, you'll need to include information about you, the author. Here's where you can really let loose and brag about what you have accomplished in life: awards, honors, education, experience—pile it on. Let everyone know about your writing experience, publishing history (if you have one), and professional success. Do you have local, statewide, or national recognition in your field? Talk about it here. Try to position yourself as someone uniquely qualified to write this book.

Are you a skilled public speaker or presenter? Do you hold seminars or classes that relate to your book? The publisher needs to be reassured that you are not only a qualified author, but that you can also be an effective public image for the book.

Now that you understand everything that goes into the pitch section of your proposal, you're ready to move on to the other sections.

Detailed Table of Contents

That's right, you'll need to include a detailed table of contents. Not only should you list each and every chapter, you also should include a short paragraph to describe each chapter or section. This is sometimes referred to as a chapter summary. Describe not only the purpose of each chapter, but also some of the content.

Sample Chapters

Including a good representative sample chapter is important. Not only is the writing itself important, but so is the topic. A well-chosen sample chapter can be a powerful thing. Just as the query letter was a way of introducing yourself to a stranger (and presenting yourself in the best possible light), so too is the sample chapter. It gives you the opportunity to influence the way you are perceived. It's important that the chapter you include is representative of the rest of the book in style, content, and length. It's not unusual to include Chapter 1, but if Chapter 1 is not representative, replace it with one that is. Better yet, include Chapter 1 plus a later representative chapter. We'll give you a great example.

Write What They'd Enjoy Reading

When we were trying to get the contract to write this very book, *The Complete Idiot's Guide to Getting Published,* we needed to write and submit a sample chapter. With all the possible aspects of getting published to choose from, which do you think we chose? Publicity. We wrote a sample chapter about book publicity and how important it is for authors to work hard to publicize their books. We included lots of information about how hardworking authors can make a big difference in the sales success of their books.

Send an Upbeat Message

Why did we choose that topic? Because we wanted to send a positive message to the publisher: that these two women, Sheree Bykofsky and Jennifer Basye Sander, know what they are doing. They understand how to make a book sell. They will work their tails off to make this book succeed.

Why choose a chapter with a negative tone (like one that talks about the high rate of book returns, or the changes afoot in the publishing business) when we could do something positive? Not only was the chapter on an upbeat topic, but it positioned us as go-getters. Hey, we got the contract, didn't we?

So what should you choose for your sample chapter? Choose something that will help the reader. And the reader, in this case, is not the general reading public, but the agent or editor reading your proposal. Give that person a sample chapter that will make him feel great or learn something new. Don't choose a chapter that will leave him depressed and reaching for a box of tissues. Here is an excellent opportunity to make him feel good about you and your ideas.

The Kitchen Sink

The very last thing that goes into your proposal is important: evidence of your credibility and that of your book. Here is an opportunity to include all the media attention you and/or your topic have gotten and that you've been saving up. With an impressive bundle of clippings, you can establish yourself as an expert, and you can establish your topic as big.

Newspaper and Magazine Articles

Did we say *recent* articles? It is important to include only articles from the last five years. If all your clips date from years ago, an agent or editor will wonder what happened to your career in the meantime.

It is also important that the articles you include about your topic be recent. If you include dated material, it might appear that the topic itself is old news and that the book would not sell.

Be careful about the quality of the clippings you send. Ripped, smudged, or messy-looking clippings will do you no good. You are a professional, and you need to look like one. Make sure that you include only clear copies that are readable, neatly presented, and of a reasonable length. It is better to send nice new copies rather than large original clippings from a newspaper. And because you will be making many copies of your proposal, it is cheaper than buying up 20 copies of the newspaper on the day you appeared.

Slush Pile

No gimmicky presents should accompany your proposal unless they relate to the book itself. So, a proposal for a book on chocolate truffles probably won't be harmed by sending along a box of samples. But don't send a box of truffles with your proposal for a book about world peace.

Video Clips

Videotapes of you being interviewed on a major television program are great to include as well. Short clips are best, though. Don't go overboard, as agents and editors will rarely watch an hour-long video. A professionally edited and labeled video clip is best. Worst is sending the wrong tape, like the one of your children in the bathtub. Be sure to label your tape clearly with your name and address, in case it gets separated from your proposal.

Hot Off the Press

"It sometimes seems like agents are on the frontline of weirdness," agent Natasha Kern says. "We get even more kooky stuff from strangers than publishers do. What are these people thinking when they send off such things? One guy sent me a picture of himself in his underwear. Come on!" One prospective author sent Sheree a pair of used shoes. So, not only should you not send silly gifts to agents, but refrain from sending overly personal things. Agents are looking for talented, hard-working authors to represent, not for relationships.

Proposing Your Self-Published Book

If you have a self-published book that you are now trying to sell to a publisher, you must include a copy. Also include a brutally honest description of the sales and distribution of your self-published book. Did we say "brutally honest"? We mean it. Be sure to specify not only how well your own edition sold, but where and how you sold it—whether out of the trunk of your car or at Barnes and Noble. Under no circumstances should you fudge, puff up, or exaggerate how well (or how not well) it sold. Trust us, if you lie, you will be caught. And that will be the end of your chances of selling the book. It may work to your advantage if your book sold well to a limited audience (for example, through your newsletter) but never made it to the major bookstore chains. That way, if a publisher *does* release your book, it will appear fresh to a bookstore buyer, not seem like old news.

Time to Get Writing!

Do you have a good handle on what goes into a book proposal now? We have included as an appendix the entire book proposal for one of co-author Jennifer's books, *Christmas Miracles*. Was it a successful proposal? Heck, yes. This proposal was so well received that the rights to this book were auctioned for a healthy six-figure advance. So get to work on your proposal, and you, too, might hit the jackpot!

The Least You Need to Know

➤ A book proposal is a 10- to 20-page description of the book, with supporting information.

➤ Professional nonfiction writers write a book proposal first; if it sells, then they write the book. You can do the same.

➤ The more compelling the information you provide about the market, the greater your chance of finding a publisher.

➤ Choose a sample chapter on a topic that will leave the reader (the editor or agent) with a good feeling.

➤ Include clean copies of recent newspaper and magazine articles about yourself and your topic.

➤ Do not send gifts or attention-getters with your proposal.

Chapter 9

Fun with Fiction

In This Chapter

➤ You've got to write the whole book first!

➤ Ready, set, query

➤ Writing a novel synopsis

➤ Now you've got an agent on the line!

➤ Summarizing your novel

When writing nonfiction, you can sell your book before you write it. No such luck with fiction. Fiction is a different ballgame with a more complex set of rules. It's harder to play and harder to win. In this chapter, we'll tell you how to write query letters and book proposals for fiction. But before we do, let's look more in depth at the wide world of fiction.

So, I Have to Write the Whole Book First?

Yes, to sell a work of fiction, you have to write the entire book first. Why? Because fiction requires more craftsmanship.

To write nonfiction, you need to know how to organize information in a clear and entertaining way. But writing fiction requires a mastery of myriad fiction techniques. From pacing to character, plotting to dialogue, more skill is required to pull it off. Moreover, a novel has a beginning, a middle, and an end—and lots of complications along the way. Publishers can't tell from an outline and a sample chapter alone if you can sustain a narrative and keep readers turning the pages for 250, 500, or maybe even 1,000 pages.

You have to supply them with proof, which is in the completed manuscript. You need to have written an entire novel before you can approach an agent to represent you. Agents, too, need to know that you can keep it up for hundreds of pages. Then, with masterpiece in hand, you can prove you've written a page-turner. You might become the successful novelist that you—and your mother—always dreamed you could be.

Want Support? Mingle with Other Writers

Writing may be a lonely business, but getting published doesn't have to be. Join a writers' organization so that you can keep abreast of new markets and trends and make valuable contacts with agents and editors.

If you are completely antisocial, don't despair. Many of the organizations in Appendix B, "More Good Resources," have online chapters you can join. You can cybernetwork without leaving the privacy of your own computer.

Hot Off the Press

"Belonging to Sisters in Crime has meant so much to me," says Terris Grimes, award-winning mystery book author. "The other writers are so open, so encouraging. Without their support, I wouldn't have had the starch to go on and finish my first book. It's important for creative people to get together in a group—if only a group of two!"

And Then I Have to Write the Whole Book, Again?

You and your mother are not alone. Agents and publishers like nothing better than successful novelists. Like the Energizer Bunny, successful novelists just keep on going and going and going. They sell, sell, sell. New York literary agent Ethan Ellenberg, who represents fiction writers in all genres, puts it this way: "A successful novelist can write 10 or 20 books over 10 or 20 years."

That's the long haul, and the long haul is what publishers are looking for when it comes to fiction. It takes time and money to build an audience for a new novelist.

Once that audience exists, though, the sky's the limit. People who read fiction read their favorite writers. And when they find a new favorite writer, they read everything that writer ever wrote—as well as everything he or she goes on to write in the future.

This makes successful novelists an excellent investment for publishers. It more than makes up for the initial investment required to build an author's name.

But Can You Do It Again?

That's why it's not enough to show the publishing world that you can write one great novel: You have to convince 'em that you can do it over and over and over that you, too, are in it for the long haul and that you can keep 'em turning pages through 8 or 12 books over 10 or 20 years.

Most important, you have to convince 'em that you aren't just a good writer, but that you're also a good storyteller.

The Never-Ending Story

Literary agent Don Maass, author of 14 novels as well as *The Career Novelist: A Literary Agent Offers Strategies for Success,* advises aspiring novelists to make the distinction between good writing and good storytelling. Artful language does not make good storytelling. Conflict does.

"John Grisham is not known as a great stylist, but he's a great storyteller," says Maass. "Take the opening scene of *The Firm*. It's just a job interview, but it's riveting because of the conflict. In a Grisham novel, there's conflict on every page, and conflict keeps readers turning the page."

Slush Pile

Difficult as it is to get a first novel published, the real make-it-or-break-it book is usually the second novel. A novelist's career depends on showing everyone—from the publishing folk, to the media, to the readers—that the first book was not a fluke.

Hot Off the Press

John Grisham is once again breaking new ground, this time by serializing his latest work. Instead of being published in hardcover, Grisham's *A Painted House* will be published over the span of a year in his literary magazine, *The Oxford American*. His agent, David Gernert, describes the book as being "so unlike his major books that we thought we should do something different with it."

Forget Dickens!

According to Maass, the biggest mistake many fiction writers make is to rely on nineteenth-century storytelling techniques—techniques that no longer engage today's fiction reader.

"I see so many manuscripts that begin with long, rambling descriptions, descriptions that would be great in a novel published in 1890, but not in a novel published in this era of MTV," says Maass.

Read, Read, Read

So where do you go to learn twenty-first–century storytelling techniques? Surprise! Go to a bookstore.

"The best course is also the least expensive," says Maass. He advises his clients to study today's great storytellers. "Read, study, and analyze. Then write your own powerful stories—stories with conflict on every page. Tell the best damn stories that you can."

Ready, Set, Query

Okay, so you, the great storyteller, have written a great novel with an engaging protagonist. There's conflict on every page. The ending not only satisfies your readers, but it leaves them screaming for a sequel. You pounded out several hundred pages that readers won't be able to turn fast enough.

Congratulations, you wrote a novel. Now take that 12-pound doorstop and put it away where you can't see it (and the dog can't eat it).

What? After we insist that you write the whole novel first, now we tell you to put it away?

Exactly. The last thing anyone in publishing wants to do is read a 12-pound manuscript from an unknown writer. Agents and editors are drowning in them. All those publishing cartoons you've seen in *The New Yorker,* the ones with the editor sitting behind a desk mounded high with papers, are true. You have to sell these people on the idea of reading your hefty tome. That's where your query letter comes in.

Did you read Chapter 7, "Query Letters That Sell Nonfiction," and Chapter 8, "Bulletproof Nonfiction Book Proposals"? They were good introductions to what comes next, especially for you.

Introducing the Mighty You

Your query letter is your major sales tool. It's a one-page letter that sells an agent on taking a chance on you. Your query must convince your quarry to invest several minutes, hours, and even days evaluating your novel—all this on the off-chance that the time invested will pay off. Remember, no one pays agents a salary. They invest hundreds of hours looking at stuff in the hopes that they can find a writer who will someday bring in the dough.

All that in one page, huh? It can be done. The trick is to keep the query simple, sweet, and sell, sell, sell. Here's how you break it down.

First Paragraph: What Kind of Book You've Written

You've written a 55,000-word mystery set in Jamaica at a Club Med entitled *Dead Men Don't Date*. Skip the cute introductions; get straight to the point by describing the genre, your concept, and a sentence or two about the plot. The only exception is if you've met the agent at a writers' conference or you've been referred by a mutual friend or colleague. If so, mention that first. As with every business, publishing is a business of people. Any kind of personal connection counts.

Second Paragraph: What Your Book Is About

Dead Men Don't Date is a story about young, unpublished romance novelist Melissa Manhattan, who escapes the cold, slushy, January streets of her native New York City in search of sun, sex, and a multibook contract at a writer's conference in Aruba—only to wake up and find the publishing industry's leading sleaze-bag agent dead in her king-size Club Med bed. Through a combination of wits, pluck, and an uncommon knowledge of deadly voodoo poisons, our girl Melissa solves the murder, saves the life of the biggest independent romance publisher in the business, and lands a six-figure contract as well as a very attractive and well-connected publicist—not to mention bringing the murderer (a disturbed ghostwriter driven to the edge after years of putting his sexy prose into lesser writers' mouths) to justice.

Third Paragraph: Why Only You Could Write This

You grew up in New York, where your mother worked as a secretary at a big publishing house. You spent your summers in the Caribbean helping your father with his life's work, the cataloging and classifying of voodoo poisons. You have met a sleaze-bag agent and personally know two ghostwriters committed to mental institutions for the foreseeable future.

Fourth Paragraph: Other Impressive Stuff

You studied creative writing in college and wrote your master's thesis on "The Importance of Poisons in Agatha Christie's Poirot Novels." After school, you worked for a couple years as a reporter for the *Bronx Cheer*. You have published a number of short stories in the mystery magazines, both print and online. You serve as president of your local Sisters in Crime chapter. You are already hard at work on book two of the Melissa Manhattan series, *Dead Men Don't Call You Back*.

Fifth Paragraph: How to Reach You

You would be happy to send a copy of the manuscript for review; feel free to contact you at home or at work anytime. You have also enclosed an SASE. You look forward to hearing from them.

Slush Pile

You won't make it very far if you do any of the following: handwrite your query letter, fail to send it to an agent who represents fiction, spell the agent's name wrong, or spell anything wrong. And, please, don't say "fiction novel." It's repetitively redundant.

How Hard Can That Be?

Writing an effective query letter ultimately depends on salesmanship. For some reason, many people who can write great novels cannot write a decent sales letter. So, if you feel that your efforts to sell yourself and your work on paper fall flat, don't despair. Enlist the help of a copywriter friend or colleague to help you punch up your pitch. If you don't know anyone with that skill, hire someone. Look in The Yellow Pages for freelance advertising copywriters.

Remember, this one-page query letter is your foot in the door. It's worth investing more than a little time and money on perfecting your query. So, when the door opens up a crack, you want to slip in a Gucci loafer, not those old sneakers you wore to paint the front room.

Also be sure to enclose an SASE, and sign all the query letters yourself.

An Invitation for a Proposal!

You come home from a hard day at work to see the message light blinking on your phone. Could this be the call? Has your query letter hooked an agent?

"I'd really like to see more," the agent says. "Can you send me a proposal?"

A proposal for a novel? If you read the chapter on nonfiction proposals, you now know all the different types of information that goes into one of those. But what on earth do you put into a fiction proposal?

Very little, actually. Here is what goes into a fiction proposal:

➤ A synopsis of the novel
➤ The first 50 pages of the novel, or the first three chapters, whichever is longer
➤ Information about the author

Unlike a nonfiction proposal, you won't have to spend countless hours analyzing the competing titles. Novels are generally understood to stand on their own, not to compete directly with similar novels on similar themes. You won't have to do research and include data on the market for the novel. The market is understood—it's people who read fiction.

So, let's see how to put together a *synopsis*.

Summarize, Please

Why do you need to write a synopsis if you've already written the whole novel? Here again, it is a question of time. Agents and editors aren't going to plow through your 12-pound manuscript to see if your plot is full of holes. They can figure it out by skimming a 1- to 10-page synopsis. They also don't have room in those cluttered offices for an extra 30 chapters when they can tell in 50 pages or less that your characters play like cardboard cutouts and that your pacing is wildly uneven.

Like the query, writing a synopsis is an art all its own, with its own set of rules.

Bookmarks

Before an agent or editor will read your whole novel, he will want to read your **synopsis.** A synopsis is a 10-page long summary of your novel, written in the present tense, in the third person. It spells out the plot of your novel in an effective and readable way.

Hook 'Em Again?

Entertaining and scintillating? How can you condense an entire novel into a few pages, much less be entertaining and scintillating? Granted, it's not easy to breathe life into such a stilted narrative, but it can be done. Many writers spice up their synopses with snippets of dialogue and small bits of scenes. Whatever you can think of doing to add flair to your synopsis, do it.

Sample Synopses

Did you join the local writer's group for your genre? Do you attend workshops as part of a romance writers group or a mystery writers group? Or, do you meet with a group of local writers at the Starbucks down the street to swap tales? Ask your friends if they have sample synopses you could see. Study these synopses, and then write one for your book that outshines them all!

If they're interested, some agents, like co-author Sheree, will request the whole manuscript in lieu of a proposal. Even then, it's necessary to include at least a one-page synopsis and bio. Sheree likes to request the whole book for several reasons: 1) so that she can finish the book while it's still fresh in her mind if it's got her hooked after Chapter 3; 2) so that she can be sure the novel is complete; and 3) so that she can be sure the novel keeps her attention through the end.

Exclusivity

When an agent asks for exclusivity, it means she wants to be the only agent to consider your manuscript. If an agent does ask for exclusivity, be sure that she gives you a reasonable time frame for a response. Sheree usually offers a four-week turnaround for a proposal or manuscript in exchange for an exclusive first look at a manuscript. Giving an agent exclusivity does not mean that you are then required to use that agent if the agent likes your manuscript. She is still going to have to click with you. The agent should show some passion for your project, should offer you terms for representation that you find reasonable, should be able to give you references, and should be able to do whatever is reasonably necessary to make you comfortable that the agent is the best person for you. If not, on to the next!

Bookmarks

The **slush pile** is where all the unsolicited manuscripts are piled, waiting to be returned.

Hot Off the Press

You've heard the stories. An author sends in an unsolicited manuscript to the top publishing house, and a young assistant finds it in the slush pile. The assistant and the writer go on to great literary glory. On rare occasions, one will be found, read, and published. Judith Guest's *Ordinary People* was one such slush-pile discovery.

The Least You Need to Know

➤ With fiction, you must write the entire novel before trying to get an agent or a publisher.

➤ Never send the entire manuscript unsolicited; try first with a short query letter.

➤ Your query letter should include a short description of your novel.

➤ Your proposal should include a 1- to 10-page summary of the novel, and either the first 50 pages of the manuscript or three complete chapters.

Part 3

Romancing the Stone: How to Get a Book Contract

Whether your goal is to find an agent first or to go directly to a publisher yourself, the information is all here. You'll find great tips on how to find agents, and even how to get agents to find you! But if that doesn't work, you'll learn the protocol for approaching publishers without an agent. Whether with children's publishers, university publishers, or even self-publishing, there is much to be learned about the different styles of publishing books.

We'll also help you understand two critical areas of the publishing process: what goes on in an editorial meeting, and how to understand a standard publishing contract.

Chapter 10

What's an Agent For, Anyway?

In This Chapter

➤ Why writers use agents

➤ Why agents and editors do lunch

➤ How agents negotiate contracts

➤ Some common contract pitfalls

➤ How agents help you stay on the publisher's good side

Hey, I Did All the Work!

You've written a tantalizing query letter, and your bulletproof book proposal is put together. The outline for the book (or the entire novel itself) is solid and waiting for a buyer. You're ready to go. But wait! You worked darn hard on all this—why should you cut an agent in on the deal now? Because writers write, and agents sell.

Whether you write fiction or nonfiction, it's hard enough going about the business of writing without also having to deal with the actual business end of it. Very few writers are really equipped to both let their imaginations soar on the blank page and at the same time concentrate on trying to market their work.

Here are a few quick reasons that writers use agents:

➤ Contacts

➤ Contracts

➤ Money

➤ Guidance

Hot Off the Press

You don't need to live in New York to be a published writer, and agents don't need to live in New York to be literary agents. Like writers, agents are spread out all over the country. In Dallas you'll find Jan Miller, and San Francisco has Michael Larsen, Elizabeth Pomada, Fred Hill, and a host of other agents. Bill Adler Jr. is in Washington, D.C.; Martha Casselman lives in California's wine country; Michael Snell lives in Truro, Massachusetts; and Elizabeth Wales drinks lots of Starbucks Coffee up in Seattle. Jacqueline Turner Banks is in Sacramento, California, and Jane Jordan Brown is in downtown Chicago. So look around carefully—there might be a literary agent in your town, too!

Bookmarks

The editors who are responsible for bringing in new books are called **acquisitions editors.** They are often called senior editors, but they may also be editors or editors-at-large. The titles vary from house to house and generally depend on the level of responsibility or the amount of experience an editor has.

Friends in High Places

Agents devote much of their time to cultivating contacts with editors and publishers. They do lunch, they circulate at book parties, they attend conferences, they share cabs. Agents make it their business to get to know *acquisitions editors* at all the major publishing houses. Agents learn what kinds of books each and every editor likes and, more important, just what kind of book each editor never wants to see again!

Each publishing house has its specialties. Some large houses publish a vast array of books on a vast array of topics. Random House, for instance, has a mind-boggling number of imprints, each with a different personality and focus. A smaller publisher such as Avery, on the other hand, is known for alternative health titles. Agents keep track of who publishes what, who went out of business, and even which publishing companies seem to be nicer to their authors than others. This is the sort of specialized knowledge that an agent can use to sell your book to the right publisher.

What Gets Done When Agents and Editors Do Lunch?

Lucky for agents—particularly poor, starving agents—this is the only business around where the buyer wines and dines the seller. This expensive practice alone should help convince you of the important role that agents play in the publishing business.

Publishers value the knowledge, judgment, and wisdom of agents enough to ply them with meals. Just as authors can't effectively do their job of writing while also being their own agents, publishers can't do their jobs of acquiring and editing while at the same time screening a million writers and projects.

When an editor agrees to take a look at a project that an agent is representing, she knows that this is a professional project worth considering. The editor is relying on the fact that an agent is not likely to take on a project (investing hours of his own time, office help, and supplies) that he doesn't believe to be of the highest quality. Editors rely on agents to do quite a bit of the screening and selecting for them.

What do they find to talk about during these long publishing lunches? That is where all your hard homework, all the information you dug up about the audience, the market, and the potential for your book comes in. The agent works to sell the editor on the potential of your book, combining her knowledge with the information you've supplied. In the publishing business, unwritten books are the stuff of dreams. Who knows where the next big thing will come from? Every agent, every editor, and every publisher hopes that she has found it.

Experts Say

But if agents and editors are friends, how can they negotiate contracts? "In my experience, *many agents do become my friends over a period of time,*" says Susan Schwartz, former senior editor at NTC/Contemporary Publishing Group. "But I knew them as agents first, so that relationship is primary and doesn't change. It is a professional arrangement, and we behave accordingly."

Experts Say

Why does Daylle Deanna Schwartz, the author of several books (including *All Men Are Jerks Until Proven Otherwise*), need an agent? "With an agent, I get taken more seriously by publishers. My contracts are negotiated properly. Agents have a vested interest in what's earned through that contract, so they work hard! I like having one savvy person take care of everything so I can write in peace!"

A Hope and a Prayer

Does a book have an intrinsic value? Well, no. The value of an *intellectual property* is determined purely by taste (the editor's) and perceived need. It isn't like a diamond or a vacuum cleaner, something that has an expected value in the marketplace.

A book is more like Jackie O's toilet brush: It's worth whatever someone is willing to pay. So, over lunch, agents get editors excited about the books they have for sale. Agents also listen closely as the editor describes the kind of books he hopes to find.

"Is That the Best You Can Do?"

Well, the lunch meeting between your agent and the prospective editor was a great success. Eventually the editor calls your agent to make an offer. This doesn't happen that same afternoon, however.

Profit or Loss?

In Chapter 14, "Behind Closed Doors," you'll get an inside look at what happens during editorial meetings. But before then, we'll just say that the editor needs to get the support and approval of a whole bunch of other folks—and to do what's known as a *P and L* (profit and loss statement) before he makes that call to your agent.

This profit and loss statement is used to estimate in advance what a publisher can expect to earn from the publication of a book.

Any Other Takers?

Publishers sometimes wait to see if other publishers are interested in the same book. Let's pretend that the agent has submitted your brilliant proposal to editors A, B, and C. Editors C and B are polite, but editor A is the only one who calls the agent with an offer. Editor A wants to make sure, then, that he is not "bidding against himself." If there is only one bid on the table, the agent does not have much leverage to get it raised. Agents do have a trick or two up their sleeves to try to maximize the publishers' offer and get the best possible deal for their author.

Let's not forget that an agent's work is done on "spec"—his income is solely based on *commission*. No sale, no commission; low sale, low commission. Your agent earns no money at all from representing you until your book is sold to a publisher. Then, depending on your agreement, she receives anywhere from 10 to 15 percent of your royalties and 15 percent of your advance. So, it is possible for an agent to work long and hard, only to not earn a penny if your book is not sold. You can see why an agent will always try to get the best deal possible for the author—because it is at the same time his deal, too.

Money, Money, Money

So, the editor wants your book. Great. You get the call from your agent and begin dancing around the room shouting, "Show me the money!"

Just how much money can you expect?

This is a sticky subject. Sadly, most American writers have rather small average yearly incomes. Around $10,000 a year is typical, and that may reflect a number of different income sources (magazine and newspaper articles, freelance copywriting) in addition to book royalties.

How much money you can expect depends. We've seen first-time advances for most nonfiction books range anywhere from as low as $5,000 to as high as $100,000. If you really have a great background—a platform that includes a large speaking schedule, a newspaper column, a high-profile name, or a tremendous idea—the number could be higher.

Megamarkets

The number could also be higher if you establish a ready market for your book. With *Christmas*

Bookmarks

A **P and L** stands for a profit and loss statement, which takes into account all the money that must be spent on a book, balanced against the money that can be expected from potential sales. It is hoped that the P column outweighs the L column by a desired profit margin.

Experts Say

Life in New York has become so frantic that the traditional leisurely lunch hours have become a time to cram in as many meetings as possible. According to *The New York Times*, some agents and editors are doing multiple lunches in an effort to find that big book before someone else does. How does it work? A big agent will set himself up at the table, meet with one editor over the salad course, another editor over the main course, and yet another editor for dessert and coffee!

Bookmarks

Literary agents work solely on **commission,** a percentage of the book's income.

Bookmarks

The money paid to an author upon signing a contract is called an **advance against future royalties.** That's money up front that will have to be earned back once the book is available for sale. An author's royalty account starts as a negative figure that reflects the advance. Once the royalties earned surpass the amount advanced, an author begins to receive more money.

Miracles, co-author Jennifer was able to establish how well Christmas books sold, how well books on miracles sold, and how well inspirational short-story books such as *Chicken Soup for the Soul* did. All that research paid off.

Advances for Fiction

Advances for first-time novelists are generally on the low side, but if your book is perceived as a bestseller candidate and an auction ensues, the advance could go off the charts. From time to time, an unknown writer hits the million-dollar jackpot. It happens.

Double Indemnity

When agents negotiate contracts, the size of the advance is just one of many complicated issues. In Chapter 15, "The Party of the First Part," you'll walk through a typical publishing contract piece by piece.

Rely on Your Agent

Although agents negotiate contracts on behalf of the author, the agent does not sign the contract. The author does. But you shouldn't sign the contract until the agent is happy with it, until you have read it completely, and until you understand it. Your agent is there to explain the quirks of the contract. Don't be afraid to ask about any and all details.

Publishing agreements are sticky wickets, but thankfully (for agents and authors), they are all pretty much the same. An experienced agent is aware of the traditional traps and loopholes. Nobody, including most lawyers, knows publishing contracts like an agent. Agents know just when to push and when to back off.

Let's Do Another One, Just Like the Other One

Agents sometimes maintain boilerplate contracts with the publishing houses with which they do business. What does this mean to you? On other contracts, the agent has already gotten the house to agree to more free copies or a better royalty rate on special sales, or he's eliminated the option clause. The editor likely will knock these things out of your contract, too.

After the Deal Is Done

So, your contract has been negotiated and signed. You and your editor have a direct relationship. Your editor will now guide you through the publishing process. Is your agent's job finished? Not by a long shot.

An agent is an experienced publishing player. He can help you learn the ropes so that you, too, will be an experienced player. After the contract is filed in a drawer, the agent will take on these tasks:

➤ Learn how to get the most from the publicity department

➤ Examine your royalty statements

➤ Make sure that you get paid properly

➤ Sell subrights and licenses for your book

➤ Be your book's greatest advocate

Good Cop/Bad Cop

And the best part of all is that your agent can be the bad guy. As an author, you want to be loved by your editor. You want to shy away from any kind of behavior that could damage your relationship with your editor (more on this later, in Chapter 19, "Proper Care and Feeding of Your Editor"). But what if you aren't happy?

Your agent can do the job! Call and tell him your concern, and ask him to speak on your behalf. You can sit back and let your agent air your complaints in such a way that you don't jeopardize your relationship with your publisher. Your agent is the bad cop. The agent will do the yelling (about the crummy cover design, the lack of a publicity campaign, or the slow royalty checks) while you sit back and bat your eyelashes.

Publishers are people, too. Even if your book is the best thing since *Gone with the Wind,* those with the power to help you will not put forth their best efforts if you alienate them. At any given time, a

Experts Say

Author and former lawyer Tim Perrin says that whenever you receive a first offer from a publisher, you should always say, "Oh? Is that all? I was thinking more like ...." Then name a figure substantially higher than what you've just been offered. "It's never failed for me," says Perrin. "I don't often get double or triple the amount first offered, but I always get a substantial increase. I make more money in those 10 seconds than I do in any part of writing."

Slush Pile

So your agent has gotten an editor interested? An offer is on the table and a contract is in the works? *Mazel tov.* But don't ever pick up the phone and call the editor directly about a contract issue. This will make both your editor and your agent angry. Relax, and let your agent do his job.

publishing house has lots of different books to peddle, so don't give it a reason to spend less time on yours. Your second most important job as a writer (after writing the best book you can) is to make the publisher love you and your book. Be as pleasant as you can. Let your agent do the unpleasant things.

Hot Off the Press

Most editor/author relationships start off nicely. The trick is to keep them that way. In some cases, by the time a book is published, the editor hopes never to hear from the author again. How does this happen? In their enthusiasm, some authors can overdo it with frequent calls to the editor, to the publicity department, or even to the publisher. If you have a complaint, let your agent make the call. If you have a compliment, send a short note. If you have a suggestion (or two or three), start it off by saying, "You have probably already thought of this, but how about ...." And it never hurts to send flowers.

Get Thee an Agent

Now you know the full story. An agent's role goes far beyond brokering a profitable deal with a publisher.

We're not saying that you need an agent because co-author Sheree is one (and we're not saying that because Sheree is Jennifer's agent, either!). We're both writers, and we know a lot of other writers. We have seen all that can happen to writers in the rough-and-tumble world of book publishing. Get yourself a good agent, and you will have less to worry about.

How the heck do you find an agent? Move on to the next chapter, and we'll show you where they hide!

The Least You Need to Know

➤ Agents do many things, from negotiating a contract to guiding you through the publishing maze.

➤ Agents get to know editors and what kinds of books they want to publish.

➤ Books are intellectual properties and are worth what the highest bidder will pay. An agent is better placed to handle the bidding.

➤ Standard boilerplate publishing contracts favor the publisher, not the author. An agent knows the ins and outs.

➤ Agents can help you maintain a good relationship with your editor and publisher.

Chapter 11

Finding and Working with an Agent

In This Chapter

➤ Where do they hide, those agents?

➤ Choosing among the many

➤ Fiction or nonfiction?

➤ Agent etiquette

➤ Landing a live one!

With any luck, we convinced you in Chapter 10, "What's an Agent For, Anyway?" that you need an agent, particularly if you are a first-time author and want to sell your book idea to a large national publisher. In this chapter, we'll tell you how to find a good one.

Members of the Club

So how do you tell if an agent is the real thing? A large percentage of established agents in the business are members of the Association of Author's Representatives (AAR). This is the largest professional association of literary and dramatic agents for authors. Its address is P.O. Box 237201, Ansonia Station, New York, NY 10023. To get a list of all its members, send your request with a self-addressed, stamped (totaling 55 cents) envelope and $7 to cover photocopying and handling, or take a look at the association's free Web site at www.aar-online.org.

Hot Off the Press

In its Canon of Ethics, the members of AAR pledge loyal service to their clients' needs. A member's accounts must be open to the client at all times with respect to the client's transactions, and members promise not to represent both buyer and seller in the same transaction. The AAR believes that the practice of agents charging clients or potential clients for reading and evaluating literary works (including outlines, proposals, and manuscripts) is subject to serious abuse that reflects adversely on the profession. Current and future members may not charge for reading and evaluating literary works and may not benefit from the charging of such fees by any other person or entity.

What will this list tell you? That the agents listed are what they say they are: experienced literary agents. To become a member of the AAR, you must be a well-established agent with several contracts negotiated on behalf of authors with major publishing houses. In addition, you must agree to abide by a strict Canon of Ethics. You must also pass a rigorous application and screening process.

Hot Off the Press

"Book doctors should respect your confidentiality," says Jerry Gross, a book doctor himself. If you use a book doctor, no one needs to know about it. Other than the confidentiality question, what else should you ask a book doctor before hiring one? First and foremost, make sure that he is skilled in your area. "If you are writing a sci-fi novel, make sure that the book doctor has written sci-fi novels, too. You don't want someone with an expertise in romance novels." Ask for references—and check them! And always be suspicious of someone who "guarantees" that if you work with them, they will get you an agent or a publisher.

Just How Much Is This Gonna Cost?

It costs nothing to have an agent who's a member of AAR read your material. Other agents may charge reading fees. Most of the reference books that list agents will note whether they charge a reading fee, and if so, how much.

Reading Fees? No

The fact that an agent charges a reading fee does not necessarily mean that he is taking advantage of you. In fact, if you ever got a glimpse at the towering stack of unsolicited material that floods into agents' offices every day, you might understand the idea behind a reading fee. Remember, agents don't make any money at all until they sell your project.

But the AAR believes that reading fees can easily lead to corrupt practices, so do try to stay away from paying a reading fee.

They're Agents, Not Readers

Not only do most literary agents not charge reading fees, but they also do not provide "reader's reports." An agent will simply tell you whether your manuscript is suited to his agency. If the manuscript doesn't interest him enough to represent it, he certainly won't take the time to tell you what he thinks is wrong with it. But if he does want to represent your book, he will take the time to help you make it better.

The hard truth is this: If all the agents that you approach who don't charge fees turn you and your project down, it is pretty likely that the publishers are going to have the same reaction. So, if this happens, spend your money on a good book doctor, a writing class or seminar, or an independent editor. All of these will help you to improve your work and its chances of someday being published.

Slush Pile

Rather than paying reading fees to an agent, hire yourself an independent editor, or sign up for a writing class if you want your writing evaluated. Agents will either represent you or not represent you. We don't think you need to pay someone to evaluate your work in exchange for representation. And by all means, do not pay an agent a fee to represent you or to place your manuscript with a publisher. Agents collect commissions, not fees.

Slush Pile

You owe it to yourself and your book to be rigorous in your evaluation of a potential agent. Do most of your early research through books and any personal sources you might have. Don't call and ask agents for their biographies or the names of potential clients until they have offered to represent you. Once they have offered to represent you, it is perfectly proper to ask questions.

Where to Find Help (!)

Many good book doctors and freelance editors can help you with your proposal, and agents sometimes can give you the names of such people. So might members of local writers' groups. Then there's the Editorial Freelance Association (EFA), a nonprofit organization whose members are all freelance editors. Check out EFA's Web site at www.the-efa.org, or call 212-929-5400.

Screening Agents

Are all good agents members of the AAR? Are all members of the AAR good agents? Many good agents are not members of the AAR and don't charge fees. But evaluating them may prove difficult without checking with an association.

After an agent has offered to represent you, but before you sign up, feel free to ask for names and phone numbers of other clients. The agent should happily let you speak to some of his clients to get a better sense of who they are. If an agent is reluctant to hook you up with any other clients, take this as a red flag.

Not sure what kinds of questions you should ask an agent before agreeing to let him represent you? Here are a few questions that will help you sound him out:

➤ How long have you been in business as an agent?

➤ Do you have specialists at your agency who handle television and movie rights?

➤ Do you represent other authors in my area of interest?

➤ What is your commission?

➤ Do you issue 1099 tax forms at the end of the year?

➤ What kinds of books have you sold lately?

Where to Look for Agents?

So where else do they hide, these agents? Co-author Sheree would like to say that all the good agents have offices in New York City (guess where she has an office?), but she would be lying. New York agents might have an easier time accessing New York editors face-to-face, but excellent agents live all around the country. Agents outside the Big Apple make frequent trips into New York. They pack their appetites in their carry-ons and gang up their breakfasts, lunch, dinner, drinks, and coffee dates with as many publishers as they can.

Besides checking the membership list of the AAR, there are several other ways to find agents.

Look in a Book

Three great books list agents: *Literary Market Place (LMP)*, *Writer's Guide to Book Publishers, Editors, and Literary Agents*, and *The Writer's Digest Guide to Literary Agents*.

We talked about the *LMP* in Chapter 4, "Super-Stealth Market Research Techniques"; it's an expensive professional reference. Though it's full of information, only one of the many sections in it is devoted to agents. The agent listings in the *LMP* don't give any information beyond name, address, and phone number, and whether the agent is a member of the AAR.

The *Writer's Guide to Book Publishers, Editors, and Literary Agents* is put together by an actual literary agent, Jeff Herman. He's been doing it for the last 10 years or so, and he includes lots of personal and professional information about the agents he lists. Each agent listing includes the agent's description of the type of book he or she likes to represent, and the type of book he or she never wants to see again. If you are just beginning your search for an agent, Herman's book is great. Be sure to get the most current edition available because the listings change every year.

The *Writer's Digest's Guide to Literary Agents* lists more than 500 agents who "sell what you write." It's concise, is kept up-to-date, and is an excellent resource not just for finding agents, but also for learning about the publishing industry.

Face to Face

A great way to find an agent is through a recommendation from a friend or colleague, particularly a published friend or colleague. But what if you don't know any other writers? Get thee to a writers' conference!

In any given month, somewhere around the country, a writers' conference is being held. Most organizers of writers' conferences arrange to have a few agents on hand for you to meet. These meetings are invaluable. Not only do they give you a chance to stick out your hand and shake with a live agent, but you also can often arrange for personal appointments with agents to discuss your project. This is time that you wouldn't be able to get from them on the phone with a cold call. If you are serious about writing, writers' conferences are never a waste of time. The Guide to Writers Conferences & Workshops at www.shawguides.com is a fabulous source for writers. It provides more than 600 detailed conference and workshop descriptions, including upcoming dates, faculty, and programs. In Appendix H we've listed some conferences, many of which co-authors Sheree and Jennifer have addressed.

"I'd Like to Thank My Agent"

Don't know any writers? Can't get to a writers' conference? Well, you can open a book, right? That is a great place to find agents! Take a book, any book, off the shelf. Open it to the acknowledgments page. Not all books have such a page, but

Bookmarks

When authors write to a number of agents at one time, this is called a **multiple query.** You are approaching a number of agents at once to try to get them interested in requesting your proposal, chapters, or manuscript. This is an accepted practice in publishing.

many (if not most) do. This is where the author thanks his family for their patience, his editor for her guidance, and his agent for all those lunches.

Looking in the acknowledgments is a great tactic, particularly when you need to find an agent who represents books in your area. Writing a health book? Look inside the health books that you admire. Writing a romance novel? Check out recently published romances. This method helps you find the agent that might be open to your type of writing. Does the author thank everyone in the world but her agent? Hmmm … must have been an oversight.

Eeny, Meeny, Miney, Mo …

So, you've looked inside your favorite books. Your list has arrived from the AAR, and you met eight great agents at a writers' conference last weekend. You've highlighted, cross-checked, and pondered the selections. You know which agents represent your area, and the list is longer than Madonna's little black book. Do you have to just choose one? No! You're in luck. It is perfectly acceptable to send queries to more than one agent at one time.

Still, you want to be somewhat selective about whom you send your precious queries to. What if they all responded at once, and they all said "Yes"? Select your hottest prospects first.

Exclusive Territory

When an agent does respond and request more material from you, she might also ask for an "exclusive" for a limited amount of time. Three to four weeks is standard. What does this mean? It means that for the next three to four weeks she can study your material closely and not have to worry that you might be swiped out from under her by another agent.

If an agent chooses you, do you have to choose her? No. But, realistically, if someone does want to represent you and offers you a reasonable author/agent agreement (and if she doesn't seem obnoxious), well, why not? Don't try to interest an agent that you really don't want. You will waste both your time and hers.

The Good Agent

The best things to look for in an agent include these:

➤ An established reputation

➤ A reputation for selling books in your field

➤ Accessibility by phone (once she's become your agent)

➤ A manner that lends itself to comfortable communication

➤ A passion about her work—and about yours

If you can't find all these qualities in an agent who responds to you, move on down your list until you do.

Are You Really Ready?

How do you know when you are ready to begin querying agents? You're ready if you have the following: a well-written query letter, and a polished proposal for nonfiction or a polished manuscript for fiction. If these elements are in place, get started!

Slush Pile

No matter how brilliant you think your book idea is, if you don't have the written material to back it up, you will fail. Do not approach an agent or a publisher with an idea for a book until you have something in writing—your writing!

Fiction

If it's fiction you're writing, don't even think about querying agents until you are satisfied that your novel is the best it can be. You'll hear from time to time about first-time novelists selling a novel for a million dollars. It happens, but rarely. What you might not realize, though, is that although this is the first book that writer has sold, it is probably not the first book he has written. Many writers write 2, 3, or 10 novels before selling one.

Novelists write and write, regardless of whether they'll get published. True novelists usually get published, eventually. But don't send something to an agent just because you worked hard on it. Send it because it's good. Don't ask an agent to decide whether it's good; ask discriminating colleagues, teachers, and editors for their honest opinions first. Take praise from family and friends (who may be biased or who don't want to hurt your feelings) with a large grain of salt.

Sometimes novelists need to put their novels aside and let them sit for a while. Then they go back to them with a fresh perspective and re-evaluate them. Very often authors come back to their very first novels years later and say, "Oh my gosh, what was I thinking?"

Nonfiction

For nonfiction, you can submit before you've got the entire book written. As you learned in Chapter 8, "Bulletproof Nonfiction Book Proposals," nonfiction is usually sold on the basis of a book proposal, a table of contents, and a representative sample chapter. If a publishing house likes what it sees in a proposal and decides to publish it, you have a deal. The publisher will pay half the advance upon signing a contract and half upon receipt of an acceptable manuscript. A manuscript is deemed acceptable when it matches the promises in your proposal, as reflected in the contract description.

When you have a good nonfiction proposal together, go ahead and start querying agents. If you haven't yet started your sample chapter, don't worry. Start it soon, but don't let it hold you back. If an agent is interested in your query and then asks to see more, you don't want her to have to wait too long. She might forget you!

Slush Pile

Although most nonfiction books require only a book proposal, there is one instance in which you will need more. Creative nonfiction books that are literary memoirs (such as *Angela's Ashes*) require a more fiction-like approach. You can't sell creative nonfiction with a bare bones nonfiction proposal. Like a novel, you might need to write the whole book or a substantial portion first.

Try, Try Again

What if an agent looks at your proposal and tells you it still needs more work? She might tell you exactly where she thinks it is weak and how to improve it. Or, she might think your proposal is so weak that you need to hire help, and she might suggest that you work with a book doctor (see more on book doctors earlier in this chapter and also in Chapter 8).

Big Name, Superb Credentials

You might not have to wait until a proposal is done before querying agents. If you have such superb professional credentials, such as a recognizable name, you might not have to wait. Write a strong query letter and see what kind of reaction you get from agents. It might be that an agent will be able to link you up with a co-writer for the project. The agent might also be able to guide you in the proposal process.

Blue Light Special

If you decide to try to place your book first without an agent, don't shop the project to all the publishers in town and then try to find an agent. If you try this, you will make it very hard to get yourself an agent later, no matter how good your project is. Agents can't go back to the same publishers; if a publisher has passed on a project already, an agent will feel awfully foolish when the editor points it out—and it will come back to haunt you. Come clean with agents about which publishers have passed.

Return to Sender

Don't send your unsolicited query letter via certified or registered mail. The agent will think he's being sued! Seriously, you don't want to look over-cautious or paranoid. Portray yourself like the professional you are.

Once again, we will remind you of the importance of including a self-addressed, stamped envelope with your correspondence to agents. It is a simple step that can make all the difference in hearing back. If you leave out the SASE, the agent will assume that you need no reply if the agent isn't interested. If that's the case, it's better to say so than to look sloppy.

Hold My Calls, Please

Unless (and until) you have an agent/author agreement with an agent, do not try to call a prospective agent on the phone. It will backfire. Approach agents the way they want to be approached: with a query and an SASE.

Agents need to evaluate your writing, not your speaking. So give them what they need and more: a great query letter that will pique their interest right away.

You Hooked One!

An agent received your query letter, read it, and then picked up the phone and called you! Hurrah! This is a good sign. But don't jump the gun and start writing your Pulitzer Prize acceptance speech yet. When an agent is intrigued by your query, she might call you to find out more about the project. She might be calling to learn more about you as a person.

Slush Pile

If you use a book doctor or other kind of professional in preparing your proposal, and the book finds a publisher, you need to make sure that your finished book does not disappoint the publisher. If the publisher bought your project based on a proposal that had help, make extra sure that your book itself meets or exceeds the expectations set in that proposal. Don't promise one thing and deliver another. Many publishers have been burned by books that didn't match the quality or content of the proposal.

Bookmarks

When only one agent is considering your proposal, this is called an **exclusive submission.** If an agent asks for an exclusive submission, be sure to set a time limit. Three to four weeks is reasonable.

If the agent does want to go further, she might ask for an *exclusive*. Remember, this is when you assure her that she is the only one considering your project for a particular length of time. It is hard to say no to an agent on the phone, and that's why it is so important for you to have done your research before deciding which agents to query. You don't want to go to the dance with the wrong partner!

Another Darn SASE?

When an agent responds to your query and asks to see more material, include an SASE with your proposal. There is more at stake here, in fact. You are sending a lot of material, and you want it back if the agent decides to pass. To be sure that your package was received, send it via an express service such as FedEx or UPS. You can track it by phone without calling the literary agent and looking anxious. The good old U.S. mail is just fine, too. According to statistics, 99.9999 percent of all mail is delivered properly.

For packages that weigh more than 1 pound, include return postage, either loose stamps for the proper postage or a check to cover the cost of an express service.

The Least You Need to Know

➤ Members of the Association of Author's Representatives abide by a professional code of ethics and don't charge a reading fee.

➤ Find an agent through the membership of AAR, directories that list agents, or writers' conferences.

➤ Looking in the acknowledgments section of books you admire could lead you to a great agent, too.

➤ With nonfiction, query agents when your proposal is finished; with fiction, query when your novel is finished.

➤ Always include a self-addressed, stamped envelope with any correspondence to an agent.

Chapter 12

What You Can Expect from an Agent

In This Chapter

➤ When an agent calls to represent you, what then?

➤ The agency/author agreement

➤ Is it okay to call now?

➤ Dealing with rejection letters

➤ Every author's first question

➤ How agents sell books

Was that a dream? Did an agent actually call and say, "I want to represent you?" You wrote a good query letter and you have a great idea, so stop pinching yourself! And put down that champagne glass—you have more work to do.

99 Percent Ready

It is rare that the manuscript or book proposal that you sent is 100 percent ready to go. Chances are, the agent will want to discuss some fine-tuning and changes. At the very least, you'll need to change the cover page to your manuscript or proposal. Remember, it has your name and address on the bottom. Now that you've got an agent, you'll need to drop your own information and add his.

"I Really Like it, But ..."

Fixing the cover page—that's no problem. But is this agent passionate about your project? Does she believe in your book? It is imperative that the person who is going to represent you to publishers feels confident about your book's prospects. If the agent has any doubts going in, you want to know about it.

Let's say that the agent does love your project, but maybe she also has some changes she needs you to make before sending your book out to publishers. After all, what an agent sends out is her calling card. She must maintain a good reputation with publishers to stay active in the business. You must make your work as perfect as possible.

Be Open to Changes

The agent might feel that your competition section needs work. This might mean that you need to strengthen your facts or do a quick double-check to make sure that you haven't left out major titles.

She might also feel that you've been too hard on the competing titles and might risk alienating the publishers of those books you've maligned (who might have otherwise become your publisher).

Your new agent might also make recommendations on your author biography section. Perhaps you've been too humble about your accomplishments. Or, perhaps you've been a touch arrogant and need to tone it down.

Slush Pile

With the advent of "spell check," there is just no excuse for finding misspelled words in your manuscript or book proposal. Use it.

Hot Off the Press

Agent Laurie Liss has had a strong streak of finding bestselling authors in the past few years. Her finds include Richard Paul Evans (*The Christmas Box*) and the author of *The Bridges of Madison County*, Robert James Waller. More recently, she represented a book called *Ten Fun Things to Do Before You Die*, written by a nun. Hyperion bought it based in part on Liss's strong record.

Your Best Interests Are at Stake

Whatever the agent suggests, feel free to discuss it with her. This is very important. Discuss all changes. If an agent makes suggestions to your manuscript (about combining chapters, say, or dropping a section), you don't have to agree. Do not make any changes to your work that you don't feel 100 percent good about. If you can't get the agent to see things your way, or vice versa, then perhaps this is not the agent for you. True, you've both wasted your time, but thank heaven you discovered it early.

On the other hand, the agent does have quite a bit of experience in this area. Do try to be open-minded and understand what is being suggested (and why). The agent has your best interests in mind and is trying to make your project as salable as possible because you really have only one shot at it. If the agent sends out a project that wasn't quite ready to go and it is turned down by every-one who sees it, that is the end of the road. Publishers seldom want to see the same project twice.

Love at First Sight

Now let's say that you and your agent are com-pletely sympatico. You see eye to eye about the book and agree on what is necessary to touch it up and make it ready. The conversation you had about your book energized both of you. You like the agent's manner. You can talk to her. She listens. Great, so what's next?

Call Other Authors

The agent might suggest that you call one or two of her other clients for a reference. This is a great way to learn more about what the agent is like to work with on a long-term basis. Take the numbers; it wouldn't hurt to call. In fact, if the agent doesn't offer this, you should bring it up.

Great Expectations

This is also a great time to find out more about how that agent works. Ask the agent to describe how she plans to sell your book. What is the process? And what more does she need from you? Here are a number of good questions to ask:

Slush Pile

So, one agent hasn't been able to sell your work, and you got an-other agent. Tell the second agent which publishers have already seen (and rejected) the proposal. If you don't, it will backfire. Editors who see the same proposal twice from two different agents will call the agent and tell him. Believe us, the agent will not be happy with you as a result. Remember, editors and agents know each other and often share much information.

Bookmarks

When an editor declines to pur-sue a book project, she sends out a **rejection letter.** Rejection letters sent directly to authors say little more than "no thanks." But rejection letters sent to agents might contain more information about why the editor turned it down.

➤ Will you need to make copies of your proposal or manuscript? How many copies?

➤ How many publishers does the agent plan to contact?

➤ Will you get copies of the rejection letters?

➤ Does the agent call the publishers to let them know your proposal is coming?

➤ Does the agent plan to submit to several publishers at once, or only one at a time (exclusively)?

Are there any wrong answers to these questions? Not really. But it is better to ask in advance about how the agent works than to grumble about it later.

Who Does What?

The answers to this question might be found in the agent/author contract. This is an agreement that the agent will send to you after you have agreed that he may represent your book.

Most times, the agent/author agreement covers just the one book. Ideally, an author hopes that one perfect agent will represent him forever. Just as ideally, agents long for clients whom they can represent profitably forever. But at this stage of the game, take it one book at a time.

In many ways, this is a trial run with an agent—an engagement, not a marriage. Maybe you're really just dating for a while. Hopefully, the relationship will turn out well—the agent will sell your book, and you two will get along famously. But you'll also want to continue to monitor the relationship after your book is successfully sold. Is the agent still communicating? Is she still passing along information as she receives it? If not, maybe the relationship should end.

Read the Fine Print

Examine the agent/author agreement carefully before you sign it. Make sure that you understand all the terms and that they are acceptable to you. (You might want to look right now at the sample agreement in Appendix D, "Sample Author/Agent Agreement."

Office Fees

One of the things that you might notice is that there is typically a charge for expenses such as postage, messengers, copying, and other office expenses. What's up with that?

Most agents require that the author pay for these expenses. This charge is not to be confused with the reading fees discussed in Chapter 11, "Finding and Working with an Agent." Some agents put a cap on such expenses. For instance, co-author Sheree caps these fees at $150. Realistically, however, it could cost an agent several hundred dollars to sell a single book.

How are these fees collected? If your agent sells your book and receives an advance check from the publisher, the office fees will be deducted (along with the agent's commission) before a check is sent on to you. And if an agent hasn't had any luck selling your book after trying for a year or so, don't be surprised if you receive a bill in the mail one day.

So make sure that you know what the fees could be. If the agreement doesn't mention office fees, ask.

"Hello, It's Your Author!"

You shouldn't call agents during the query process, but now that it's official, go ahead and call. You have a right to expect reasonable access to your agent, not to just shoot the breeze, but to be kept informed of everything the agent does on your behalf. Expect progress reports from time to time.

Your agent will be pleased if you respect his time. Call only when you need to, and try to group your questions together. Better yet, send a fax (or e-mail) with all your questions, and ask your agent to call you.

Do we make agents sound scary? They aren't really. But they are busy people who, like us all, have developed particular ways of working. You will get along nicely with your agent if you just accept that fact.

So, What Do You Think?

Up to this point in your writing career, you have been in control. But from the time an agent starts to try to sell your project, the agent is now pretty much in control of what happens.

Here is what you hope is happening: The agent is calling editors to pitch your book. He's talking you and your book up as he lunches with editors. Throwing humility to the winds, he has all the top editors clamoring to see what you've written. He has written a glowing cover letter, which accompanies your proposal as it goes out to publishers that request it.

Time in a Bottle

How long does the process take? It takes several weeks for editors to respond. The cover letter that your agent sent along with your material might have requested a response within a certain time period. Sometimes agents include a sentence similar to this: "I'd like to have all offers in by January 30th." But even with a clock ticking, editors tend to move slowly. (In Chapter 14, "Behind Closed Doors," you'll get a glimpse at the inner workings of a publishing house to better understand the process.)

What is your agent doing while the days slip by without an answer? Making follow-up calls to check that the proposal arrived. The real purpose of the phone calls is to remind editors of their early interest in the project, of course. But so as not to appear pushy, more subtle tactics are employed.

Ante Up

If a publisher calls to express an interest in acquiring your book, the agent will once again work the phones. Calls will be placed to all the publishers that received the proposal, and the agent will say: "Publisher X is interested in that book you liked so much, and I wondered if your house was still interested." This way, the editors are once again prodded into action. And such news might result in a larger offer because the second (or third or fourth) bidder has to beat what is already on the table.

The Rejection Blues

Realistically, most responses will be in the form of rejection letters. Even the best writers get rejection letters, so if it's any consolation, you're in fine company.

Kissing the Boo Boo

An agent can help you overcome the sting of rejection letters. Plain and simple, those letters hurt. They hurt you as the author, and no matter how many rejection letters your agent has seen in her career, they hurt her, too. Talk about it with your agent.

Those Wicked Letters

Should you even see your rejection letters? Yes. Here is what you can learn from them:

➤ How many publishers have seen your work

➤ Which publishers have seen your work

➤ What kind of a relationship your agent has with publishers

➤ What kinds of criticism your project is receiving

All this information will help you get better and will help increase your chances of getting published in the future. Are all the letters saying the same thing? If all editors say that they don't see a market for your book, that might tell you something. If all the editors say that there are too many similar titles already out there, that, too, might be sending you a message. And if it makes you feel better, pin your rejections up on the wall and toss darts at them.

One of Sheree's clients once asked for the original copies of two of his rejection letters. In one, the publisher said that the proposed book was "too specific." In the other, the publisher said that the book was "too general." He framed the letters side by side in his office. You'll be pleased to know that this story has a happy ending: Another publisher thought that his proposal was just right, and his book was published!

No matter what you wind up doing with them, try to learn from those letters—and learn to deal with rejection. Consider it a personal growth experience.

Going Once, Going Twice ... Sold!

What if several publishers let your agent know that they plan to make an offer for your book? To get the best price for it (in other words, the biggest advance), your agent will plan an *auction.*

Here is how an auction works:

➤ Your agent will choose a date and alert the interested publishers.

➤ Your agent may establish a *floor,* a minimum bid, or reserve the right to decline unacceptable bids.

➤ On the day of the auction, your agent will call the editors for their bids. (Not all editors will end up bidding.)

➤ As the number rises, the agent will continue to call editors and inform them of the latest price.

➤ At the end of the day (or days), the editor with the highest bid gets your book.

An auction day can be very exciting for both the agent and the author. You'll find it hard not to call your agent every few minutes to check on things. Let your agent call you, though. She needs to keep those phone lines clear for editors with big checkbooks!

Slush Pile

Rejections do hurt. But don't respond with a rebuttal in writing or a nasty message on the phone. You can easily make enemies in the publishing world with such loose-cannon behavior. Your agent will not be pleased, and editors will not be pleased. Try a big bowl of ice cream instead.

Bookmarks

When an agent has all interested publishers submit their bids on the same day, it's called an **auction.** This is the best way to get a high advance. The agent might also specify a minimum bid, called the **floor.**

"How Much Can I Expect?"

This is the dreaded first question every new author asks an agent. And it's a question that's impossible to answer. The size of an advance depends entirely on the perceived size of the book's audience. It depends on how much the publishing house loves your book. It depends on how unique your book is. It depends on how many publishers are interested in your book. It depends on the timing of your book, too, and how many competing titles there are out there.

Other factors that can affect the size of an advance include whether the publishing industry is on an upswing or a downswing. The size and power of the publishing house that wants to buy your book figures in, too. Another factor may be whether that publishing house had a good year or a bad year. It may also depend on whether the publisher had a fight with his spouse or whether it is raining outside. Who knows?

Nibbles

If an editor is interested in your book, chances are she'll call your agent before making a formal offer. This lets the agent know that you've hooked at least one fish! Chapter 14 is filled with material about how editors pull together information before making an offer, but in this chapter, let's just say that the first offer is never the best offer. Your agent will work hard to try to get the offer increased.

Reeling 'Em In

As the author, you should be included on the action surrounding your book. Your agent will want to keep you abreast of interest, offers forthcoming or on the table, and any anticipated closing date. You should definitely be included in the conversation about money. This does not mean that you, too, will talk to the editor. Money talk goes on between an agent and an editor; it does not include the author. But you do get to approve the final deal—congratulations!

The Least You Need to Know

➤ Know what you can expect from an agent who wants to represent you.

➤ Familiarize yourself with an agent/author agreement.

➤ An agent might ask you to make changes to your work, but you don't have to agree.

➤ Rejection letters sometimes have much useful information you can learn from.

➤ The size of an advance is totally unpredictable, but what is for certain is that your agent will work to get as large an advance as possible.

Chapter 13

Submitting Without an Agent

In This Chapter

➤ If you can't get an agent—or don't want one

➤ University presses

➤ Submitting directly to small publishers

➤ Niche publishing

➤ The world of children's books

➤ Basic submission guidelines

➤ Should you self-publish?

What do you do if you can't get an agent? Or what if you simply don't want to use one? Can you try to work directly with a publisher without the extra layer of an agent? Sure. In this chapter, you'll discover some of the specialized situations in which agents aren't required. You'll also learn how to make a professional submission without an agent.

It is entirely possible to get published without the help of an agent. Many writers have done it. In fact, there are some areas of the publishing business in which agents rarely, if ever, are used. Where? At university presses, scholarly publishers, regional publishers, some small presses, and many children's publishers.

Let's take a quick look at the world of academia first.

The Ivy Leagues

University presses are a world unto their own, with specialized methods of editorial selection and approval. Acquisitions editors who work for university presses crisscross the country attending professional conferences of all sorts—literary, anthropological, medical, sociological, and the like—to stay on top of what the issues are and who is tops in the field. When they familiarize themselves with the leading scholars in their field of publishing specialty, the editors cultivate relationships with them in the hopes that these experts will someday write for them. To put it bluntly, in most cases you don't call such editors; they call you.

You can submit without being "summoned." How do you do it? First send a query letter to the acquisitions editor describing yourself and your book, and then wait for the editor to respond. All the same rules for writing query letters (as you learned in Chapter 7, "Query Letters That Sell Nonfiction") apply. Do not leave out your self-addressed, stamped envelope. University presses have even less money than other publishers and surely cannot afford to pay the postage on all the unsolicited material they receive!

Experts Say

"Once a university press editor asks for your proposal, it should be an exclusive submission," a professor told us. "Etiquette dictates that, even if you never hear back, you wait at least six months before trying another publisher. Multiple queries are all right, but the in-house review process is so long with the proposal that you need to give them the exclusive."

Curriculum Vitae

An editor at a university press will take a long, hard look at your educational and scholarly credentials. If you do not have the right ones to back up your book, the chances are slim that a university press will take you on.

If an acquisitions editor does respond to your query, she might ask you to send in a "prospectus." Don't panic—that's just a book proposal by another name. Why the world of scholarly presses uses it is unclear; perhaps it just sounds more scholarly.

Bookmarks

University presses use **readers,** or **referees,** to help with the acquisitions process. These folks judge manuscripts in their fields of expertise. They either are paid a fee or are paid in kind with free books from the press.

Readers and Referees

Unlike a trade publisher with its pub board and editorial meetings, folks outside the university press primarily judge the fate of a proposal.

If the editor likes what she sees in your prospectus, and if your credentials are up to snuff, your material will then be sent to a reader. *Readers* are also known as *referees*. These are well-known professors and other experts who are qualified to judge your material from a professional standpoint. As the editor is seldom academically qualified to pass judgment on a manuscript, readers perform this critical task.

How many readers or referees will see your material? Perhaps only one, or as many as three or four. It depends on the topic and the input from the first reader. Readers might sometimes recommend your book "with reservations." The editor will then go back to the author and ask for changes or a response to the reservations.

Read More About It

The average print run from university presses is lower than a trade publisher, but you might find that university presses have a longer-term commitment to keeping their books in print.

An excellent way to learn more about the world of university presses is through a book published by the Modern Language Association. Known as the *MLA Style Manual and Guide to Scholarly Publishing,* this is the standard guide for graduate students preparing theses. Over the years, it has grown to include information on how to get published.

Small Is Beautiful

Some of the success stories coming out of small publishing companies show that small can indeed be beautiful. Don't kid yourself—New York is not the only place where book publishing gets done. There are thriving presses all over the country, from Tennessee and Louisiana to Washington and Vermont, and from New Mexico to Colorado. One of the strongest-selling business books in recent history, *The Millionaire Next Door,* didn't come from Random House or Simon & Schuster. It came from the Longstreet Press in Atlanta, Georgia. The publisher behind the multimillion-copy *Chicken Soup for the Soul* series is Health Communications in Deerfield Beach, Florida. Both *small publishers?* Technically, yes.

Slush Pile

If you are submitting without an agent because you couldn't get one interested in your project, keep that information to yourself. Never send a letter to a publisher that begins: "I couldn't get an agent to represent me, so I am writing to you myself." Yikes! The publisher will figure that you couldn't get an agent because your project wasn't viable and will put your letter on the stack to be returned with a polite note or form letter.

Bookmarks

How small is small? Instead, ask how large is small, as the case may sometimes be. The term **small publisher,** or **small press,** is used loosely but generally is applied to publishing houses with sales of less than $10 million a year. Mini-majors are publishers with $20 million to $50 million in annual sales.

"Mini-majors," a new term in publishing, refers to publishers such as Running Press in Philadelphia; Prima Publishing in Roseville, California; and Workman Publishing in New York. They're not big publishers with sales of hundreds of millions of dollars, but they're medium-size companies with solid sales in the $20 million to $50 million range.

Small publishers and the mini-majors are generally more open to dealing directly with authors than the New York houses are. And it can be somewhat less intimidating for a first-time author. Many a big-name author (including Tom Deepak Chopra) got started with a small publisher before achieving fame with a larger house (much to the chagrin of the smaller publisher, who took a chance on an unknown).

When you work with a publisher that has a small staff, you can sometimes have a closer relationship with the editor, publicist, and other people working with your book.

The Name Game

The best way to get your query letter read is to address it to an actual editor. How do you find out who the editors are at these small presses? Here are three ways:

➤ Look on the acknowledgments page of other books from that publisher; authors often thank their editors.

➤ Look in the *Writer's Guide to Book Editors, Publishers, and Literary Agents;* or in *Literary Marketplace* (*LMP*).

➤ Call the publishing house and ask which acquisitions editors acquire books in your genre.

Query an Editor

The query letter you should use with a small publisher is essentially the same as outlined in Chapter 7. The only difference is that you're not trying to sell an agent; you are trying to sell an editor.

Review the advice in Chapter 7. Remember to keep your query letter short and to the point. But also remember that the purpose of a query letter is to sell yourself and your project. Talk up the market, and talk up your commitment to seeing the book work. Also include an SASE.

Will you hear back from an editor at a small publisher? Yes, if you have included an SASE. How long it will take to hear back is anyone's guess. But if you neglect to include an SASE and your query doesn't interest the editor, you will never hear back. Your letter will be tossed, and you will wonder forever if it ever even arrived. Resist the temptation to call and ask whether your query letter got there. Even at small presses, an editor's day is hectic, often with no time to return phone calls about unsolicited queries, proposals, and manuscripts.

Negotiating on Your Own

If an editor responds to your query and requests a copy of your proposal or your manuscript, you are one step closer to success. What happens then is described at length in Chapter 14, "Behind Closed Doors." The acquisitions process for a small publisher is the same as that for a large publisher.

If the small publisher makes you an offer, then what? You can negotiate on your own, but if you decide to do so, you'll need to learn a lot in a hurry. An excellent book by Mark Levine, called *How to Negotiate a Book Contract,* can help you.

Chapter 15, "The Party of the First Part," walks you through some of the basic points in a publishing contract. Some editors are also quite patient in explaining contract points to first-time authors.

Experts Say

Have you been dropped by your agent, who was unable to sell your project after a year or so? You're not alone. Mark Victor Hansen and Jack Canfield were dropped by their agent, too, just before the *Chicken Soup for the Soul* book sold to Health Communications. "Biggest mistake he ever made," they laugh.

An Agent, at This Point?

If you have an offer in hand, getting an agent should be no trouble now! Those same folks who weren't interested in helping you before would be happy to help you now that there's an offer on the table. But do you need an agent?

Hot Off the Press

One of the bestselling book categories today is alternative health. It took decades before big publishers began to publish folks like Deepak Chopra and Andrew Weil. It was the small publishers who built public awareness and brought out well-researched information on topics such as herbal medicine, vegetarianism, and yoga. Companies such as The Book Publishing Company, Avery Publishing Group, and Shambhala Publications are well-established publishers with great distribution in both bookstores and health food stores. There are dozens more as well. "Mainstream acceptance of our books has exploded in the last few years," says Bob Holzapfel, publisher of The Book Publishing Company. "It is a great reward after 20 years of work!"

If you don't think you can do a good job of negotiating on your own behalf, perhaps you should get an agent involved. At this point, the editor may be happy to refer you to an agent she's worked with before. Ask if the agent is willing to take a lower commission, though, since you got the deal on your own.

If the publisher tells you that it doesn't like to work with agents, be on your guard.

The Hunt Is On

Small publishers and mini-majors sound great, but how do you find them? They're right there on the shelf next to the big boys! As you spend time in bookstores familiarizing yourself with the players in your category, you will begin to spot the small publishers on your own. Many of them are listed in *Writer's Guide to Book Editors, Publishers, and Literary Agents,* and in *LMP.*

If you're game, give it a try; small publishers just might be right for you.

Tight Niches

A discussion of small publishers has to include the "niche" publishers, the ones that specialize in one tight niche market. A niche market can be anything from mountain-climbing books (The Mountaineers Press) to books on the occult (Samuel Weiser, Inc.), and from Northwest travel books (Sasquatch Books in Seattle) to Southern travel books (Pelican Publishing Company). The more familiar you become with your area of specialty, the more you will notice niche publishers who cater directly to your market.

Bookmarks

There are several different types of **children's books:** illustrated books, easy readers, and chapter books. Illustrated books are the lovely big picture books that small children love to "read" over and over again. Easy readers are books of the "see Jane run" variety, and chapter books are longer books for more experienced readers.

Don't spin your wheels trying to interest a large publisher when you can go directly to a small niche publisher that specializes in your area. These are the experts in the marketplace and will understand right away whether your book is marketable and how best to do it. Niche publishers are very careful about the books they publish. The decision process will be slow, but if your book is published by a smart niche publisher, the sales could be steady for years to come.

Once Upon a Time

Children's books are another area in which you can deal directly with a publisher. Some agents specialize in representing children's books, of course, but a large portion of children's authors do not have agents.

How do you approach a children's book publisher about your idea? With a query letter! Look for the names of editors in *Writer's Guide to Book Editors,*

Publishers, and Literary Agents or in *LMP,* or call the publisher to ask for the names of its acquisitions editors and their areas of specialty. But if you do call, just get the name from the receptionist and politely hang up. Resist the urge to ask to speak to an editor directly at this point. Remember, the early stages of getting published are all done by written letters, not phone conversations. You must first prove that you can write.

You may also call the company and request its submissions guidelines. When you receive the guidelines, follow them down to the letter. Do not get fancy and decide to try another approach. Guidelines have been developed over many years of publishing experience and should be heeded.

Be warned, however, that many children's publishers have ceased accepting unsolicited manuscripts altogether. These companies still will accept query letters from first-time authors, though.

Poetry

Poetry is still one more category that usually does not require an agent—and most agents do not represent poetry. If you would like to have your poetry published, our best advice is to scour the writer's shelf in the library or bookstore, and read more than one book on getting poetry published. Identify appropriate magazine, journal, and poetry book publishers, and query them according to their specific guidelines. Some books list appropriate publishers, but an even better technique is to read books and magazines of poetry. Ask poetry teachers as well as published poets for advice. Don't get discouraged before you start. Poetry gets published all the time—just not very often via agents.

Experts Say

"I recommend so many writers to the Society of Children's Book Writers and Illustrators, it should pay me a commission!" laughs author Debra Keller. "The benefits of membership are tremendous: a list every August of all children's book publishers, the names of their editors, the submissions guidelines, and what they are looking for." You don't need to have been previously published to join. Contact the SCBWI at 323-782-1010.

To Self-Publish or Not to Self-Publish

If you've had no luck with agents and no luck submitting directly to publishers, what options are left? Is the only way your book will ever see its way into print if you pay for it to be printed and bound?

Self-publishing is an old and honorable pursuit. (Even Benjamin Franklin did it!) But how can you decide if it is right for you? After all, writing a book is an art. Self-publishing a book is a business.

Hot Off the Press

When Debra Keller wrote her book *The Trouble with Mister*, she sent it out to 16 children's book publishers, carefully following the guidelines for each. Fourteen publishers rejected it, but one expressed an interest and asked if it could hang on to the book and consider it more carefully. Months passed, and Debra suddenly remembered that she had never heard anything at all from the 16th publisher, Chronicle Books in San Francisco. She sent a follow-up letter asking about the fate of her manuscript. She heard back right away—not only had it been received, but that publisher wanted to publish it!

A Means to My End?

To decide if self-publishing is the right route for you, go back to a question in Chapter 1, "So, Why Write?": Why do you want to write a book?

➤ I'm compelled to write.

➤ I want the personal satisfaction of being published.

➤ I hope to advance my cause.

➤ I want to share my knowledge.

➤ I'd like to advance my career.

➤ I'd like to achieve fame.

➤ I'd like to earn a fortune.

➤ All of the above.

Which of these goals can be satisfied by self-publishing your book? Pretty much all of them except fame and fortune. Sure, it has happened that a self-publisher has gone on to fame and fortune, but it is a fluke.

Do You Have What It Takes?

Not everyone is cut out to be a self-publisher. It requires lots of money, creativity, ingenuity, dedication, and entrepreneurial zeal. Do you have what it takes? Asking yourself these five questions might help you find out:

Slush Pile

Do not send an illustrated manuscript. Illustrated manuscripts go first to the art department to be evaluated, not to the editor. If it doesn't meet with the art director's approval, it is rejected. Your actual words themselves will never be seen or read. Submit only a manuscript.

➤ Is publishing my book so important to me that I am willing to pay thousands of dollars to see it happen?

➤ Am I willing to accept the fact that I will probably never see that money again?

➤ Once my book is published, am I willing to invest countless hours attempting to distribute, publicize, and market my book?

➤ Am I thick-skinned enough to take it if my book is criticized, ignored, or rejected by booksellers and/or the media?

➤ Am I persistent enough to keep going if I get that kind of treatment?

Hot Off the Press

Emeline Howe Malpas was angry. A former overseas Red Cross Hospital Worker, she watched in disbelief for 50 years as the good work of 35,000 WACs, Red Cross, and Army nurses who volunteered for duty during World War II was ignored. Her book, *Run Away to War*, is a moving account of Malpas' experiences in war-time Paris. An agent was unsuccessful in selling it to publishers. But Malpas wanted the book to be published before President Clinton dedicated a memorial to all women who served, so she self-published her book. "I'll have to sell 1,000 copies before I break even," says 85-year-old Malpas. "But now the story has not been lost."

Speaking of Speaking ...

One of the best reasons to self-publish a book is to augment your speaking career. If you are already giving talks to rooms full of people, it might be quite easy to sell them a book you just happened to bring with you. Skip the headache of bookstore distribution, and keep all the money. Sounds great! And it can be done with a self-published book.

Several excellent books are already available on how to self-publish a book. We really don't have enough room here to do a thorough job of covering the process, but here's a quick look at the steps you will need to go through.

1. Find a copy editor and a proofreader.
2. Get the book designed and typeset.

3. Have a cover designed.

4. Find an affordable short-run printer.

5. Arrange for your book's distribution.

6. Market and publicize the book.

Proof Positive

If your self-published book is a success, can you sell it to a larger publisher? Certainly! You have to stop selling it yourself then. If you can show a solid record of sales success with a self-published book, both agents and publishers will take you very seriously.

On the other hand, bestselling self-publishers have sometimes just stuck it out for the ride instead of selling to a larger publisher. They might also ride it to the very top in order to cut a bigger deal with a large publisher. *Rich Dad, Poor Dad* spent month after month on the business bestseller lists at the end of 1999 and into 2000. The author continued to publish under his own imprint, pocketing the larger portion of the proceeds himself instead of taking a royalty arrangement from a publisher. The book itself attempts to teach lessons in wealth-creation—apparently the author had learned the lessons pretty well because when he finally did sell to Warner Books, he made quite a bundle!

Experts Say

Why not learn from the best? Bestselling author Mark Victor Hansen periodically teaches a seminar called "How to Build a Speaking and Writing Empire." And he should know—millions and millions of people bought his *Chicken Soup* books. For information on scheduling, or to purchase an audio of the event, call 949-759-9304.

Oh, Don't Be Vain!

Self-publishing is a fine and honorable pursuit, but we think vanity presses are a rip-off. We recommend staying away from anyone called a "subsidy publisher," or anyone who acts like he's willing to publish your book as long as you pay the costs.

The contract from a vanity press looks just like a standard publishing contract, but with one critical difference: A clause states that you have to pay for producing the book. If you are offered something like this, run!

The Electronic Edge

Many adventurous writers are experimenting with new forms of self-publishing: e-books and on-demand printing. Companies such as Fatbrain and iUniverse have set up systems whereby writers can either make their materials available online to prospective purchasers, or print up smaller quantities than would be possible with most printers.

Like traditional self-publishing, though, it remains the responsibility of the author to create sales for what he has written. Just because your work is available online as an e-book doesn't mean that a reader is going to buy it, unless you somehow create demand through publicity.

These companies have even more to offer: online classes and seminars taught by publishing professionals. Check out the Web sites www.fatbrain.com and www.iuniverse.com.

As with the rest of the online world, what happens there changes with blinding speed. So, even if this route never occurred to you, go and check out these companies anyway. Who knows what services they are offering today?

Hot Off the Press

Barnes & Noble bookseller bought a 49-percent stake in iUniverse. Does that mean that writers who use iUniverse can get their books into B&N? It can happen, but it is not guaranteed. It happened for Natasha Munson, though, and her self-published book *Life Lessons for Black Girls*. The book became a frontlist title at B&N and a part of an iUniverse advertising campaign.

You're on Your Own

You now know many of the circumstances in which you can try to get your work published without an agent. When submitting on your own behalf to any kind of publisher (whether a children's publisher, a niche publisher, or a small publisher), be as businesslike as possible. Review the chapters on queries and proposals before you begin to compile your materials, keeping in mind that you are directing your information to a book editor, not an agent.

An editor has the same concerns as an agent: the potential market for the book, the author's credentials, and the uniqueness of the idea. Just as an agent's career depends on finding successful authors, so too does the editor's career flourish when she finds great writers whose books sell well. Editors are looking for new writers. Help them find you!

The Least You Need to Know

➤ It is possible—and quite common—to approach university presses, children's publishers, and small publishers without an agent.

➤ Learn the names of the editors, and approach them directly with short query letters.

➤ Respect the system: queries first, and proposals later (if requested). Do not try to call editors directly before they've had a chance to review something from you in writing.

➤ Once you have a deal in hand, you will be able to get an agent, but ask for a reduced commission.

➤ Self-publishing requires both money and dedication, but it can be emotionally rewarding and can perhaps help boost your career.

Chapter 14

Behind Closed Doors

> **In This Chapter**
>
> ➤ Getting past the first hurdle: the editor
>
> ➤ The pub board meeting
>
> ➤ Competition and sales projections
>
> ➤ Production costs and P and Ls

So far, on your mission to get published you wrote a great query letter and a superb book proposal. An agent called you up and offered to represent you. Or, no agents called and you decided to take up the task yourself. Twelve copies of your proposal have been sent to 12 editors at the 12 publishing houses best suited for your book. Your fingers are crossed, and you are saying your prayers nightly. What happens now?

Hurry Up and Wait

Several things could happen:

> ➤ The editor opens her mail one day and discovers your proposal. Intrigued after reading just a few paragraphs, she sets it aside on a stack of material she plans to take home and read more thoroughly.
>
> ➤ Your agent may have placed a call to the editor to get him excited about the proposal in advance. It arrives in the mail, and the editor thinks, "Ah, yes, this is the book Mr. Agent described. I must take a look at it right away; it sounded perfect for our *list*." He glances at a few pages and sets it aside on a stack of material he plans to take home and read more thoroughly.

➤ Your agent might have gone to lunch with the editor the day before. Over a spinach salad, your agent pitched the editor a number of book projects from several clients. The editor expressed an interest in seeing one or two of them (including yours!), and the agent messengers them over that same afternoon.

The editor sets it aside on a stack of material she plans to take home and … you know the rest.

However it got there, your proposal is now inside the doors of a publishing house.

"Sorry, Not Right for Our Needs at This Time"

Sadly, the story could easily end right here. The editor might not put your proposal on the stack that she plans to take home. Perhaps she took a look at your proposal and then put it in her reject pile.

Why? Well, for any one of a number of reasons. You might not make it as far as the editorial meeting for these reasons:

➤ It is clearly not appropriate for that publishing house—your book is about the history of fighter pilots, and this publisher publishes only vegetarian cookbooks.

➤ The publishing house already has a book on that topic, and it hasn't sold well.

➤ The publishing house already has a book on that topic, and the author of that book plans to do more in that area.

➤ The editor doesn't think that a large market exists for your book.

Most rejection letters do not include any actual reason why your book was rejected. The standard line is "Thank you, but this is not right for us." Why don't editors write more? Two reasons: They don't have the time to analyze, critique, and then write to you; and they don't want to invite a response or rebuttal from you. Try to take your rejection letters in stride.

Experts Say

Editors don't read much at the office. Yes, they do read query letters, but most of the real reading gets done at home. "I've broken the straps on four book bags this year alone from the weight of the manuscripts I carry home every night," says Danielle Egan-Miller, an acquisitions editor at NTC Contemporary.

Bookmarks

The word **list** is used to describe the books that the publisher plans to publish in the near future. "It's on our list," an editor might say, or "We have a few holes on our list that need filling"—these phrases are music to an agent's ears. Perhaps *your* book is just perfect for their list!

Hot Off the Press

Publishing is a people business, and the people who work in publishing are people just like you. Sometimes they are tired, cranky, and not in the mood to buy books. If your book proposal has been rejected by an editor, do not take this as a sign that your project is doomed and will never be published by anyone. Who knows, perhaps it just was a bad day at the office when your material crossed their desks. Keep trying, and go on to the next publisher.

Consider This

But if your book does make it onto the stack to be read further, then what?

Editors do quite a bit of investigating before bringing your proposal to a meeting. An editor might call your agent to ask questions or request more material. An editor might call you directly to learn more about you, the market for the book, and your plans to promote it. Editors might also do more hands-on investigation: prowling around bookstores to examine the competing titles, asking friends in the industry how well that category is selling, or cruising the Internet to see if there is much interest in the topic.

If the editor likes what he sees in the proposal, what he hears from you, and what his own research turns up, the next step is for him to present it to his colleagues and superiors for possible publication.

Committee Decisions

As powerful as many of them are, editors do not make the decision to publish a book. That decision rests with a group of people sometimes called the *pub board* or the *editorial board*. The editor who likes

Slush Pile

The phone rings, and it's an editor asking about your book. Although the questions may all relate to the book itself, the editor might have another motive. How well you present yourself on the phone is critical to your book's future success. Editors want authors who can handle themselves easily with interviews and the media. If you are tired, distracted, or otherwise unprepared to sound good on the phone, it is better to beg off and reschedule the conversation.

your book is only one voting member of this group. Other members include other editors, the publisher, and folks from the sales, marketing, and publicity departments. The process works something like this:

Bookmarks

Unless it is a one-person publishing house, your proposal will be presented to an **editorial board,** or **pub board.** This is a group of people who collectively make the decision about what titles to publish.

➤ An editor is intrigued by your proposal and decides to present it to the pub board.

➤ The editor brings your proposal to a meeting.

➤ The editor makes a short presentation about your book and attempts to drum up interest and enthusiasm.

➤ The editor answers questions from other members of the group. Sometimes the editor needs to do further research and will present the book in more detail at a future meeting.

So, that's it. The fate of your book can be decided in about 10 minutes. But if you get past this point, then what happens? Does the editor call to say that he wants to make an offer? No, not yet.

Hot Off the Press

"Editors had to do a lot of homework before presenting a title for a publication decision," explains Carol Hupping, former executive editor of Peterson's. They had to fill out a long "proposal to publish" form. It included an overview, content description, a chapter outline, strong selling points, the editor's take on the market, descriptions of competing titles, and an author bio. The editor also had to provide the specs for the book: information on the proposed size and shape of the book, number of pages, and whether it had photos or illustrations. Each presentation took about 10 minutes, although the discussion might stretch to a half-hour.

How's It Gonna Sell?

Even if an editor has successfully lined up support in the meeting, there is still more work to be done. Remember, publishing is a business, and in business, the bottom line is king. So, the editor has to work up the numbers to see whether publishing your book will pay off. How is this done?

Editors ask the sales department for help. Experienced sales folks can help the editor figure out what the typical orders would be for the proposed book. How many copies would Borders buy? Barnes & Noble? Target? Small independent bookstores across the country? They add up all these numbers and hope that the result is big.

The publicity department may also be polled at this point. The editor will talk with the publicity folks about whether the topic of the book (or the name of the author) lends itself to publicity.

The editor might also pay a visit to the production department to check on the typical production costs for a book of this type.

All these numbers are plugged into the P and L, the profit and loss statement. If the numbers look good, the editor reports back to the pub board. And then maybe, just maybe, the editor will get the go-ahead to make an offer.

Slush Pile

The power and influence of the publishing sales department has grown in the last decade. Although in years past, the typical sales department wouldn't find out what was on the list until the sales conference, it is now included in the front-end decisions about what to publish. If the sales department doesn't think it can sell a book to its customers, the book does not get published. End of story.

Money, Money, Money, Money

The editor doesn't make the decision to publish on her own, nor does she decide the size of the offer on her own. In the pub board discussion or in a one-on-one with the publisher, all decision-makers determine the range of the advance. The editor then has the authority to call either the agent or the author (if there is no agent involved) to make the offer.

The Meeting Begins

Let's take a close look at what goes on in one of these meetings. This will give you a good idea how all the information you dredged up for your proposal comes into play.

It is a Tuesday afternoon at Big Publishing Company, Inc., and all the members of the pub board are gathered in a conference room. The editors carry armloads of book proposals and other materials. In any given meeting, the fate of 10 or more books is decided. Each editor has high hopes for the books he has decided to champion.

Batter Up!

Editor 1 leads off with her first proposal: a book of affirmations and prayers for breast cancer survivors. She describes the focus of the book, the reason that the world needs this book, the qualifications of the woman who put it together, and the impact the book could have on the women who read it.

The sales manager speaks up with a question: "How many books already exist on this topic? And just how large is the market? What are the current figures on breast cancer occurrence?"

The editor has carefully read the proposal and knows the answers to those questions because the author did her research well. It was all right there.

The publisher wants to know: "There is a strong title already on the subject from another publisher. How will this book be different enough to find an audience? I worry that the bookstores won't see a need to order another similar title."

Once again the editor answers the questions and concerns with authority. The author of this book has researched the competing titles, talked to bookstore managers about the need, and lined up the support of a major breast cancer survivors group. A solid proposal has all the answers.

So, the pub board is interested in considering this title. What happens then? The editor spends the next few days making the rounds of the departments to gather more information on how much it would cost to produce this book and how many copies they can expect to sell. She calls the agent or the author with any questions about the proposal that she couldn't answer herself. She distributes copies of the proposal to those interested in reading.

When the editor has rounded up all the answers, she once again makes a short presentation at a pub board meeting. If the numbers are right, the group will decide to go on to the next phase: making an offer to publish the book.

Next Up!

Editor 2 gets a turn. He begins his presentation on a book about the history of baseball cards. "This will be the first-ever book on the topic," he says proudly, pointing with confidence at that claim in the proposal.

"Oh, come on!" says the publicity manager. "I am a collector myself and own at least two books on the history of baseball cards."

The editor stammers and flips quickly through the pages of the proposal, looking for something to salvage the situation. "Ah, but this is the first time that the cards themselves will be organized by player position rather than team! That is really unique!"

"Just like the book I have on my shelf," the publicity manager snickers.

Another book bites the dust.

Hot Off the Press

The worst thing you can do in a book proposal is lie. If you lie or fib about your qualifications, if you lie about the competing books, or if you lie about the sales history of your other books, you are headed for disaster. Editors never forget and will certainly not forget if they are made to look foolish with information that you supplied. Think you can try to fool one editor at one house and then move on to the next if that fails? Don't be surprised if your first editor moves, too. A bad reputation spreads quickly and is hard to shed. Always play straight.

Let's Pretend

You can see how critical the information that you provide in your proposal is to your future success. When compiling a proposal, pretend that you, too, are a member of a pub board. Put yourself in that person's shoes, and try to anticipate all the negative or hard-hitting questions that might be asked. Then supply the answers in your proposal. Give the editor something to work with.

Second Chances?

Is there ever a second chance? If an editor flops with your proposal once, can he ever try it again? Seldom, but it happens. It has nothing to do with begging or pleading on your part, though.

If the editor has truly fallen in love with your book project, he might go back to square one. He might poke around some more in the marketplace, ask more questions of friends in the industry, and try to gather ammunition that will convince the skeptics that this book would succeed. If the information he gathers is compelling enough, and if his own commitment to the book is strong enough, it just might work the second time around.

Try, Try Again

But if the answer was "No" and the editor doesn't have the heart or the interest to re-pitch the project, you have come to the end of the road—the end of the road with that publisher, anyway. Don't try another editor at the same house.

Congratulations are in order, though. Only a tiny fraction of book projects ever make it to the pub board stage, so you have succeeded. Keep trying. If one editor was interested enough to pitch it, another one will be, too.

They Like Me! They Really Do!

What if the answer is "Yes"? Go ahead and pop open the bottle of champagne. The editor succeeded with the pub board and got the go-ahead to make you an offer—way to go! Now what happens?

The editor will call you, or your agent, if you have one. The conversation will sound something like this: "I've got good news! We'd like to publish your book. I'd like to make you an offer of an advance against future royalties of ...."

The Numbers Game

The size of the advance could vary from small to large. Who knows? There is no way to predict exactly how much you'll be offered. If you have an agent, chances are that she will immediately ask for a larger figure (remember, the more you make, the more your agent makes). If you don't have an agent, should you ask for a bigger number, too?

It never hurts to ask, but ask for a reasonable increase over what is being offered. You might also risk looking like an egotist if you counter with what the editor thinks is an unreasonable sum. And you only risk being told "No, we won't go any higher." On the other hand, if you are just thrilled that someone wants to publish your book, take the offer.

Congratulations, you are getting published!

The Least You Need to Know

➤ Editors present proposals to a pub board made up of representatives from several different departments.

➤ If the sales department is not enthusiastic about a book idea, it will seldom go any further.

➤ The better the information in your proposal, the easier it is for an editor to gain support for your book.

➤ Never lie, exaggerate, or exclude important information from your proposal; it can only hurt you.

➤ If you get a "Yes," you'll be offered an advance, which you (or your agent) might be able to negotiate upward.

Chapter 15

The Party of the First Part

In This Chapter

➤ Boilerplate contract clauses

➤ "Half and half" advances

➤ The 12 major flex points

➤ Rights, royalties, and remainders

➤ Bonuses and other contract sweeteners

An offer is in and a contract is coming. Your book project is becoming more real by the moment. Someday you really will be able to walk into a bookstore and see your book on the shelf.

But first, you have to sign a contract.

We are not lawyers. After working with hundreds of contracts over the years, however, we do have a fairly good handle on what it all means. In this chapter, you will learn the meaning behind many of the standard clauses found in a publishing contract. Then we'll give you the inside scoop on which clauses we have found to be more negotiable than others.

Whereas and Therefore

Regardless of the size of the publishing company, most contracts are essentially the same. Some are considerably longer than others (40 pages is the longest we've seen), but the basic points are the same.

What is the purpose of a book contract? A publishing company wants to publish a work that you wrote and needs to have a legal document that does the following:

➤ Gives the company the right to publish and sell your material in an agreed-upon territory

➤ Outlines the monetary arrangements

➤ Establishes your right to grant the company the rights

➤ Spells out the responsibilities of the author and the publisher

➤ States a time length for the agreement

Pretty simple, isn't it? Then why does it take so many darn pages to establish those simple facts? Is that because lawyers bill by the hour? Perhaps. But the business world grows more complicated by the decade, and new legal issues crop up all the time. Let's take a close look at 15 major clauses in a publishing contract.

Slush Pile

So, you don't have an agent. Do you need a lawyer? Actually, most lawyers have little knowledge about the quirks found in publishing contracts. An editor will not be pleased to hear from your lawyer, either, if he or she is not familiar with a publishing contract. To find a lawyer who specializes in publishing, contact the Author's Guild (see Appendix B, "More Good Resources").

The Work

One of the early paragraphs in a contract will define what is generally called the "Work." This, of course, is your book. Your book will henceforth be referred to as the "Work." You get to be the "Author." The company is forever known in contracts as the "Publisher."

In this paragraph, the subject matter of the work will be defined. If you are writing a novel, it will be defined as a work of fiction, and the general focus of the book will be mentioned. If you are writing a nonfiction book, the work will be described as "a Work of nonfiction whose subject matter is as follows ...." The expected length of your finished manuscript will also be stated.

Why is this here? The publishing company needs to make sure that the book you turn in is the book that it had in mind when it signed you up. This clause protects the publisher from signing you up to write a novel about the Civil War, only to have you turn in a nonfiction memoir about your childhood in New Orleans.

Copyright

Standard publishing contracts state that the publisher will register the copyright to the work in the name of the author. Beware any contract that asks you to assign all rights to the publisher, or one that stipulates that the publisher is the copyright holder. Unless the author gives the right away, he or she owns the copyright by virtue of having written the material. In fact, the minute that you put pen to paper and write something original, it is copyrighted material without you even so much as filling out a form.

Hot Off the Press

Writers who agree to a flat fee for their work are performing what is known as "work for hire." Under a work-for-hire agreement, the writer does not own the copyright to his work and receives no royalties for books sold.

Tentatively Titled

This section of the contract might also contain a zinger, a phrase that refers to the book as "tentatively titled." Tentatively titled? But you thought of that title years ago, and it is all over your queries and proposals. How can the publisher refer to it as tentatively titled?

Sorry, but most publishing contracts allow the publisher the right to change the title of your book. Some will state that the title can be changed only "by mutual agreement."

Your delivery date (the day that your manuscript is due) will also appear in this early section of the contract.

The Advance

Ah, the money part. This is where the publisher spells out exactly how much of an advance you will receive. The language will read something like this: "As an advance against all monies accruing or payable to the Author under this Agreement, the Publisher will pay to the Author the sum of _____, payable as follows ...." Payable as follows?

Experts Say

As the author, you are not selling your book rights to the publisher; you're merely licensing the rights. When you license a right, you continue to own it for the life of your copyright, which is 95 years. The publisher may exercise certain rights that you grant him only for the term of the license. Once that term has expired, those rights revert back to you.

Regardless of the size of your advance, do not expect to receive it in one lump sum. The standard arrangement is for two payments: one payment on signing the contract, and the second tied to the completion of the final manuscript. The language and terms for the final payment vary widely, with some publishers paying when you turn the manuscript in on your delivery date, and other publishers not paying until the manuscript has been edited. Those are the most common advance payouts, but not the only ones. A few publishers have gone to three payments of one third each, with the final payment upon publication of the book. Others pay one third upon signing, the second third upon receipt of one half of the manuscript, and the final third upon receipt of the remainder of the manuscript.

Why won't they just write you a check for the whole sum? The publisher needs to know that you will follow through and turn in a manuscript on the topic and in the style that you promised in your book proposal. The best way to do this is to hold back part of the money until that happens. The publisher also wants to make sure that what you turn in is publishable—hence, the second payment is generally linked to receipt of an acceptable manuscript.

Grant of Rights

This is where you, as the author, grant and assign the rights to your work to the publisher. This is what gives the publisher the legal right to publish and sell your book. In addition to the right to sell your book in bookstores and other retail outlets, this clause may also grant the publisher the right to do these things:

➤ License the work to book clubs

➤ Sell the English-language book in foreign countries

➤ License foreign-language editions of the work

➤ Produce or license electronic versions or multimedia versions

➤ Produce or license audio book versions

➤ Produce or license hardcover, trade paperback, or mass market paperback versions

➤ License newspaper and magazine excerpts or serializations

➤ License movie rights

➤ License commercial or merchandising rights (maybe even coffee cups and T-shirts)

➤ Produce other sundry items, such as Braille versions or a play based on your book

Sounds like a lot of rights, right? This is a complicated section, one that agents love to tackle in detail. Publishers believe that they should be granted all these rights to be given a chance to earn back the money invested in your book. On the other hand, agents like to retain as many rights as possible on behalf of the author to obtain extra income for both of you!

Royalties

In the royalty section of the contract, the publisher defines exactly what the author will receive from the sale of the book. There are two different ways to calculate royalties:

➤ As a percentage of the retail price printed on the book

➤ As a percentage of the publisher's net, the actual cash the publisher receives from the sale of the book after discounts have been deducted

Royalties based on the retail price range from 7 to 15 percent or more. Royalties based on net usually start higher, at 10 percent, and escalate from there. Your contract should clearly state what type of royalties you will receive for each copy of your book sold.

The royalties clause might also be where you will find information on what share (or "split") the author will receive of any subsidiary rights income if any of the rights that the publisher is granted earlier in the contract (book clubs, mass market paperback, and so on) are sold.

Bookmarks

The publisher's standard contract is referred to as a **boilerplate contract.** It's the standard contract that's always used, and it has not (yet) been modified with any changes that you might request.

Hot Off the Press

By its very definition, negotiating can involve conflict and disagreement. Every time someone wins, someone else might lose. What if you, the author, feel that you have lost? It can make for a rocky start with a publishing company. That is one of the primary reasons that writers like to use agents. The agent can be the hard-nosed contract negotiator, and the relationship between the editor and the author can stay friendly. If you're negotiating on your own, consider your every paragraph carefully. You will need to work with your editor for a long time, and you don't want the relationship to go sour right from the start.

You will also find information on how many free copies of the book the author will receive once it is published, and whether the author can buy more copies at an author's discount.

Delivery of Manuscript and Corrections

The hard, cold truth is revealed here: the date by which you must turn in your completed manuscript. It may be a few short months, or it may be years away.

What happens if the date arrives and the publisher does not receive your finished work? The contract will include language to the effect that the publisher has the right to terminate the contract, generally upon written notification of the author by the publisher. If this happens, the contract states, the author will be obligated to repay the publisher any sums advanced to the author.

The contract will also include language that allows the publisher to reject the work as unpublishable, or to request specific changes to the manuscript. The contract should state a process by which the author can address the changes. If the publisher still feels that the manuscript is unacceptable, the contract can be terminated.

Once again, this is included because the publisher needs to be protected against receiving a shoddy product. In the case of nonfiction books, the publishing house probably made its decision based on only a proposal and a sample chapter. If the book ultimately turned in does not offer the proper information or isn't written professionally, a publisher will pull the plug.

Other Deliverables

The contract will outline the publisher's expectations regarding photographs, illustrations, maps, and charts. Who pays and when it needs to be turned in will be spelled out in this section.

Bookmarks

Most contracts contain an **option clause** for the author's next work. This means that the publisher gets first crack at the next book you write, or the next book of the same type.

Options

Publishers are taking a chance on your book. If it becomes a success, the house might want to publish more of your work. In the *option clause,* the contract will state that the publisher gets the first crack at your next work, the book you write after the book under contract. The language gives your publisher the exclusive right to consider your next work and describes how long the publisher has to make an offer. It may also say that if your publisher bids on the next work, you cannot sell the next work to another publisher for a lesser sum. It will also specify the earliest date that the next work can be submitted for consideration.

The clause might also cover competing works. The publisher will not want you to publish a similar book with a different publisher that would compete with this one.

The option clause and the noncompete clause can sometimes cause trouble for working writers. Later in this chapter, you'll find some ways to deal with this issue.

Author's Representations, Warranties, and Indemnity

In this clause, you, as the author, are assuring the publisher that the work is original and that you have the "sole and exclusive right to make the grant of rights set forth herein ...." You also are assuring the publisher that you are not slandering, libeling, or invading anyone's privacy with your work.

If legal action arises from the publication of your book, this clause allows the publisher to stand aside and point directly to you. "He's the one you want, he wrote the words. We just printed the darn thing." This clause might also outline the legal procedure if a lawsuit arises. Some publishers carry libel insurance; some do not.

Obligations of the Publisher

You have promised to deliver a manuscript by a certain date, and in this clause the publisher promises to publish the manuscript by a certain date. Other than exceptions mentioned in the contract (such as labor strikes, acts of God, or other circumstances beyond the publisher's control), if the publisher does not publish it, what then? There should be language that allows the author to terminate the agreement and keep the advance.

Accounting

You have already been informed about the amount of royalties you will receive, but when exactly will this be paid to you? The contract will have a paragraph that outlines the schedule. Some publishers pay twice a year; some pay only once a year. This section should also include language on what happens in the case of overpayment (if the publisher's accounting department accidentally sends you too much money!) or audits are requested by the author.

Bookmarks

When a book ends up being sold at a steeply discounted price, it is called **remaindering.** Books are sold for pennies on the dollar to remainder companies (who then sell them back to bookstores for the bargain tables). Before a book is remaindered, most publishers offer the author the chance to buy copies at bargain prices.

Overstock, Out of Print, or Reversion of Rights

If your book goes out of print, or if the sales dwindle down to nothing, what then? The answers will be found here. Most contracts state that if the book goes out of print for a particular length of time, the rights revert back to the author.

This clause also gives the publisher the right to sell your book at *remainder* prices, if need be.

Assignment

Once you sign the contract, your heirs will be legally bound by it as well. This means that if you die, the publisher still has the rights to the book. This clause also allows the publisher to assign the rights to your book to a new company if your publisher sells the business.

Bankruptcy

This clause covers the possibility of the publisher's bankruptcy, not yours. According to most contracts, if the publisher goes bankrupt, the author may buy back the rights to the book. But it leaves the publisher the right to sell any remaining copies of the book in inventory without paying any royalties.

Agency Clause

If you are represented by an agent, there will be an agency clause in your contract. If you are not using an agent, this clause won't appear.

The agency clause names the agent as the person to whom the publisher should send all monies accruing to this book. The agent will then subtract her percentage and pass the balance on to you. As long as the book remains under contract to this publisher, the agent will receive the royalty check.

Electronic Rights

The term "electronic rights" is very broad. Several things are meant when one speaks of electronic rights, so it is important to look at each right individually:

1. **Verbatim electronic rights**—The right to make a book available online, non-interactively, or using a hand-held device such as an e-Rocket book. This is also known as "electronic display rights."

2. **Database**—An electronic collection of writings (such as an anthology or a cookbook).

3. **Interactive**—An electronic version of the book that is enhanced by a third party (the publisher, for example) with material such as audio or video elements or

illustrations that allows the reader to manipulate the text. Publishers increasingly either are insisting on keeping this right or retain the first option of exploiting it. Even when an author does keep this right, it is important not to compete with the published version of the book. The publisher might get mad and might have cause to litigate, and it is not necessarily beneficial to the author.

4. **Print on demand**—This refers to short-run printing. New technology has made it possible to use an electronic file to print a small number of copies of the book as and when they are needed, relatively inexpensively. In the past, it was very expensive to print a small number of books; even a thousand was considered small. Now books can be printed one or a few at a time. When publishers control print on demand, they either use it to authorize wholesalers or retailers to print copies as needed, or do so themselves. When authors control print on demand, they can publish books themselves through services such as those offered by iuniverse.com. Authors cannot hold back print on demand, however, when they sell to a publisher. It is really only useful once the rights to a book have reverted back to the author.

Is It Worth It?

For the average unpublished writer, self-publishing, whether through electronic print on demand or otherwise, will not bring you income, nor will it establish you as a successful writer—and you may end up with a garage full of books. Print on demand, therefore, seems to be most valuable to published authors whose books no longer generate enough sales to warrant standard print runs, but who have found an audience. Another value to print on demand applies to promotional speakers or people who make a living giving seminars: These authors can sell books from a table in the back of the room. This is a cheap way to make professional-looking books available.

So, Is Anything Negotiable?

Hey, most things in life are negotiable, including (sometimes) contracts. As we mentioned before, we've each spent hundreds of hours working with publishing contracts, so we know a thing or two about where publishers might be willing to make changes. Don't take this as legal advice, but rather as guidance from two learned colleagues. Here are the 12 major flex points:

➤ Who pays for the index

➤ Who pays for illustrations, photos, and similar parts

➤ What sales territory the publisher has the rights to

➤ Various subrights issues

➤ Commercial and dramatic rights

➤ How many free copies the author receives

➤ The delivery date

➤ The author's expense budgets

➤ High-discount/reduced royalties clauses

➤ Joint accounting

➤ Next work and option clauses

➤ Reversion of rights

We have seen publishers make concessions in these clauses many times. Let's examine them closely.

Who Pays for the Index?

Most contracts call for the author either to provide the index or to pay for a professional index. Ever tried to do an index? Forget it. We recommend asking that the publisher pay for the index, or at least split the cost with the author. Indexing can cost several dollars a page, so the bill can be steep. If the publisher won't pay the entire amount or won't split the cost, ask for a cap on the cost. If you end up having to pay for the cost of the index, make sure that it comes out of your future royalties so that you don't have to pay for it out of your advance or out of your pocket.

Who Pays for Illustrations, Photographs, and Other Such Things?

For books in which photographs play a central part, the cost is usually borne by the author. When designing the book, if the publisher thinks that photographs will add to the book (food photography, for instance), the publisher should pay. Illustrations that decorate the book usually are paid for by the publisher, but illustrations for necessary charts are paid for by the author.

Make sure that you understand who pays for what, and feel free to ask the publisher to pay a larger share. Sometimes the author needs to deliver only what is known as scrap art: rough sketches of suggested art for the publisher to have drawn professionally.

The Sales Territory

The publisher will, quite literally, ask to publish the book in every language throughout the whole world—not just the United States and Canada, but tiny territories you've never even heard of. It wants the right to publish the book in the English language throughout the whole world, and it also requests the right to license foreign publishers to translate the book into other languages.

Some publishers do exploit these foreign rights well; others routinely distribute in the United States and Canada and let all the other territories languish. If you have an agent, your agent might want to keep foreign rights on your behalf and try to sell them directly to foreign publishers, so she will try to retain this right for you.

When publishers license translation rights, they split the monies received from foreign publishers with the author. If you don't have an agent, at least ask if there is any flexibility regarding the split. Some publisher's contracts call for a 50/50 split between the publisher and the author on the money from the sale of these rights, but you can always ask for a better cut. "How about 75/25, with 75 percent going to the author?"

Splits and Serials

As with the size of the territory, there are two questions with regard to serial rights. One, who controls the rights? Two, what is the split? If you have an agent, she might want to try to keep control of the *serialization* rights. But if you (or your agent) don't have the contacts to try to sell *first serial* rights to a magazine or newspaper, you might as well let the publisher's rights department try. But again, ask about the split. It is not unusual for the author to receive 90 percent of the money from a first serial rights sale.

> **Bookmarks**
>
> When an excerpt from the book appears just before the book is published, this is a **first serial.** Any excerpts that appear after the book has been published are known as **second serials.** These strange-sounding terms come from the word **serialization.**

Commercial and Dramatic Rights

These are the movie and play rights. Do you see your book as a perfect movie-of-the-week? Or as the basis for a Broadway musical? Then either fight to control these rights all yourself, or reduce the publisher's split.

Free Author's Copies

Most publishing contracts give the author a scant 5 or 10 free copies. Hey, you've got a big family! Your mom wants one, your great-aunt, your old next-door-neighbor .... You need more free books, and you can probably get them. This is an easy place for an editor to give up a little something. Ask for 25, anyway, and see what you get.

Publishers usually are generous with free copies used for publicity or review purposes, so if you have good opportunities for promoting the book yourself, ask for some free review copies.

Try to get at least a 50-percent discount on the cover price for any additional books that you want to buy. If you plan to give lots of speeches and sell books, try to get an even better quantity discount.

The Delivery Date

By the time you get to the contract stage, the publishing company might already have a pub date in mind. But you can always try to get a little extra time here—a few weeks or an extra month or so. Be kind to your editor, though. If you don't need the extra time, don't ask for it.

Bookmarks

If you are using material to which you do not own the copyright, you need to secure the proper **permissions.** To quote or reprint from newspaper, magazines, or other book, you must contact that company's permissions department. Sometimes there is a fee involved, which generally falls on the author.

Slush Pile

This chapter is not all you need to negotiate a contract. If you don't have an agent, then consult a literary lawyer, or at least a good book, such as *How to Negotiate a Book Contract*, by Mark Levine. The Author's Guild in New York can also be a good resource, if you wish to join.

Expense Budgets

These are fairly rare. Sometimes cookbook authors get baking allowances to help with the cost of buying ingredients. And sometimes the authors of anthologies or compilations can get a *permissions* budget. It never hurts to try, though.

High-Discount/Reduced Royalty Clauses

These are tough. Publishers claim that the deep discounts so prevalent today have cut into their margins and that they need to reduce royalties to stay in business. Agents (and authors) claim that it reduces royalties to practically nothing. Always try to get some concessions in this area. Publishers will also ask for reduced royalty rates on small print runs. You can try to negotiate the size of the print run that triggers this.

If your royalties are based on net and not list price of the book (see the section on royalties, earlier in this chapter), you or your agent may want to ask for a higher starting royalty rate. Or, perhaps ask that the royalty rate escalate as the book sells more copies—for example, a starting percentage on the first 10,000 copies sold, a higher percent on the next 5,000 copies, and the highest percentage on all copies sold in excess of 15,000.

Joint Accounting

Joint accounting? What's that mean? It means nothing on your first book. It means a great deal if you publish a second book with the same publisher, however. With joint accounting, all monies from both of your books go into the same big pot. So, if you haven't earned out the advance on your first book and your second book does really well, the publisher will ding your account for the negative royalty balance on the first one. We think each book should stand on its own, and we recommend asking to get this clause eliminated.

Options Clauses

If you and your publisher get along well, you will want to work together again. If you don't get along, you don't want to be legally bound to offer it your next book.

If you are a working writer with lots of books in the works and in various stages of publication, this needs to be stated in the contract. Some contracts actually seek to prevent you from signing another contract with another publisher until this book is published—and publication can be months (even years) after you've completed the manuscript. If this is a problem, speak up.

Electronic Rights

Unfortunately, as the field of electronic publishing is changing so rapidly and rights appear to be more lucrative, publishers are becoming less willing to budge from their very stringent boilerplates on the matter. They want to keep a great big bag full of rights. Following is an electronic clause that we feel is fair to the author.

"Electronic book" rights, which for the purposes of this agreement shall be limited to the right to digitize, reproduce, transmit, display, download or otherwise transfer, manufacture, publish, distribute, and/or sell the verbatim text of the Work, or a portion thereof, in an electronic format in any media and by any means, on any platform now known or hereafter developed, but without enhancement (such as video, extrinsic illustrations, audio or any other contributions not present in the printed edition of the Work). Any such display, transmission, or transfer of more than a single chapter of the Work must be encrypted to prevent unauthorized reproduction. Publisher acknowledges and agrees that such grant of electronic display rights does not include any grant of electronic version or interactive multimedia rights, and that such rights are expressly reserved to Author.

Experts Say

Publishing lawyer Bob Stein says, "Authors should look very, very carefully at all electronic rights clauses to ensure that they are compensated for any uses made or authorized by the publisher." He adds, knowingly, "Publishers vary considerably in their willingness to negotiate these provisions."

Reversion of Rights

Some contracts state that as long as the publisher keeps the book in print somewhere (even if it's available only in New Zealand), the rights will not revert to the author.

It is generally in the best interest of the writer that the rights to the book revert when the book is out of print in book form in the United States. Ask and see.

It's becoming more important to note that the availability of print on demand copies or electronic copies have the potential to keep a contract in effect forever if it is not expressly excluded from the definition of "in print."

Publishers might say that this is beneficial to the author, but it prevents the author from having the book reissued by another publisher who might promote it, which actually might happen if a new book by the author becomes successful. In any case, it is just as easy for an author to make her book available through print on demand as it is for the publisher, and the author can keep 100 percent of the profits without having to earn out an advance.

If you can neither keep the print on demand rights nor get the publisher to exclude print on demand from the out-of-print clause, then at least request vociferously that a clause be added stating that unless the book sells a certain number of copies (for example, 250) in a royalty period, then the work shall be considered out of print. Many publishers are finding this to be a fair compromise.

The Least You Need to Know

➤ A publishing contract grants the publisher the right to publish and sell your book.

➤ You should receive a small payment, a royalty, on every copy of your book that is sold.

➤ Exactly what rights are granted to the publisher is open to negotiation.

➤ Under most contracts, the publisher has the final decision regarding the book's actual title and the cover artwork.

➤ Some contract terms are more negotiable than others, such as free copies to the author, first serial rights, and merchandising rights.

➤ If you plan to negotiate on your own, get help from a literary lawyer, or get a good book on publishing contracts. The family lawyer probably won't be much help here.

Part 4

War and Peace: Working with a Publisher

Congratulations, you've got a publisher! But now what happens? In this section, you'll get a complete overview of the actual book publishing process and learn about how to work effectively with all the players. From meeting deadlines to formatting disks, from keeping an editor happy to understanding the retail book process, it's all here.

You'll also learn the basics of book publicity, a critical element in the future success of your book.

I Signed a Contract— Now What?

Now you've done it—you've signed a book publishing contract. That means now you will have to produce a manuscript. No more talking about how someday you plan to write a book; now you have to. In fact, you are legally obligated to write one. This was the very thing you sought so hard, but now that it has happened, it can be intimidating.

Allow us to repeat what we believe is the central message of this book: The book publishing business is a business, and to succeed in book publishing as an author, you must be businesslike.

You wrote a businesslike query letter. You put together a businesslike proposal. You conducted contract negotiations in a businesslike manner. Now you must continue to behave in a professional manner during the next phases of the process. No artistic suffering, no writer's block—and the dog won't eat your manuscript. Remember to use professional behavior at all times and in all interactions with your publisher.

Deadlines Loom

Deadlines can sound so final—and they are. When a contract specifies a deadline for a completed manuscript, it is not just an arbitrary date. It's a date that needs to be met because of these reasons:

➤ You need to maintain a good working relationship with your editor and publisher.

➤ Deadlines allow your book to be published in a timely fashion.

➤ If you do not meet the deadline, your chances to be published might disappear.

Think back to those idyllic days when you first decided to write a book. You were completely in charge of the schedule for the project. You decided when you would sit down and write, when you would wander down to the bookstore for a low-fat cappuccino and a little bit of research, and when you'd finish up the query letter.

But those leisurely days are behind you. Once you sign a contract with a publishing house, you may no longer do things at your own pace. You must meet the deadline specified in the contract.

Bookmarks

Some contracts will specify a **word count** for the completed manuscript. This is the minimum number of words that your manuscript should contain to live up to the contract. Some contracts might specify a **page count,** the minimum number of pages that must be in the manuscript. And sometimes there is a maximum word count or page count, which means that you don't promise *Life's Little Instruction Book* and deliver *War and Peace.*

Ready, Set ...

Why is meeting deadlines so important? The minute a book is scheduled for an upcoming season, the following wheels are set into motion:

➤ The book is scheduled for publication.

➤ The catalog copy writers begin to write.

➤ The cover designer begins to design.

➤ The accountants begin to forecast costs and expenses.

➤ The sales department starts planning the best way to sell your book.

➤ The publicity department begins to think about publicizing your book.

➤ Your editor makes plans for editing your book.

So, as you can see, this is no longer just a solitary endeavor for you, your imagination, or your computer. A large structure has just been put into place that depends on the timely arrival of your fully completed manuscript.

We'll examine some of these things more closely in later chapters so that you have a better understanding of the sales process, the publicity process, and the editorial process. But for right now, keep that image in your mind—the image of a cast and crew of several people all waiting anxiously to begin working on your book.

This image is not meant to scare you. But on those days when you just don't feel like working (even if you know that it will set the project back a week or two), remember what is happening inside the publishing house. The entire house is expecting you to meet a deadline.

More Time, Please?

You tried hard to meet the deadline, but the book just won't be done on time. What can you do? You can ask your editor for an extension on the deadline—that is, an officially sanctioned excuse note.

"Don't wait until the last minute to ask for an extension," warns editor Steve Martin of Prima Publishing. "Better to recognize your need for extra time as early as possible and ask accordingly." If you don't warn your editor that you won't make the deadline and then call the day your book is due … well, this is not a good thing. No editor wants to hear bad news at the very last minute. Plan ahead, but don't count on an extension. Never ask for an extension of an extension. And try to get your editor to put the extension in writing. Be warned—at many houses the failure to meet a new deadline is grounds for cancellation.

Where's My Advance?

You signed a contract promising to deliver a completed manuscript by a certain date. The publishing company signed that contract, too, and promised to send you an advance. But it's been weeks, and the money isn't here. You have to meet a deadline; shouldn't there be some deadline they have to meet, too?

Slush Pile

Bear in mind that if you need to ask for an extension on your deadline, the reason is immaterial. The editor doesn't really care if your computer crashed, your house was destroyed in a mudslide, or there has been a death in the family. This sounds cruel, but it is true. One excuse is no better than another. If the book is late, the editor is in trouble. It doesn't matter why.

Slush Pile

Editors don't cut checks; the royalty department generally does. Understand that no matter how sympathetic your editor is that you have not yet received a check, she cannot write one for you. She can walk down the hall and ask, nudge, or lobby, but she cannot write the check. So don't hold your editor responsible for the fact that the check hasn't arrived yet.

Welcome to the world of business. The simple answer is "no." The company should be timely, but it can take many months sometimes to see the first of your money.

It seems awfully unfair, doesn't it? Yes, but try to be businesslike about it. If you have an agent, let your agent nudge the editor about when the first payment will arrive. If you don't have an agent, tread as gently on the topic as you can. You are just starting out in your relationship with your editor—don't jeopardize it now. Should you threaten to stop working on the book until you get your first check? Once again, the simple answer is, "no." Yes, it stinks that you are working hard to meet a deadline and that the money hasn't yet shown up. But it is better for your book (and your career) to keep working. If you threaten to stop working, you will hurt only yourself.

The Sizzle for Your Steak

You and your editor have had a conversation or two about your book, and she has asked you for quite a bit of material. This might seem to you as unimportant stuff. Shouldn't you concentrate on writing and not have to worry about sending off the bunch of newspaper clippings and magazine articles she's asked for?

As you learned a few paragraphs ago, much is happening at the publishing house while you work away on your book. One of those things is hype.

The fate of your book may depend on several things:

➤ How excited the sales people are

➤ How sexy the catalog copy is

➤ How jazzed up your editor is

Bend Over Backward

While you're working hard to meet your manuscript deadlines, you also need to work hard to supply the things that these folks need—particularly when they need it. If someone from the publicity department calls for a copy of the newspaper profile that you included in your proposal, get another copy made and send it. Don't ask to get a copy from your editor. If someone from the editorial department calls and asks about where you went to school, answer the question. Don't tell the caller that the answer can be found in your proposal.

Will You Say "I Love It"?

Your editor (or the copywriter, or the publicist) might also ask you about endorsements. Your proposal bragged about an endorsement or two, and now you need to produce them! Why do they need endorsements so long before the book is being published? Endorsements aren't just used on the back of the book or in advertisements—they are sometimes used in catalog copy as well.

You need to spend time and energy rounding up endorsements for your book, often both professional and celebrity ones. But you will be amazed at how the words, "I'm under contract to Publisher X to write a book ..." helps you open doors and get responses to requests for endorsements. You'll find that this is a great time to expand your personal and professional network.

You're Excited, They're Excited

Understand that publishing people will ask you all kinds of silly questions and will ask for all kinds of silly stuff. Just smile and provide the answers and materials they need. The easier you make it for them, the more excited they will be about you and your book. Conversely, the less cooperative you are with them, the more their excitement will dim.

The more enthusiasm that builds around you and your book, the better your chances for strong sales. And you can help to create the excitement and enthusiasm by supplying your publisher with as much information as possible to create a *buzz*, the impression that you and your book are destined for greatness.

But I Haven't Heard from My Editor in Months!

You are working diligently to meet your deadline. You have created a writing schedule, and you sit down to do it every day, regardless of whether you feel creative. You take your contract deadline seriously. So why haven't you heard from your editor in a while? Has she forgotten about you?

No. No one will forget about you. But yes, there may be long stretches when you will not hear from anyone.

Another reality check from the world of publishing: Your editor is responsible for many books at once, perhaps as few as a dozen or as many as 30. It depends on the size of the publishing house and how many editors are on staff. What's more, all the

Bookmarks

The word-of-mouth publicity created before a book is actually published is the **buzz.** You want a lot of buzz for your book, from the publicity department to the sales department. The more buzz, the better.

Experts Say

"There were two different periods of silence while I wrote my book," says Ellen Reid Smith, author of *E-Loyalty: How to Keep Customers Coming Back to Your Website* (Harper Business). "First, it was unnerving that I was almost finished with the book and the contract still hadn't arrived. Then you turn the book in and the silence starts again. You worry that maybe they hate it because you've heard nothing; then weeks later they call to say they love it!"

books the editor oversees are in different stages—acquisitions, contract negotiation, manuscript review, typesetting, publicity—so her attention is sometimes fragmented.

Experts Say

"Even though I have never given an author cover approval in the contract, I would never put a cover on a book that an author couldn't live with. It's self-defeating," says Michael Denneny, senior editor at St. Martin's Press. "It's really an author's book, and the same goes for the title. After all, they're going to live with it longer than the publisher."

Slush Pile

You might find yourself talking to someone from the publishing company who knows very little about your book. Perhaps it's the copywriter, or a publicity person, or an editorial assistant. If this happens (and it probably will), don't be snippy. Understand that yours is just one of many books. Be polite, and use this as an opportunity to educate, not attack.

Speaking as a former editor, I can assure you not to worry about the long absences. If an editor leaves you alone for a while, take it as a sign of trust. The editor trusts that you are a professional who is working away at home, not needing constant encouragement and reinforcement from her. Editors adore writers who don't need constant attention.

What's Going on with My Book?

You are writing easily and are pleased with the progress you've made so far. Your check for the first half of the advance arrived, and your editor has expressed his confidence in your ability to do the job. Let's leave you alone for a moment and check in to see what's happening at the publishing house.

You aren't alone. It may seem that way as you write deep into the night, with your computer screen glowing in the darkness. But you are not alone. Much is happening with your book.

What's in a Name?

You learned in Chapter 15, "The Party of the First Part," that the publisher has the final say over your book title. If the publisher does change your book's title, it will not be a casual decision. The title of your book will be discussed again and again. In every meeting on any marketing issue—from catalog copy to cover design and everything in between—the title will be re-examined.

When a group of people cluster around a table to see the sketches for your book's cover, the title will be questioned.

When a group of people sit together to examine the sales department issues for your book, the title will be questioned.

When your book is presented to the sales department (more about that in a future chapter), the title will be questioned.

Why does everyone care so much about what your book is eventually named? Because a good name can make a book, and a lousy name can kill it.

Catalog Copy

Using your own book proposal as a basis, a copywriter is struggling away to describe your book in 100 words or less for the catalog that the sales representatives use. On rare occasions, a copywriter may call the author to learn more about the book. The more he knows, the easier it is to choose the most important points that must be included in the 100-word description.

Hot Off the Press

"It's great if the author takes a stab at writing the catalog description for his book," a copy manager at Chronicle Books told us. "Catalogs are written early, so the copywriter may not have even seen the manuscript when he's writing the copy. But if the author sends me catalog copy, I can get a much better sense of the book's true strength." If you write up some catalog copy, will the publisher use it? Perhaps, perhaps not. Copywriting is a form of sales, and not everyone has the knack. But it can help someone else understand the key strengths of your book.

Judging a Book by Its Cover

Another busy person at the publishing company is the cover designer. This person's title might vary somewhat, from art director to cover coordinator. But somewhere, someone is working on designing a cover for your book.

The same group of people who met to decide whether to publish your book might also be getting together to discuss the cover ideas. Or, it might be a group that includes more folks from sales and marketing and fewer from editorial. Regardless of the group's makeup, its task is a critical one: to decide how to best convey your book's message in such a way that it accomplishes these points:

➤ The cover is eye-catching and unique.
➤ The title can be read from a distance.
➤ The purpose of the book is immediately clear.

This is easier said than done. The proper solution for each book is different.

Will these cover folks include you in their discussion? Possibly. Another harsh fact (are there more?) is that, as with the title, the publisher has the contractual right to determine what the cover will say and what it will look like. As the author, you might be included as a courtesy (this is called "consultation"), but it is not guaranteed.

The Good, the Bad, and the Ugly

What if you don't like the cover? If your editor sends you a copy of the cover-in-the-works (not all do) and you think it stinks, do not react immediately. Count to 10. Count to 20 if you still aren't cooled down. Never make a phone call to your publishing house in the heat of the moment.

The best way to convey your thoughts about the cover is on paper. Write a measured, professional letter in which you offer alternative suggestions. Don't just offer criticism in your letter. Make useful suggestions, too. If you have an agent, let the agent know how you feel about the cover. With your agent to back you up, the publisher just might make some changes.

A Busy Crew

So while you are writing away alone in your spare bedroom, rest assured that people are talking about your book. People are thinking about your book. Work is being done on your book.

Experts Say

"When writing a book, your estimate of your ability to finish by a certain date is almost always overly optimistic. It's probably going to be a much larger job than you imagined. Give yourself 25 percent more time than your worst-case estimate," advises Washington, D.C., author Mike Tidwell. He should know—he has had three book deadlines already, the most recent of which resulted in *Amazon Stranger*.

The Clock's Ticking

But enough about these other people—let's get back to you and your computer again. The time is ticking away, and the deadline looms closer ….

Although this is a book about getting published, not about actually writing a book, we can't resist offering you a few suggestions. Here are nine ways to meet a deadline:

➤ Write every day, even if it is for just 15 minutes.

➤ Set small goals, and reward yourself when you meet them.

➤ Turn off the phone, fax machine, television, and radio.

➤ Take yourself away for a weekend to write in solitude.

➤ If you find yourself stuck on writing, go do research for a little while instead; then come back to your writing.

➤ If you are stuck on Chapter 3, work on Chapter 5 instead.

➤ Write your ending first, and fill in everything that comes before it.

➤ Call your mom, and ask her to scold you into writing.

➤ Find a buddy writer, or join a group, and report regularly on your progress.

Remember the old writing adage: If you write just one page a day, in one year you will have a 365-page book. We hope that your deadline leaves you that much time!

Hot Off the Press

Just like schoolteachers and the endless excuses they've heard for missing homework assignments, editors all have tales to tell about the excuses they've gotten for late manuscripts. Co-author Jennifer's favorite was a Northern California author who claimed that his computer (and presumably the disks as well) had been ruined during a mudslide. Another author would call periodically and pretend that he was on the road, "Oh, my manuscript hasn't arrived yet? Gosh, I sent it before I left ... and I don't plan to be home for several weeks." Turned out he was home all the time, frantically writing the book. Did she ever sign either of these authors to another book? No.

The Least You Need to Know

➤ Maintain your businesslike attitude, particularly about meeting manuscript deadlines.

➤ If you're going to miss a deadline, give your editor as much warning as possible; don't wait until the last minute to ask for an extension.

➤ Long before your book is published, you will need to provide material for the sales, marketing, and publicity departments.

➤ There'll be long periods of time when you don't hear from anyone at your publisher; don't worry, you've not been forgotten.

➤ While you are writing the book, other people are also working on your book, including the cover designer and the catalog copywriter.

➤ Keep seeking endorsements for your book while you are writing.

Chapter 17

Saying Goodbye to Your Baby

In This Chapter

➤ The best software; proper formatting

➤ Garbage in, garbage out

➤ What about the pictures?

➤ Why do they need so many copies?

➤ I'd like to thank my first grade teacher ...

➤ Bye, bye book!

You met your deadline, and with pounding heart you prepare to send off your manuscript. Is there a right way and a wrong way to submit it?

To keep your editor happy (and don't you just love the phrase "your editor"?), you need to submit a clean and polished manuscript prepared according to the rules of the house. These rules are known as the manuscript guidelines.

Simon Says

Typical manuscript guidelines stipulate things such as these:

➤ What type of word-processing software is acceptable, such as the most current version of Word Perfect or Microsoft's Word for Windows.

➤ What type of disk to send, most often $3^1/_2$-inch

➤ How many copies of the actual manuscript to send

➤ What kind of printer to use when printing the hard copies of the manuscript (such as laser printer or ink jet, not a dot matrix)

Disks? Formats? Say what? If these terms are unfamiliar to you, you might be—dare we say it—computer illiterate. In this age of cyberspace, hard drives, and virtual poetry, a writer must be as well versed in computers as she is in English. Traditionalists might object, but get over it. That is just the way it is. As in other parts of the business world, publishing has embraced technology, too.

Bookmarks

Manuscript guidelines pertain to the actual disk preparation, formatting, and hard copy requirements of the final manuscript. These guidelines vary among publishing houses and sometimes among editors within a house. Make sure you have a copy of the manuscript guidelines in hand before you start to prepare your manuscript.

Slush Pile

Andy Rooney, Danielle Steel, and a few diehard newspaper columnists still use old manual typewriters. But don't think that you, as a first-time writer, can turn in a typewritten manuscript. Those days are behind us now. Plug in your computer and get to typing!

Why not simply pound out your masterpiece on your trusted old Underwood manual typewriter and then pay someone to input it on a computer for you?

You could. But by the time you pay a typist to not only input your manuscript but also make any corrections that come up later in the editing and production phases, heck, you could buy a pretty fancy computer—and hire someone to train you.

E-Mail, Anyone?

Besides, as you'll learn in later chapters, submitting your manuscript on a disk may not be enough. You may be asked to communicate and even submit electronically, via e-mail. So, not only will you need a computer, but you may also need a modem and an e-mail account.

Pencil Nubs

Write your first draft in longhand if you must, but then do your second draft on your computer. Be sure that your word-processing program is acceptable to your publisher. Some ancient word-processing programs no one will accept, dinosaurs such as Kaypro and Wordstar.

The Best Software

By definition, the best software is the software stipulated in the manuscript guidelines. But when you first started writing so many months (or years) ago, who knew what publisher you would end up with and what kind of software that publisher would require or recommend?

Your best bet, then, is to stick with the largest and most popular programs. Word for Windows, Microsoft Works, or WordPerfect are acceptable to almost all publishers. Most editors work on PCs, not on Macintosh. As a general rule, the more current the version of your program, the better.

Hot Off the Press

Working with a co-author or several contributors? It might go quite smoothly computer-wise, or it might not. In our case, it was a bit of a hassle. Jennifer, who writes in an old version of Word for Windows, couldn't read her co-author Sheree's files written in WordPerfect. We tried saving files and then e-mailing files in a variety of different file formats, but no luck. So, we resorted to long faxes flying back and forth. If you are not writing alone, one author needs to take the lead in preparing the manuscript. Work this out before you get too far into the project to avoid misunderstandings.

Translate, Please

So you go ahead and write your Great American Novel in a given program—and then you find out that your publisher requires some other kind of software!

Don't panic. You can usually translate from one computer language to another. You might have software that enables you to save your computer files in another language. Check in the manual that came with your program.

At the very least, you should be able to save your files as text files, which makes the text generic enough for most programs (unless one of you is on a PC and the other on Mac). The downside is that with text files, you can lose most of your *formatting*. That might not be acceptable to your editor.

Bookmarks

Formatting refers to the set of instructions that determines the way the printed words appear on the page, including things such as margins, indents, type size, and font.

Get Help If You Need It

One good bet is to head over to your local Kinko's, or a similar establishment that rents computer time and has knowledgeable personnel to help you. Take a copy of your computer disk (a copy, never the only one you have) with the files that need translating. You can use the computers there to take advantage of more sophisticated translation options. This way you should be able to translate your work into the word-processing program that your publishing house requires. It can be costly, though, as much as several dollars per file.

Even if you work on a Macintosh and your publisher is totally PC-based, you should be able to hash it out at one of these computer service centers.

Experts Say

"Getting wired means having access to e-mail and the Internet," says freelance editor Paula Lee. "Don't worry, be happy—you'll soon learn that the Internet is a writer's best friend."

Bookmarks

A **heading** (often called a **head**) is the title introducing a chapter or subdivision of the text. It's distinguished by a style and/or size that varies from the text. Typically, there is a hierarchy of different sized headings throughout the book, designated as Head 1, Head 2, or Head A, B, and C.

Proper Formatting

Back in the days before computers, formatting was pretty straightforward. Your editor would ask you to submit your manuscript neatly typewritten (with a new ribbon!), on standard white 8½-by-11-inch high-quality bond paper. Margins were to measure 1 inch all around, and text was to be double-spaced with half-inch indentations.

It was quite simple, actually. The tricky stuff such as italics, bold, *headings*, and the like, were left to the typesetter.

Those days (and the typesetters) are gone at many, if not most, publishing houses. In the age of computerized publishing, the rules have changed considerably, for both the publisher and the writer. Now, formatting requirements are designed to facilitate the production process.

Standard Formatting

As you've learned, most writers are asked to submit computer disks as well as hard copy (a printed manuscript). How the writer is asked to format the text on those disks varies somewhat from publisher to publisher. It depends entirely on the publisher's computer sophistication and editorial conventions.

Standard formatting requirements are as follows:

➤ 1-inch margins around the page

➤ Standard 12-point type in a typewriter font, such as Courier or Times Roman

➤ Single-line spaces between paragraphs, rather than indents

➤ Double-spaced copy

➤ Unjustified text

➤ No double hard returns

➤ One computer file per chapter, named according to the house's naming convention

➤ Printed on a desk jet or laser-quality printer, on good 8½-by-11-inch white paper

➤ No double spaces after periods

Most publishing houses have prepared very detailed formatting guidelines for writers under contract. These guidelines often specify particular coding for various design elements such as headings.

This coding (which is often alphanumeric) identifies these elements in the manuscript for the copy editor and/or production department. As we worked on the manuscript for this book, we incorporated the coding as specified by our publisher.

For example, when we wrote a heading (such as the one that begins this section on formatting), we coded it like this:

(c)Proper Formatting

That (c) designation lets the production department know that it should look like this:

Proper Formatting

And when a phrase is intended to be set off with a bullet, we coded it this way:

[lb]   1-inch margins around the page

That [lb] lets the production department know that the finished product should look like this:

➤ 1-inch margins around the page

Slush Pile

Don't make the mistake of turning in a disk with one enormous file on it (unless it has been pre-approved). Your editor will not be happy. At one unnamed publishing company, faced with a 340-page manuscript all written in one file (instead of saved one chapter per file), the editor had to hire a freelancer to electronically break up the file chapter by chapter.

Slush Pile

Don't use one of those old daisy-wheel printers for your final manuscript (the kind where you had to break the pages apart). If you don't have a good printer, take the disk with your manuscript to a computer service center like a Kinko's, and print it out there.

Your publisher will likely have similar coding requirements. Be sure to request a copy of the formatting guidelines from your publisher as early as you can to save yourself from later redoing your own formatting. Many publishers send these guidelines out when they return the signed contract. Don't wait for that—as you know from Chapter 16, "I Signed a Contract—Now What?" you might have finished the book before the signed contract comes!

Slush Pile

Don't forget to number the pages on your manuscript before sending it in. There are horror stories of large manuscripts accidentally dropped on the floor, with pages flying everywhere, only to find that—yikes—the pages weren't numbered. Don't let this happen to your editor!

Experts Say

The Chicago Manual of Style is the book publishing bible and every writer's best friend. It's a veritable treasure of information that addresses all the spelling, grammar, and language usage issues you're likely to encounter in a lifetime of writing. "Using *The Chicago Manual of Style* as your guide marks you as a professional and impresses your editor," says book doctor John Waters. The book is available in the reference section of the bookstore.

Garbage In, Garbage Out

GIGO is tech-talk for the phrase "garbage in, garbage out," an expression as applicable to publishing as it is to computers. The cleaner the manuscript you send to your publisher, the cleaner the book that comes out from your publisher.

Writers often complain about the finished product, as if that product were completely out of their hands. Particularly loathsome to writers are unnecessary tinkering by copy editors, typos, and formatting bloopers.

Yet, as the writer, you have more control over this process than you might think. If you turn in a manuscript riddled with grammatical errors, typos, and formatting inconsistencies, you're asking for trouble.

So, polish your prose. Check your grammar and your spelling. Follow your publisher's formatting guidelines to the letter. You'll be glad you did (and you'll impress your editor, to boot!). If you've forgotten everything you learned in English class, take a look at *The Complete Idiot's Guide to Grammar and Style* for a refresher course.

What About the Pictures?

Many book projects include interior art, a term that in book publishing refers to the photographs, illustrations, maps, and cartoons that might appear on the pages of the book. If your book does have interior art, you will need to find out exactly what your responsibilities are concerning it.

Some publishers—particularly the larger ones—provide all the art, and they like it that way. If this is the case, you, as the author, may be encouraged to contribute ideas for possible art. Or, you might well be discouraged from contributing art ideas. Check your book contract to see what your publisher expects from you.

What to Send

What if you're responsible for providing art? You'll have to provide it in the proper way. Here again, this varies from publisher to publisher. Most often, it depends on the production department's technical sophistication.

Here are a few possible scenarios:

➤ If you're providing black-and-white photographs, you may be asked to provide simple 8-by-10-inch black-and-white glossies. Or, you may be asked to provide color slides, or electronic versions that you've scanned and delivered electronically in GIF or JPEG files.

➤ If you're providing maps, you may be asked to provide simple sketches that the publisher's art department can use to render final art. Or, you might be asked to deliver *camera-ready,* professional-quality maps.

➤ If you're providing actual illustrations (this is unlikely), then you may be asked to deliver the originals or the camera-ready versions of those originals.

May I?

Regardless of the form, remember that you must also obtain written permission to reprint any art that's not your own or that's not in the *public domain.*

Why so Many Copies?

Most publishing contracts specify that you submit your book on disk, along with at least two hard copies of the entire manuscript. This may seem excessive to you (especially at 5 cents or more a page for copying), but it is still required. Having more than one copy of the manuscript is critical for the production process. Here's why …

As soon as your manuscript arrives at the publisher, your editor opens it with great expectations. Typically, she hands your computer disk right off to an editorial assistant. The editorial assistant makes an extra copy of the disk for the design and production departments.

The editor keeps one hard copy of your manuscript for herself to read; the other copy of the manuscript goes to the editorial assistant. It is this extra copy that in turn is copied and copied and

Bookmarks

Camera-ready art refers to the finished artwork that is ready to be photographed, without alteration, for reproduction. Sometimes it's called **mechanicals.**

Slush Pile

Including art in a book can increase its production cost—and thus its price—considerably. So, despite your opinion, if the publisher decides not to include art in the book, try to understand and be gracious. This is a business decision, not an emotional one.

copied in-house. Copies of your manuscript may end up in the hands of any other editor in line to read your book—everyone from other acquisitions editors who are curious about it to developmental editors, production editors, publicists, and other folks you haven't heard of yet. But you'll learn who all these folks are in the next chapter.

Without two copies, each ready to initiate the editorial and production processes, delays could occur. And you wouldn't want that. So cough up the 5 cents a page and be done with it.

Bookmarks

Written works or artwork that is no longer protected by copyright law is in the **public domain** and can be used without permission or cost by anyone. Artwork that is free to be used by anyone without obtaining permission is called **clip art.**

I'd Like to Thank My First Grade Teacher ...

Ah, the acknowledgments section. Here is your chance to tell the world where you learned to write, who has influenced you in your life, and to whom you will feel eternally grateful.

Many writers turn in the acknowledgments section of their manuscript last. And it sometimes seems to the editor that the author has spent the most time writing this section of the book—it can be quite lengthy.

Again, we would like to impress upon you that the most businesslike and professional approach to the acknowledgments section is to keep it short, perhaps just a few paragraphs. Understand that if you turn in a long one, you just may be asked to cut it.

Bye, Bye Book!

Good job. You've prepared your manuscript in strict accordance with the publisher's guidelines. Your manuscript is now ready to begin the labyrinthine journey known as the editorial and production process. It's ready to become a book. Read on to learn exactly how this happens.

The Least You Need to Know

➤ Computer illiteracy is not acceptable in today's publishing world; you must learn how to use a computer if you don't already know how.

➤ Very few publishers still accept manuscripts on paper only; most require a disk version as well.

➤ Save each chapter in an individual file; never write a book as one long file.

➤ Ask your publisher early on for manuscript guidelines.

➤ Number the pages, make several copies, hold your breath, and send your manuscript on its way!

175

Chapter 18

Welcome to the Home Team!

> ## In This Chapter
>
> ➤ Book production, step by step
>
> ➤ Responding to editorial queries and changes
>
> ➤ Cover copy and design
>
> ➤ Interior design and paper
>
> ➤ Page proofs and bluelines

Much is often made of the solitary nature of the writer's life. Some writers—loners and dreamers at heart—like it that way.

Well, writing a book may be a solo act, but making a book is a collaborative one. Making a book requires that the author put aside her artistic, sensitive, prideful self and join forces with the cast of folks needed to produce a bound book. For maybe the first time since you started writing your book, you've joined a team.

The process of producing a book is by no means simple. You, the writer, have provided the text of the book. But a book is much more than simply text. It's a product that must be polished, designed, manufactured, marketed, promoted, sold and shipped into retail outlets all over the country, and finally, sold to readers.

Production in a Nutshell

The steps to producing a book include these:

➤ Developmental edit

➤ Copy edit

➤ Interior design

➤ Front, spine, and back cover copy and design

➤ Final page proofs and proofreading

➤ *Bluelines*

➤ *F&Gs*

Bookmarks

The term **bluelines,** sometimes called blues, refers to the cheap proof—the test run off the press that's usually blue (hence the name)—that the printer sends to the publisher before proceeding with the actual printing.

Bookmarks

The **F&Gs** are the sheets of a book that have been "folded and gathered" in preparation for printing. In the rush to market, many publishers do not bother to review F&Gs, having already reviewed the bluelines. A notable exception to this is heavily illustrated books.

Join the Team

You are now part of a team of talented and resourceful publishing professionals whose contribution—be it the copy edit or the cover illustration—is as important to them as your words are to you. Let's meet this team and learn how you can make yourself a welcome addition to it.

We'll introduce you to these publishing professionals in the order you are most likely to meet them—or hear of them, as the case may be.

The Acquisitions Editor

The first person to read your final manuscript is usually your old friend, the acquisitions editor. By definition, this person is already a big fan of yours, having had the wisdom and foresight to offer you a book contract in the first place.

But I Thought You Liked It!

At this point in the process, however, your biggest fan may become your worst critic, all in the name of making the best book possible. She'll take a big-picture look at your manuscript, performing what's called a content edit. She'll be reviewing your manuscript for the following:

➤ Content

➤ Style

➤ Voice

➤ Structure

➤ Pacing, and more

Especially for Fiction

If the book is fiction or creative nonfiction, the acquisitions editor will also be looking to see how you've handled these elements:

➤ Setting

➤ Plot

➤ Characterization

➤ Dialogue

➤ Point(s) of view

➤ Narrative

➤ Theme, and more

Once your editor has completed her review, typically she'll write up her comments, proposed changes, and questions and then forward them on to you. As we'll discuss in a later chapter, it will be your job to incorporate all your changes with grace, professionalism, and speed—especially if you want to get your hands on that acceptance check. (The acceptance check doesn't come until these changes are made to your acquisitions editor's satisfaction.)

The Developmental Editor

If your acquisitions editor believes that substantial changes must be made to your manuscript before approving it for publication, she may assign your project to a developmental editor. In some houses, the acquisitions editor and developmental editor are the same person. Developmental editors work on actual content, helping you rework your manuscript to the publishing house's expectations.

If you are for any reason unable or unwilling to make the changes requested, the developmental editor may serve as a book doctor, rewriting your book as she and the acquisitions editor see fit. The fee for this developmental editing either will be paid by the publisher outright at no cost to you, or will be paid by the publisher and then charged back to you against your royalties.

The Production Editor

When you and your acquisitions editor have ironed out all the big-picture issues, you and your manuscript will be handed off to the production editor, who'll run your manuscript through the next lap in this publishing relay.

As your acquisitions editor has seen you safely through the acquisitions process (from query letter to signed contract to acceptance of the final manuscript), so will your production editor see you safely through the production process (from copy edit to final proofs to bluelines).

Note: In some publishing houses, the production editor also assumes responsibility for the content editing, either doing the edit or sending it out to a freelance developmental editor.

The Copy Editor

The way some writers rant and rave about copy editors, you'd think they were insensitive, intolerant, inflexible … well, you get the picture.

Wrong! Copy editors can be a writer's best friend. Sure, they're a little picky, but then, they're paid to be picky. Who else will catch all your inadvertent misspellings, erroneous grammar, questionable punctuation, and inconsistent capitalization? Not to mention all those other things you didn't even know that those meticulous copy editors check, including these elements:

➤ Pagination

➤ Illustrations

➤ Front and back matter

➤ Contradictions and ambiguities

➤ Parochialisms and anachronisms

➤ Abbreviations and contractions

➤ Accuracy of names, dates, and places

➤ Cross-references

➤ Coding for headings, illustrations, and the like

Who (and where) your copy editor will be varies according to the publishing house. At some houses, the production editor does the copy editing herself. At other houses, the production editor sends the manuscript to the copy editing department, where an in-house copy editor does the job. At still others, the production editor sends your manuscript out to a freelance copy editor.

No matter where she comes from, the copy editor deserves your respect, and maybe even your undying love.

The Art Director

The art director is the person responsible for the way your book will look, both inside and out. In large houses, the art director heads up a design department that creates the interior and cover designs for each title. In smaller houses, the art director may create the designs herself or send them out to freelance designers.

Interior Design

Interior design varies greatly in its complexity, depending on the type of book you have written. Novels, made up primarily of *text,* typically require very simple interior designs. Nonfiction books can run the gamut, from simple text to highly illustrated, to books like the one you hold in your hands. This nonfiction book, *The Complete Idiot's Guide to Getting Published,* incorporates a number of design elements such as *sidebars,* bullets, and numbered lists. If the design of your book dictates that text be arranged in a certain way (like this one does), you may be asked to write the text accordingly (like we were).

Bookmarks

Words on a page are called **text.** Text that is set aside in a box or that runs down the side in a smaller size type is a **sidebar.** Sidebars are like little asides in a conversation.

Cover Design

You may not be able to tell a book by its cover, but you can sell a book by one! The cover is a book's major sales tool. As you've learned in other chapters, that is why the publisher usually states flatly in the contract that the cover text and design is its decision, not yours. Moreover, the cover is usually the most expensive piece of the production process—it typically costs thousands of dollars for even the most basic cover and can cost thousands more if the cover includes an illustration or photograph. For a how-to book, the art director may choose a straightforward type solution, with no illustration. For books such as novels, the illustration is paramount.

The art director will present his designs for your book's interior and front and back covers to a panel that includes your editor, the marketing director, and the publisher.

The Copywriter

The copywriter writes the copy that appears on the cover of your book (front and back) as well as the inside flaps on a hardcover book. The cover copy must work with the cover design to entice the bookstore browser to pick up your book and buy it, right then and there. In effect, this is sales copy.

At some houses, the acquisitions editors write the copy for the books they acquire; at other houses, the copy is written by in-house copywriters in the marketing department. No matter who writes it, this sort of copy is an art form.

Will this be the same copywriter who wrote the description of your book for the catalog? It might be. But it might also be someone who is new to the project, so be kind and patient if that person calls you for information.

The Proofreader

The proofreader is the last person to read the formatted book pages before they're shipped off to the printer for manufacturing. The proofreader's job is to catch glaring mistakes only, such as typos, pagination problems, and so forth. Think of proofreading as a last-ditch quality-control effort.

Here again, who does the proofreading depends on the house. At larger houses, in-house proofreaders in the proofreading department perform this function; in smaller houses, the proofreading may be done by editorial assistants or may be sent out to freelancers.

The Manufacturing Manager

The manufacturing manager is your publishing house's liaison with the printers. He's typically in charge of buying the paper on which to print the books and decides which printing company to use. In this age of escalating paper prices, many manufacturing managers are buying cheaper paper to keep costs down. As an author, you should know that paper is the most expensive component of the book, something like 70 percent. Complain to your editor if you like, but there may be nothing your editor can do about it, to his frustration as much as to yours!

Over to You, Now

Okay, now you've met the major players in the editorial and production processes at most publishing houses. Let's take you step by step through the interactions you'll have with some of these people as your book is produced.

As we've tried to make clear in the last several pages, much of what goes on at your publishing house is out of your control and is in the hands of your team members. But when the ball does bounce back into your court, you want to make sure you do your part to keep the process going smoothly.

Responding to Your Editor's Comments

Your part first comes into play when your acquisitions editor reads your final manuscript and delivers her content editing comments.

No matter how pristine your manuscript, you can expect revision suggestions that include these:

➤ Cuts (where you run too long)

➤ Additions (where you leave too much unsaid)

➤ Clarifications (where you might confuse the reader)

➤ Rearrangements (where your structure falters)

➤ Rethinking of sections (where you veer off track)

Especially for Fiction

If you're writing fiction, you can also expect comments concerning these factors:

➤ Characters who work, characters who don't

➤ Holes in the plot

➤ Milking certain scenes, eliminating others

➤ Building suspense, stepping up the pace

➤ Dramatizing your beginning

➤ Sustaining interest in your middle

➤ Nailing your ending

What's Best for the Book

Take these comments in the spirit in which they are given. Your editor's only interest is in making your good book even better. No one is trying to hurt your feelings. The book's success (for both you and your editor) depends on it being the best book it can possibly be.

Sometimes editors are better at seeing what is wrong than they are at seeing how to fix it. Take a hard look at the problems your editor has identified, and if you don't like her solutions, then come up with your own. Feel free to discuss these issues with your editor, but don't drive her crazy over every detail. (You'll learn more on maintaining this all-important relationship with your editor in the next chapter.)

Hot Off the Press

The publishing industry is replete with writers who have sabotaged their own book projects—and ultimately their careers—by objecting too strenuously to editorial comments. A case in point: A writer sold a book proposal to a major publisher about marriage and the devastating effect of adultery on the bonds of matrimony. When the manuscript came in, however, the editor objected to large sections in which the writer examined the feelings of the third party (the other man or woman). The editor insisted that the section be cut; it was inappropriate in a book about marriage. The writer insisted that it remain. The impasse was never resolved, and the manuscript was declared unacceptable. Deal over.

Get the job done, make the changes your editor needs, and get the manuscript back to her within the deadline she's given you. If you are slow in this step, you will jeopardize the production schedule, and your book may not be published on time. This is not a good thing.

Bookmarks

Author queries are questions the copy editor needs you, the writer, to answer before the text proceeds to the layout stage. These questions can relate to meaning, accuracy, and research, among other things.

Slush Pile

"But I gave them a perfect book," co-author Jennifer once heard an unhappy author lament. Wrong. There is no such thing as a perfect book, and that attitude will not make you any friends at your publisher. There is always room for improvement, if only a buff and polish.

Copy Editing Changes and Queries

When you've made the content changes as requested by your acquisitions editor, your manuscript is handed off to the production editor. He'll review the manuscript and choose a copy editor based upon that review. The copy editor will make her edits, which will most likely include *author queries*.

It's your job to answer these queries as completely and swiftly as possible. If the copy editor seems a little overzealous, keep in mind that, by definition, copy editors are suspicious of everybody's copy. Don't take it personally—they are merely doing their job.

Man Overboard!

Of course, there are times when copy editors really do go overboard. If you feel this is the case, first get the opinions of other publishing pros as a double-check. If they, too, agree that the edit is excessive, talk to your editor first. He may want to handle it himself. Be polite—no ranting and raving. If your editor agrees with you, he might tell the copy editor to tone it down, or he may reassign the job to someone else.

More Deadlines to Meet

After the copy editing process is completed, your manuscript is ready to go into layout. In the typesetting days of old (before computers), authors would receive galleys to review. Galleys were long proofs pulled off the machine before the copy was divided into pages. Ask your editor if you can see a sample design for the interior layout for your book. Many houses use standard designs, but some books will have custom designs created for them.

But galleys are mostly history now. What you are more likely to receive are page proofs, straight from the layout person's laser printer. These page proofs are reviewed by a number of people: the acquisitions editor, the production editor, the art director, the manufacturing manager—and, last but not least, you, the writer.

Page Proofs

As the author, you'll usually review what's known as the first pass, the first set of page proofs from the layout person. Do not go overboard on corrections or additions here; your opportunity to make big changes was during the copy editing phase. This stage is really just to catch computer errors.

Changes at this stage are very expensive. And if you make too many, you will have to pay for them. Check your contract for details; each publisher draws the line at a different place. Even if you don't get charged, you'll possibly delay publication.

Usually there are two more passes of page proofs, but the author seldom sees these. One ensures that the first-pass changes have been made, and then there's one more: the final pass read by the proofreader just before the book is shipped to the printer.

Bookmarks

Manuscripts are no longer sent off to typesetters, but rather to **compositors.** The compositor then formats the book on computer disk and gets it ready to go to the printer.

Hot Off the Press

Desktop publishing has revolutionized the editorial and production processes for much of the industry. The managing editor of a computer game book publisher described how quickly their books appear. It's crucial for the game guides to appear in the stores when the games do. "We do everything electronically," he told us. "Our writers deliver their manuscript via e-mail, chapter by chapter as they write it. The project editor reviews them and sends them on to the copy editor, again by e-mail. The same goes for design and layout. We often even send the finished book to the printer electronically—all to save time and get our books out to the marketplace as quickly as possible."

Stop the Presses!

As the printer prepares to print your book (a process known as "make ready"), he first makes a proof. This proof, as we learned earlier, is called the bluelines. Publishing pros just call them "the blues."

Will you get to see the bluelines? Probably not. Blues are meant to be reviewed post-haste by the production editor only hours before the presses actually start to roll. Although some writers may insist on reviewing the bluelines, very few are allowed to do so. Without the clout of a bestselling track record behind you, you won't see the bluelines.

Even if you could, who'd want to? Leave the last-minute quality control to the pros, and get started on your next book. There's no better feeling in the world for a writer than to have one book at the printers and another one in the computer.

The Least You Need to Know

➤ The editorial and production processes require teamwork; this means coopera-tion between the publishing staff and you, the author.

➤ Try not to take editorial criticism personally; the editor's goal is to help you write the best book possible.

➤ Make all requested changes, and answer all editorial queries promptly so that you don't delay production.

➤ The later it is in the production process, the less likely you will be allowed to make changes to your book.

Proper Care and Feeding of Your Editor

Your manuscript has now left the safety of your nurturing arms and has headed off to the big city. Its fate will now be determined by strangers, many of whom will remain strangers.

The notable exception to this is your editor. He or she is your link to this strange new world, so it's in your best interest to make this person your new friend.

Make a Friend for Life

Writers and editors as friends? It works for John Grisham.

When Grisham signed with Doubleday for his second novel—and first big hit—*The Firm,* he made sure to befriend his new editor, David Gernert. It's an association that has gone well beyond the usual editor/writer relationship.

Gernert edited (heavily, according to Grisham) the next several Grisham bestsellers. They both profited from the arrangement. Grisham went to the top of the bestseller lists, and Gernert went to the top of Doubleday as editor-in-chief.

When Grisham's agent, Jay Garon, died in 1995, Grisham asked Gernert to become his agent. Gernert, who left his job at Doubleday, acts not only as Grisham's agent, but also as his personal editor. And the bestsellers just keep on coming.

Your Book's Best Advocate—and Yours, Too!

David Gernert is literally John Grisham's advocate. And your editor, having acquired your project for the publishing house, is your book's advocate. What you want is for the editor to become your advocate, too.

Hot Off the Press

The most celebrated editor of all time was the legendary Maxwell E. Perkins of Scribner's. Editor and friend to such luminaries as Thomas Wolfe, Perkins was renowned for his ability to draw the best work out of his authors. "Do not ever defer to my judgment," he admonished Fitzgerald in one of his remarkable letters. It is worth noting that, despite Perkins's warning, Fitzgerald took his editor's comments and criticism seriously—to his and his work's great credit.

The trick is to fuel your editor's enthusiasm for you and your book as your manuscript makes its way through the editorial and production processes. Be sure to maintain your editor's enthusiasm after the book is published, too, all the way through the marketing and promotion. At every point, your editor is crucial to the success of your book.

However, while your editor's excitement was initially high when the book was signed, this may fade over time. This apparent loss of enthusiasm and/or interest in your project is more a function of workload than anything else.

Remember, at any given time, your editor is juggling three lists:

➤ The list of books currently being acquired

➤ The list of books currently being produced

➤ The list of books currently being promoted

Depending upon the house, this can add up to anywhere between 20 and 100 books. That's a lot of books to track. When it comes to your editor's interest, there is quite a bit of competition for your book.

Hot Off the Press

Most acquisitions editors toil in relative obscurity. But a handful have become industry superstars and have earned the biggest reward of all: their own imprint. When this happens, an editor's name is right up there with the publisher. And so you have Nan A. Talese Books/Doubleday and Regan Books/Harper Collins. Nan Talese is the editor of, among others, *How the Irish Saved Civilization.* Judith Regan of Regan Books vaulted to prominence with Rush Limbaugh's books, and more recently with two bestsellers from professional wrestlers. So there you have another reason to be nice to your editor: She might have her own imprint some day.

It's your job to sustain this interest and to accomplish this with grace and professionalism. This means you'll need to learn as much as you can about editors and how they operate. Let's observe an editor in the field, so to speak, and find out how she spends her time.

Editor for a Day

Your editor's day typically begins early. Although the work day may officially begin at 9 A.M., many early-bird editors are already at their desks by 8 A.M.—and many can be found at their desks long after 5 P.M.

As you have learned before, there is little time in the editor's day to do the "real" work of reading and evaluating manuscripts and proposals. You'll recall that most of this work is done on the editor's own time, either at home or on the train, subway, or carpool. Many an editor has fallen asleep at night next to a stack of manuscripts.

8 A.M.

At your editor's office, the early-bird editors are getting as much done as they can before the daily meetings start up.

Reading and Responding to E-Mail

One editor we know gets 100 e-mails a day, from authors as well as agents, other editors, and all manner of in-house staffers. As more editors and publishing houses go online, the number of e-mails will only grow.

Going Through Snail Mail

With any luck, your editor has an editorial assistant who sorts through the mail first. Still, many editors prefer to perform this formidable task themselves. Formidable? Yes. Each day the mail may bring a dozen queries, a dozen requested manuscripts and proposals, and just as many unrequested ones! That's not to mention contracts from agents, catalogs from other publishers, trade publications and newsletters, interoffice correspondence, faxes, and maybe even the occasional postcard from a long-time author.

Making Overseas and Transcontinental Phone Calls

Many editors conduct a great deal of business with foreign publishers. They evaluate projects, make deals for translations, and work together on other projects. The best time to call Europe is early in the day. Likewise, West Coast editors are calling back East as early as they can.

Writing Rejection Letters

Yes, some editors do write their own rejection letters. This is a time-consuming job, but many editors consider it a professional courtesy crucial to maintaining good writer-editor or agent-editor relations. Let it never be said that editors don't care about writer's feelings!

9 A.M.

By 9 A.M., the meetings start. Ask any editor how she spends her day, and she will likely say (with some irritation), "In meetings!"

The first meeting on the schedule is the production meeting. Here, your editor meets with the production editors to discuss the problems and issues regarding books currently in production. At today's meeting, your editor learns that a conflict concerning the copy edit of one title has arisen. The writer is unhappy with the copy edit and is dragging his heels on responding to the author queries. The production editor asks for your editor's help in resolving the issue. They agree to meet later in the day to call the writer together and work things out.

10 A.M.

By this time, the production meeting has ended and the cover meeting has begun. At a cover meeting, the art director, editors, marketing execs, and often the publisher get together to brainstorm ideas for new covers and to review covers already in the design process. At today's meeting, they discuss ideas for four new covers and review the art for front covers on four books in production.

One cover for a new cookbook gives them particular trouble. Cookbooks are expensive books to produce, especially when the front cover boasts a beautiful photograph of a savory dish. Cover photos featuring recipes from the cookbook require a photo shoot, a top photographer, a food stylist, the cooperation of the cookbook author, and, of course, the food. It's an expensive production from start to finish.

Even then, the results are not guaranteed. Maybe the final photos are not what anyone—including your editor—had hoped they would be. The art director is defensive, the marketing executive is fighting for another photo shoot, and the publisher is unhappy at the prospect of doubling the cover costs with another shoot. Your editor knows that the cookbook author (a bestselling author currently being wooed by other publishers) will not like the photo either. "If we run with this cover, we could be giving the agent the ammunition she needs to convince the author to switch houses," your editor argues. The publisher agrees and approves a new photo shoot.

Noon

By the time these and other issues are have been resolved, it's after 12 P.M. Your editor, late for a luncheon with a top agent, runs down the street to the appointed restaurant, cell phone in hand. Once there, she sits down for a quick bite (no three-martini lunch, this) with the agent. In between bites, the agent pitches a few of his clients' top projects.

As the editor pays for lunch, the agent tells her that he will be in touch with her on the projects that most piqued her interest.

1:30 P.M.

Your editor rushes into her office to check her messages before the next meeting begins. As quickly as possible, she returns the most urgent phone calls. One is to an agent about a final contract point, one to an author about a rewrite in progress, and one to a rights manager trying to close a deal with a book club.

By the time she hangs up the phone, 45 minutes have gone by. She has only 15 minutes to collect her thoughts (and her information) for the most trying meeting of the day: the acquisitions meeting with the pub board.

The meeting begins. As you already know, this is the meeting where editors try to sell their colleagues and bosses on projects they'd like to sign up for publication.

The degree of formality at these meetings may vary from house to house, but the pressure does not. Your editor, and the projects she pitches, fall under close scrutiny during these meetings. As you've read in Chapter 14, "Behind Closed Doors," each editor at the meeting presents one or more titles. This round-robin approach continues until all the books have been discussed or the time is up. Not surprisingly, acquisitions meetings often run late.

At this meeting, your editor is able to present two projects. The first, a follow-up book by an author whose first book did very well, is an easy sell. The other, an offbeat project by a first-time author that the editor loves, is not. Despite her passion for the project, she fails to convince her peers and will have to turn the writer down.

5:00 P.M.

Your editor finally returns to her office. Again, she listens to her voice mail messages and returns the most urgent calls. She checks her e-mail and her snail mail for afternoon FedEx packages. She sorts through her in-box, pulling out the catalog copy for a couple of new books left there by the copywriter, which must be reviewed and returned before she goes home. Ditto for the proofs of two covers for books due to ship to the printer the next day.

Depending on how late she works, she may also make the less urgent calls on her list and write more rejection letters. She writes a very encouraging and complimentary rejection letter to the writer whose project she was unable to sell at her acquisitions meeting earlier in the day. She recommends another editor at another house to the writer.

6:00 P.M.

She packs up the manuscripts she hopes to review at home that evening and leaves the office.

Experts Say

"There's a fine line between too much contact and too little," one weary editor admits. "The first note to strike is one of professionalism. If you treat your editor like a pro, odds are she'll return the favor."

11:30 P.M.

Your tired editor falls asleep, a stack of proposals in her lap.

Tomorrow will bring more of the same. It's a tough job, but your editor loves doing it. It's her love for her work that keeps her coming back, despite the relatively low pay and heavy workload.

Why Doesn't My Editor Ever Call Me?

Unless you slept through the last couple of pages, you now know why. She's busy—busier than you imagined. But don't panic that she hasn't called lately: Generally, no news is good news.

Still, you want to believe that your editor has not forgotten you and your book. If you need to discuss an issue, call and talk to her about it. Given the time she spends in meetings, you may often be reduced to leaving messages on her voice mail. Voice mail can be frustrating, but don't allow your frustrations to influence the message you leave. Be brief and succinct. Be sure to let her know the best time to return your call so that you two don't wind up playing phone tag.

Getting Through When You Need To

If you do not hear back from your editor in a reasonable amount of time, there are a number of things you can do:

➤ If your editor has an assistant, try getting through to him. Often he may be able to resolve the situation himself. Befriend the assistant. He can not only help you now, but he may be able to help you later—when he is an acquisitions editor himself!

➤ If you know your editor's e-mail address, try contacting her this way. Though some editors and houses are resisting e-mail, many others are finding it an increasingly efficient way to communicate.

➤ If it's an issue that has come up during the editorial or production process, try to resolve it with the production editor first. Only as a last resort should you antagonize your production editor by running around him to your acquisitions editor.

➤ The same thing goes for going over your editor's head to her boss. Before you do anything like this, talk to your agent. Let your agent talk to your editor's boss. This is one of the biggest advantages of having an agent: You get to stay pals with the editor while your agent looks like a meanie. If you don't have an agent, do the best you can to work it out with your editor. If you do go over her head (and we advise against it), proceed at your own peril.

Slush Pile

Have an attitude? Don't. One writer we know turned in a manuscript twice as long as the contract specified and then refused to speak to her editor about it by phone. The writer demanded that, from now on, the staff communicate with her only by e-mail. The book was eventually published, but by then she'd made enemies all over the building. Did she sell them another book? No.

When to Confess You're in Trouble

We've mentioned this before: Tell your editor sooner, as opposed to later. If for any reason you find yourself unable to meet your deadline, complete your rewrites, or turn around your author queries, speak up. Let your editor know as soon as possible.

The sooner she knows, the sooner she'll be able to do damage control. Damage control? Yes, your lateness will cause damage. Your editor will need to rework production schedules and perhaps postpone the publication of your book.

Writers hate to deliver bad news to editors. This is unprofessional. But the longer you wait, the fewer your editor's damage control options. You have to tell her straight away, while she can still do something to save your book! As long as you speak up soon, odds are that your editor will understand.

So Play Nice

As you've seen, editors are hard-working, underpaid people who love books and writers. They are also often job-hoppers, jumping from one publishing house to another. In New York, where much of the book publishing industry operates, switching houses is as easy as crossing the street.

This revolving-door pattern is one many writers come to hate. It's what's known as the orphan syndrome: You develop a good relationship with one editor, only to lose that editor to another house. Your new editor—often a hastily promoted assistant—may lack the experience that your departed editor had. Worse, she may lack enthusiasm for your project. Then you find that you and your book are orphans, with no strong sponsor.

What to do? Befriend the new editor as you had the former editor. Take the time to educate her about your book. Don't assume that any knowledge has been passed on from your former editor. No matter who your editor is, you need her. As your primary advocate at the publishing house, your editor is your single most important contact there. It's a relationship you must both guard and nurture.

Writers who do manage to develop strong and happy working relationships with their editors are loath to let them go. Many follow them (contracts permitting) from house to house. Of course, if you become a bestselling author, you can always do what John Grisham did: Hire your favorite editor to be your editor/agent!

The Least You Need to Know

➤ Your editor is your primary advocate at the publishing house; befriend her ASAP.

➤ Your second most important contact is your editor's assistant; befriend him as well.

➤ Respect your editor's time; she's busier than you imagine.

➤ Give your editor time to read your manuscript; remember that he does most of his reading at home.

➤ When you have bad news, deliver it early so that your editor can look for solutions.

➤ Editors come and go, so try to make as many friends as you can within the in-house staff.

Chapter 20

So, How Does My Book Get into the Stores?

In This Chapter

➤ An overview of the sales process

➤ Death of a sales conference: Do I get to go?

➤ Why won't Barnes & Noble take a display?

➤ Printing and shipping your book

➤ Should I go to the BEA?

When your book comes off the printing press, where does it go? Two places, actually. Some of the finished books are sent directly to your publisher's warehouse. Some (many, you hope) go directly to bookstores around the country.

How did that happen? When did those bookstores learn about your book? How did they know to order it? And how did they decide how many to order?

Good questions, all. What follows is a brief lesson in the sales process as practiced by the book publishing industry. The more you know about it, the less frustrated you will be later. Writers have a vested interest in how the sales process works, so here is your chance to get educated.

A Short Course in the Sales Process

As you know, the book publishing business was once a quaint pursuit, and the sales process is still more than a little quaint. The two critical elements in this process are as follows:

➤ The publisher's catalog

➤ The publisher's sales representatives

Hot Off the Press

"I might have been the first-ever sales rep hired on the basis of computer knowledge rather than book knowledge," Barbara Curtis told us. Now the president of her own book sales company, Curtis was for many years a sales rep for Simon & Schuster. "When I was interviewed for the job in 1987, I told them that they needed computer-savvy reps who could change with the changing book industry. And guess what? It wasn't long afterward that the whole book-ordering process became computerized." Reps used to travel the country lugging bags filled with covers, catalogs, and order forms in triplicate. Those same orders are now sent overnight via computer.

The Dynamic Duo: Catalogs and Sales Reps

You've read about the sales catalog in earlier chapters, so you know how important it is that your book be well-described in the catalog description. But you haven't heard much about sales representatives yet. Here's how the two critical elements—catalog and rep—come together.

Several times a year, the sales representatives make appointments with the bookstore accounts for which they're responsible. Some sales reps have large geographic territories (all the Pacific Northwest, say, or all the Midwestern states), and some sales reps have large-volume sales territories (for example, all the Barnes & Noble stores, or all the Borders bookstores).

Most large publishing houses have their own full-time sales force. Many medium and small publishing houses use commissioned reps, sales reps who handle the sales for many publishers at once and receive commissions on the sales they create.

Are You Free on Tuesday?

The sales rep makes an appointment with a book buyer. That's the person who's responsible for deciding which of all the new books published the bookstore will carry, and in what quantities. In small, independent bookstores, the book buyer is often also the owner or the manager. These folks not only make buying decisions, but they also work on the bookstore floor and are in close contact with their customers' needs. With the large national chains, however, the book buyer is a staff position based at headquarters, far from the selling floor.

The actual sales call might be either a leisurely affair over lunch or coffee (with smaller stores) or just a hurried appointment in the cubicle of a national buyer.

Let Me Show You ...

During the sales call, the publisher's sales rep presents the titles that will be published in the next few months. With the catalog between them, the sales rep and the buyer move through page by page. The rep gives a short (very short) presentation on each book. The presentation includes these points:

➤ A description of the book and its contents

➤ The publisher's plans to promote, market, and publicize the book

➤ The author's credentials, other books he has written, and sales by the account

Experts Say

Sales reps and book buyers are both critical elements in your book's success. And like editors and agents, booksellers' sales reps are very often good friends. "There's always a whole lotta lunching going on," says former sales rep Lewis Buzbee. Reps are also often writers themselves—Buzbee left Chronicle Books to write novels. If you happen to meet a sales rep, it never hurts to become friends.

Sound familiar? Except for the publisher's publicity and marketing plans, these are essentially the same things you needed to give the publisher to show that the world needed your book. Now it is your publisher's turn (through the rep) to convince the bookstores that the world needs your book.

You can see how important the material you provided is. The sales rep has just a few minutes to convince the book buyer to buy your book, and he needs the best and most compelling information possible.

The Numbers Game

If the book buyer likes your book, how many will she order? Small stores buy in quantities ranging from just 1 copy, to 10 or 20 or more for a potential bestseller.

Large chains follow pretty much this same formula per store, but the total order for the entire chain might be several thousand.

Just-in-Time Inventory

Bookstores used to order what they thought they could sell in the first 30 days. With the rise of "just-in-time" inventory management, most stores now order only what they think they can sell in the first 10 days. When those copies sell, bookstores turn to wholesale distributors (rather than the publisher) for fast reorders. The theory is that less of the bookstore's money is tied up in inventory that way.

Bookmarks

All published books have an **ISBN,** an **International Standard Book Number.** These numbers are assigned by an industry publisher, R.R. Bowker. The first series of numbers always identifies the publishing house.

Comparative Sales Can Make or Break You

Now that computers grace every office, book buyers rely on them to help with buying decisions. Imagine that the rep has just presented a cookbook on vegetarian pasta. The book buyer will turn to his computer and bring up the sales figures for other cookbooks on vegetarian pasta. If the sales look good, the buyer might order this new title, too. But if the sales look slow, chances are that he will pass on it.

Hot Off the Press

Many talented writers have written several books with only so-so sales. But what if their newest book has all the signs of a real breakout? Using the computer-driven sales guide, book buyers would place only modest orders, killing the book's chance for a fast breakout. So, why not write under another name? A bestseller in the small-novel model was a book called *Dancing at the Harvest Moon*, by an author named K.C. McKinnon. But who was K.C. McKinnon? The pen name of a well-known Southern writer whose previous books had received good reviews but only modest sales. The secret strategy worked, and the sales of the book were strong.

Can that really be true? All the hard work that you and your publisher put into writing and publishing your book, and the book buyer won't even put it on the shelf because of the slow sales of a similar book? Sad, but all too true. This is a business, and the book buyer just made what he thinks is a sound business decision.

Imagine another sales pitch, this one by an author who's been published before. "This is his second novel?" the buyer notes. "Let me see how well his first book sold for us." The book buyer punches in the ISBN from the first book the author wrote, and the buy for the author's second book will be based in large part on the success of the first. Also frightening, but also true.

Prepping the Rep

The amount of time that the book buyer listens to the sales rep talk about your book is frighteningly brief—sometimes less than a minute per title. Does the sales rep base this critical sales pitch only on what he learned from reading the catalog? Not exactly. The rep also heard about your book at the sales conference he attended.

Let's move back to that time and go to a sales conference.

Death of a Sales Conference

The traditional sales conference is a face-to-face meeting between the sales staff (who are based all around the country in their sales territory) and the editors, publicity, and marketing folk. The purpose of the sales conference is to introduce the new books for that publishing season and educate the sales reps on how to best sell them.

These meetings, sometimes held over the course of several days for the larger publishing houses, unfold like this:

➤ Each editor gives a three- to five-minute presentation on the books that he's acquired (with longer presentations for the major titles).

Experts Say

Just a handful of accounts (Barnes & Noble, Borders, Ingram, Crown, and a few others) make up most of a book's advance orders. So, if one of these passes on your title, it can affect the initial print run. If several of them pass, the publisher may reconsider publishing the book at all. On the other hand, if they really like your book, it can be an almost instant success.

Bookmarks

Although books are published year-round, the catalogs and lists are divided into at least two **seasons** (fall and spring). The larger publishers have three seasons: fall (September, October, November, and December books), winter (January, February, March, and April books), and spring/summer (May, June, July, and August books).

➤ A large color slide of the front cover for the book is shown, and maybe some inside art as well, if it's a heavily illustrated book.

➤ The sales reps ask questions during the presentation.

➤ The sales reps break up into smaller groups with the sales and marketing managers to work out how to best present each book.

➤ The editors are alerted to any potential problems with individual titles that the sales reps anticipate.

How They've Changed!

In past years, the larger sales conferences were more like big parties than business meetings, often in resort areas such as Florida or even Puerto Rico. It was seen as an opportunity to reward the tired sales staff with a little vacation treat before the next season began. But as the publishing industry changed, so have the sales conferences.

Some publishing companies have even cut the face-to-face aspect of these conferences. They use video-taped presentations of the books, with each editor talking about the titles as though sitting up at the dais in a conference room.

Do Authors Go?

Occasionally, authors are asked to attend the sales presentation. Celebrity books and other types of books driven by the author's personality are the likeliest candidates for this. When this happens and the author has charisma, it does make a difference. Having met the author, and having heard the author's own take on his book, the sales reps are often more enthusiastic about selling that title.

Should you offer to attend the sales conference? If you are a dynamite public speaker and are comfortable addressing large audiences, sure. It never hurts to ask. But don't take it personally if you're given a polite "No, thanks." Author presentations are rare these days.

Slush Pile

Sales reps are very nice people, but do not attempt to call them. They (and your editor) will not be amused if you track them down and chat them up about sales for your book. There have been many instances in which overzealous authors have soured the publisher's sales reps on pushing their book.

Getting Reps Revved Up

Short of attending in person, is there anything you can do to try to jazz up the sales reps? Over the years, many authors have tried many things. Cookbook authors have endeared themselves by sending along sweet things based on recipes in their books. Natural health authors have sent along herbal supplements. T-shirts, CDs, and all sorts of little freebies are generally welcome, but they should tie in with your book somehow. Ask your editor how he feels about the idea before you rush out to the store to buy gifts.

Dumps and Other Promotional Ideas

While the sales rep is working to convince the book buyer to order your book, he is also trying to convince her to take a number of copies. One of the best ways to do this is to package several copies of the book together in a display pack and offer it at a higher discount: "Order 12, get an extra copy," or "Order 8 copies and get this attractive counter display."

The days of dumps and displays are fading, however. The large chains seldom buy them because space in their stores is at a premium; the publishers don't get enough orders to justify producing them. But savvy publishers continue to offer multiple-copy pre-packs to encourage larger orders.

Charging for Store Exposure

Booksellers are just as anxious to make money as publishers are. One of the more ingenious ways for them to make money is to charge publishers for special displays. Let's say that Valentine's Day is approaching, and bookstore chain X is planning to build special Valentine's Day themes displays in all 500 stores. But they won't just wander around the stores pulling romance novels, sex books, and books with red or pink covers to use in the display.

These stores sometimes sell positioning. For a fee (in the range of several thousand dollars), a publisher can buy a place in the holiday display. Sometimes the display is on the *endcap,* the small area on the end of each aisle. Endcap displays are almost always paid for by the publishers.

Remember those free bookstore gift catalogs we urged you to collect for research? The publishers of the books featured in those catalogs paid for them to be there. The cost to be included in these catalogs can run into several thousand dollars per title.

Bookmarks

Several copies of the book placed in a cardboard holder can be called either a **counter display**, a **pre-pack**, or a **counter pack**. Larger displays that stand on the floor and display eight or more copies are called **dumps**.

Bookmarks

The **endcap** is the shelf at the end of an aisle. Publishers can sometimes pay booksellers for the chance to have a display of their books on the endcap.

Can't Hurt to Ask

Ask your editor about all these things. You, as the author, have no control over whether your publisher decides to offer a counter display or pay for an endcap display for your book. Depending on the subject of your book, it might not be appropriate at all. But it never hurts to ask your editor if there are any special plans for displays or in-store promotions.

Bookmarks

Just before a book is shipped to the printers, the publisher takes a close look at the advance orders received from bookstores and uses this information to decide the book's **first printing,** the number of books to be printed.

Printing and Shipping Your Baby

After leaving the account with orders in hand (or in the laptop computer, as the case may be), the sales rep transmits these orders to the main office. When all the accounts have been seen and all the advance orders for your book are in, these numbers are then used to set the size of your book's first print run, or *first printing.*

When the printer has printed and bound all your books (this takes four to six weeks, on average), it is ready to begin filling orders. Large bookstore orders often are shipped directly from the printer to the store's main warehouse, bypassing the publisher's warehouse and distribution system. Other orders may be filled from the publisher's warehouse.

Warehousing the Rest

When all advance orders have been shipped, the rest of your books will be stored in the publisher's warehouse. There they wait, hoping to be sent out to fill other orders and reorders. Depending on the size of your book's print run, the publisher may have anywhere from 500 to several thousand copies of your book in the warehouse. Smaller, more frequent printings are now the rule. The publisher hopes that demand for your book will soon deplete the stock on hand and that the book will go into a second, a third, and a fourth printing, and beyond!

If any of your books are returned unsold by the bookseller, those copies probably will rejoin the others in the warehouse. Returns affect the inventory levels and are always taken into account when a new print run is under consideration.

Book Expo

No description of the book sales process would be complete without at least mentioning the annual booksellers convention. Now known as Book Expo America, or the

BEA, it was for many years called the American Booksellers Association (ABA) trade show. You will still hear many publishing folk call it ABA instead of Book Expo.

Held once a year in late May or early June, this is the trade show for the publishing industry. Publishers take large booths and display glossy blow-ups of the covers of their top titles. Their booths are stocked with catalogs for the fall list, and many publishers have freebies to pass out to booksellers: posters, advance reading copies, pins, jelly beans, T-shirts—you name it. Some of the larger publishers hold parties to fete their big clients and their big authors.

Do Authors Go?

Yes, some authors do go to the Book Expo. Should you go? It depends.

It depends on why you want to go. Unless you are a big celebrity author, no one will make a fuss over you. It can be quite a humbling experience to be an unknown author at this big event. Long lines form for free, autographed books from well-known authors. Not-so-long lines form for authors whose books are little known. Your publisher may not be willing to invest the money or the time in having you there as one of its authors.

If you want to go to the Book Expo on your own as a visitor to learn more about the book business, go ahead. This is a great opportunity to pick up catalogs from many other publishers and to learn about new books coming out. (Your publisher may be able to get you a free pass; just ask.) You can check out the information for this year's show at www.bookexpoamerica.com.

Smaller regional booksellers conventions also are held around the country. Ask your editor if there is a regional show in your area. These shows are more likely to feature local authors.

The Least You Need to Know

➤ Bookstores order books up to six months before the book is actually available.

➤ The size of the order depends on the popularity of the topic, the popularity of the author, and the publisher's publicity plans.

➤ With computer sales information, the order process is now formulaic and takes into account the actual sales history of other books on the topic, as well as the author's previous book sales.

➤ Celebrity authors might be invited to a sales conference or a bookseller's convention, but most authors are not.

Chapter 21

Maximum Publicity for Maximum Sales

In This Chapter

➤ What's publicity, and what can it do for your book sales?

➤ What to expect from the publicity department

➤ How two big promoters became megabestselling authors

➤ Generating your own publicity

➤ The beauty of radio

➤ Honing your radio talk skills

"Publicity? But I landed a big-time publisher," you say. "Why should I have to learn about publicity?" Your publisher has a whole department that does publicity. So isn't that its job?

Yes, it is the publisher's job. But it is also your job. You should learn about publicity, and you should start learning the minute you sign the contract with the publisher. Publicity is a critical element in the success of your book. As the author, you should become publicity-savvy, just as knowledgeable about this part of publishing as you've become about all the other steps thus far.

It is never too soon to begin thinking about publicity for your book. By starting early, you can make media contacts now that you can call on in the future. You can send out copies of your proposal or manuscript-in-progress to writers and celebrities in the hopes that they will give you an endorsement. You can even watch more television and listen to more radio so that you have a better sense of which shows would be best for your book. Get started acting and thinking like a book publicist right away.

Was It Always Like This?

The role of the author has changed dramatically over the years. In times past, we hear, an author could turn in a completed manuscript, dust off her writerly hands, and allow the publisher to take it from there. Authors didn't sully themselves with commerce. The in-house publicity staff would handle all the details about the book's publicity, sending sweet and gentle notes to the author to let her know the details on the many upcoming reviews, book signings, and publicity appearances.

Bookmarks

More publishers are looking for authors who have a **platform,** a ready-made existing audience for the book. Your platform might include lectures, a radio or television show, or a widely syndicated column. These aren't the planks that hold your platform up? Better start building a bigger platform now! Become an expert somewhere, if only in your local newspaper.

Bookmarks

Books become known to the reading public through **publicity:** reviews, articles, and mentions of the book and its contents in the media.

The Reality

Today, the publisher expects the author to take a very active role in publicizing the book, possibly even taking the lead (depending on how large the publisher's publicity staff is). "Does this author have a *platform?*" is a question asked in most editorial meetings today. When evaluating the feasibility of your nonfiction project, the publisher places a great deal of weight on how hard you plan to work on the book's behalf, with speeches, newspaper editorials, local appearances, magazine columns, and the like. The publisher took all this into consideration on that fateful day in the editorial meeting when your book received the go-ahead.

Just What Is Publicity, Anyway?

According to the dictionary, *publicity* is defined as "the process of drawing attention to a person or thing." You should know, however, that in the world of publishing, publicity refers more correctly to "the process of drawing attention to a person or thing for free." Publicity is not an ad in *People* magazine; publicity is an article in *USA Today*. Publicity is not a direct mail piece sent to a million homes; publicity is your voice on the radio station broadcast to a million homes.

Why No Ads?

Print and television advertising is seldom done in the book business. Why? It has to do with the economics of advertising, the huge cost of the ad compared to the retail price of what is being advertised. General

Motors buys lots of ads to sell cars, but remember how much a car costs. If just 10 or 20 cars sell, that pays for the ad. But if a publisher bought the same ad for your book, imagine how many books he'd have to sell at $22.95 to come close to breaking even.

So, don't tell your publisher that your book would be a bestseller if only the publishing house would advertise on the "Today Show." The exception is targeted advertising (placing an ad for a massage book in a massage magazine) or paying for the book to be featured in the catalogs published and distributed by large bookstore chains.

Better to Get Unpaid Praise

Publicity is the stronger way to sell a book. Articles and interviews make you appear to be an expert and give an independent endorsement to your book.

What the Publicity Department Can Do

As dazzling as the idea of glamorous television appearances and a late-night interview with Larry King might be, it seldom happens with most books. Here is a clear-eyed view of what you, as a first-time author, can reasonably expect from the publicity department.

The actual legwork to publicize your new book begins in the publicist's office some three or so months before your book is scheduled to be released. Publicists send out *review copies* to reviewers, work on setting up book signings and local tours, and try to make sure that your book gets into the hands of the right magazine and newspaper people. The publicists also make follow-up calls to be sure that the information arrived, to gauge interest, and to arrange for book interviews. Publicist Arielle Ford calls this part of the publicity process "smiling and dialing."

Although all authors dream of a nationwide book tour, it is becoming a rare thing indeed. To avoid disappointment later, do ask your editor several

Experts Say

"We write up a press release and send it along with a review copy to our sources at all the major media," explains a publicist at William Morrow. "To be quite frank, our efforts are often dictated by the size of the book's first printing. If a book's shipping in numbers of, say, 25,000 copies and above, it'll receive greater attention and a longer publicity effort than one with smaller numbers."

Bookmarks

Free copies of books sent out from the publisher to anyone who might help promote the book are **review copies.** These include book reviewers, celebrities, television and radio producers, columnists, and the like—sometimes their mail is so heavy with free books that they need help lugging the sack inside.

months before your pub date if there are plans for a tour. You might as well find out now. If there *are* plans for a tour, you will need the advance warning to rearrange your schedule.

Novel Approaches

Publicizing fiction is a challenge. With fiction (particularly first-time fiction), a publicist can't do too much beyond sending out review copies to well-known authors in the hope of creating a stir, targeting literary review sources such as *The Bloomsbury Review,* and trying to arrange for profile pieces in an author's local newspaper. "We also try to arrange readings at well-known literary bookstores such as Elliot Bay Booksellers in Seattle or Tattered Cover in Denver," a fiction publicist explains.

Novels also can be promoted through magazine excerpts or serialization. This is arranged not by the publicity department, but rather by the rights department. If you retained first serial rights in your contract, it is your responsibility (or your agent's) to sell these rights. No matter who is selling them, this has to happen many months before the book actually is published.

Hold Your Fire

Feel the need to call the publicity department for daily check-ups on what's going on with your book? Don't. Frustrated by what you view as a lack of effort and interest? Be careful how you communicate those feelings. A cranky author can turn off the staff—and once you're viewed as a problem, people there may do even less for your book. Remember what your grandmother told you: You can catch more flies with honey ....

The Publicity Department's Full Plate

If you think that the publisher's publicity department is going to work 24 hours a day to drive your book onto the bestseller list, guess again. The folks in publicity are responsible for doing what they can for as many as 10 or 15 books at one time. Understand that there is nothing for you as an author to gain by complaining about this situation. Instead, you can use this opportunity to take your book's fate into your own hands. To avoid duplication of effort and some bad feelings all around, it's best to let the publicity department have a clear shot at your book for the first few months after it is released.

When the people in the publicity department have let you know that it's time for them to turn their attention to other books (and they will be honest with you, if you ask), that's the green light you need to roll up your sleeves and take it from there.

"We are thrilled to work with authors who have taken the time to learn the ropes about publicity and can take an active role in it," says a longtime industry publicist. Don't worry that the interest will have disappeared because the book has been out for a few months. If your book is well-written, well-researched, and well-targeted, you can promote it for years to come. Read on to hear how two guys whose first book came out a couple years ago are still on the road flogging it.

Chicken Soup for Everyone!

Mark Victor Hansen and Jack Canfield are the well-known authors of the bestselling series *Chicken Soup for the Soul,* with a mind-boggling 20 million copies in print. But were they always bestselling authors? Did their publisher (Health Communications) have a superhuman publicity department that did all the work for them? Not by a long shot. Let's see how Mark and Jack did it.

The two friends decided that they wanted their first book, *Chicken Soup for the Soul,* to be a bestseller. But instead of sitting back and waiting for a publisher to make that happen, these two took active steps to achieve their goal.

Ask the Experts

Long before their book was even published, they set out on a mission. They interviewed bestselling authors, people like John Gray of *Men Are from Mars, Women Are from Venus,* and M. Scott Peck of *The Road Less Traveled.* Mark and Jack asked each of these bestselling authors a very simple question: "How did you become a bestselling author?" Makes sense, doesn't it?

The Secret Formula

So, what did they learn on their fact-finding mission? The key to a bestseller truly is publicity, and lots of it! M. Scott Peck told Hansen and Canfield that he gives one interview a day to any radio station, regardless of size. His approach seems to have worked in a big way: *The Road Less Traveled* was on *The New York Times* bestseller list for 12 years—not 12 weeks or even months, mind you, but 12 years!

Hansen and Canfield have taken Peck's advice to heart. They not only give an interview a day, but they also let producers around the country know that they are always available as last-minute guests to fill in for a cancellation (a little trick they learned from Dr. Ruth).

It is worth noting that Hansen and Canfield pay for most of their publicity efforts themselves. They work well with their publisher's publicity department, of course, and keep the staff informed of everything that they do. But they firmly believe that it is the responsibility of the author to create demand for a book.

The Idiot's Publicity Starter Pack

So how can you put what the authors of *Chicken Soup for the Soul* learned into action? Here are ideas and suggestions to get you started planning your publicity campaign.

Press Kit Starters

Start now to gather things for your press kit. Make yourself a file in which you keep a bio, a professional picture of yourself, video tapes of your appearances or audio tapes of your speeches, and newspaper and magazine clippings of articles about you or about the topic of your book. The earlier you start to build this file, the more you will have to choose from when the time comes to assemble your press kit.

Press Release Basics

A press release is a one-page announcement sent to various members of the media. Like the query letters you now know how to write, a press release serves to catch the interest of the person reading it. We have included an example of this in Appendix F, "Sample Press Release." Follow the style shown there to learn where to place your dates, phone numbers, and other basic contact information.

Press releases start out with a catchy headline. Often these same headlines will be used in the newspaper or magazine articles that result, so choose carefully! Here are a few sample press release headlines:

➤ Authors Reveal Stunning Reasons for Juvenile Crime

➤ Rock Musicians Share Their Vegetarian Recipes for *Food Without Faces*

➤ Secrets to Surviving Your Husband's Midlife Crisis

Each of these was crafted to convince a jaded press person to keep reading and to learn more about you and your book. A press release needs to deliver the basics of who, what, when, why, and where. It also needs to have a clear purpose: Are you trying to interest the media in writing a feature article? Are you announcing a press conference? Or are you just hoping for reviews? To learn more about writing an effective press release, we recommend Marcia Yudkin's book, *Six Steps to Free Publicity*.

Useful Contacts

Draw up a list of media contacts you have now (and ask your friends who they know); work hard to expand this list by joining organizations or attending events where you might meet members of the media. The cub reporter that you befriend today may be the editor of the business section by the time your book is published!

Bookstores

Talk to your local bookstores about the fact that you will have a book coming out, and ask for advice on how to promote your book in their stores. Make it a point to attend events in many bookstores to learn what kind of event draws a crowd and what draws only the author's family members.

Newspapers and Magazines

Read papers and magazines, and take note of who writes articles on topics that relate to your book. Jot down not just the book reviewer, but also the names of reporters whom you can try to interest in writing a feature-length piece about you and your book. One author sent a note to a woman at *USA Today* years ago to let her know how much he enjoyed one of her articles; now she is in regular contact with him as an expert in that field.

Promotional Postcards

When your publisher has the finished artwork for your front cover, have a printed postcard made with the book's cover, publication, and ordering information. They make great thank-you cards or note cards and will help keep the name of your book in front of everyone's eyes. (On a similar note, co-author Jennifer and her own co-authors on *Christmas Miracles* had ink stamps made that said "I Believe in Christmas Miracles" and then used them on the outside of all their correspondence.)

That way, you can circulate the image of your book long before it appears on bookstore shelves. Of course, be sure to send a whole bunch out when your book is published to remind people to buy it.

Hot Off the Press

Arielle Ford, the La Jolla–based book publicist for many bestselling authors such as Deepak Chopra and Brian Tracy, is happy to tell authors how to get on "Oprah." She says, "All you have to do is call this number." The room falls silent as she recites the phone number: 213-385-0209. "That's the number for the Prayer Line." And she isn't just joking—she says that two of her clients did get booked after leaving prayers. The folks at the Prayer Line will pray every day for 30 days to help your request come true. Hey, it couldn't hurt!

"And Our Next Guest Is ..."

Among the best ways that authors can help to publicize their book once it's available in bookstores is to arrange radio interviews. Radio is a tremendous medium for books; of all the different types of media, it sparks the quickest response. How does it work?

Experts Say

"Authors as authors and books as books concern us not at all. Authors as experts who can talk knowledgeably about topical issues, that is what we want on the radio," says Joel Roberts, morning talk show host-turned media trainer. No producer for radio or television is really booking you to talk about your book, about why you wrote it and what's inside. She's trying to put together a show that will interest her audience, a lively and topical show that will grab and hold its attention.

Bookmarks

Radio shows that play on more than one station are **syndicated** across the country. Giving one interview to a syndicated host helps you to reach several media markets and millions of people at once.

Radio Sells

If you see an ad for something on television, you file that impression away in your mind and perhaps will act on it in the future. But countless advertising studies have shown that the information we hear on the radio sparks an immediate response. If you hear something on the radio about a book that interests you, you think to yourself, "Hey, I'm going to stop off at the bookstore on the way home tonight and pick that up!" It's a powerful way to sell books.

All those folks trapped in their cars on the roadways have nothing else to do but listen to you explain to them how much better their lives will be and how much more money (or love, or sex, or jobs) they will have if they will only rush out right now and buy a copy of your book. Make it your goal to become an expert radio talk show guest, and your book sales will shoot through the roof. But how can you get yourself booked as a guest on the radio?

Selling Yourself to Radio

There are two ways to become a guest on radio shows. The first is to call up and try to get someone interested in you. The second is to let someone get interested and call you!

All the information you need to research radio stations across the country (from the size of the station to the phone numbers and addresses of the hosts and producers) is available in a really big and heavy book called *Bacon's Media*. Try to find this reference book at your library—keep in mind, though, that the cost to buy one is well over $100. Using the information in *Bacon's*, you can draw up a list of stations you would like to target and can begin your campaign to sell yourself as a guest.

Which Stations, Which Shows?

How will you decide which stations in which markets? Ask friends and relatives across the country for advice about which radio stations in their area are the most popular and which ones have live talk shows. Make it a point when you travel to listen to the local radio stations, station-hopping along the band until you have identified a few that seem appropriate. Ask other authors you might know which stations have worked for them.

Be on the lookout for the largest stations in the area, those with the greatest broadcast area. Radio shows with *syndicated* programs (programs that play on more than one station) are gems that you that should always dig for.

Smiling and Dialing

When you have identified the likely stations, you are ready to begin your campaign. Call the station first to confirm that the information listed in *Bacon's* is still current; stations can change their format at any time. It is very important that you have the correct name for the producer, as it is the producer's responsibility to put together an interesting show.

Spend time and effort in creating your "pitch," your 30-second speech about why this particular producer should book you as a guest. If you don't come across well in those 30 seconds on the phone, the producer will not have high hopes for how you will handle yourself once you get on the air. When you are confident that your pitch is compelling, pick up the phone and call! Follow up a successful pitch with a copy of your book and that press kit you've put together.

Get Them to Come to You

So, is there an easier way to get booked? Do the producers ever call authors, instead of authors calling them? Yes. A magazine is sent each month to radio and television producers around the country to alert them to possible guests: *Radio-TV Interview Report*. Instead of calling producers around the country, you can simply buy yourself an ad in this magazine and let producers know about you and your expertise.

Not sure how to advertise yourself in a jazzy way to make producers call? Don't worry, the magazine

Experts Say

"With the Web, radio listeners can now just fire up their computers and order the book they just heard about," one author told us. "Which means that after every big radio interview nowadays, I check my sales figures on Amazon.com and can literally see the books selling from the earlier interview. It's a secret thrill!"

Slush Pile

On most radio programs, the producer is responsible for coming up with a lively show that sounds good on the air. Producers are always on the lookout for good guests. If you can present yourself and your topic in a way that sounds like it will make a good show, it won't be long before you hear the words, "You're on the air ...."

staff folks can help you position yourself and your topic to appeal to producers. For more information on rates and scheduling, call *Radio-TV Interview Report* at 610-259-1070.

A Cross-Country Whirlwind Radio Tour

One way to hit a great many stations and markets in one short period of time is to arrange a satellite tour. Satellite radio tours are prearranged interviews with a large number of stations, all done in one single morning. You can sit at home in your bathrobe and give the same short interview over and over and over again to stations from coast to coast.

This type of interview is expensive (several thousand dollars) and needs to be professionally arranged; it is not something you can do on your own. Planned Television Arts in New York (212-593-5845) is the best-known firm for satellite tours.

Should You Be Media-Trained?

Not everyone makes a natural radio guest. But learning how to get your point across quickly, how to deal with questions, and how to work the title of your book into every other sentence are all skills that can be acquired. You can do it yourself by listening carefully to radio shows and analyzing what works, or you can have someone teach you. Media trainers specialize in helping you with your communications skills and your ability to field questions and think on your feet.

If you're serious about being effective on the radio, media training can be money well spent. Training will increase your confidence and lessen your fears, and it will increase your ability to sell your book on the air. You can find the names of media trainers in the Yellow Pages, or even by asking radio producers for recommendations.

Experts Say

Media trainer Joel Roberts recommends the book *How to Get Your Point Across in Thirty Seconds or Less* to help you hone your message for radio. The host isn't asking you the right questions? Don't panic, Roberts says. "Just respond with 'That's an interesting question, but what I think is even more interesting is ...' and cut straight to what you want to say."

Three Key Points

To get your point across on the air, you must always have two or three key points at your fingertips. Write them down on index cards and have them handy while you're being interviewed. And don't forget that great politicians' trick: No matter what the question is, you can always turn it to your advantage by saying, "I'm so glad you asked that, it reminds me of something I point out in my book ...." Then you're off and running with your own agenda!

Publicity Pays Off

Now you know: Publicity sells books, and lots of publicity can sell lots of books. You've learned that you may have to do much of the publicity for your book yourself, and that it really isn't such a hard thing to do after all. If you believe in your book and can craft a message that appeals to producers, you'll be on the air in no time. In the next chapter, we explore two other avenues for book publicity: television and the Internet.

The Least You Need to Know

➤ Publicity sells books better than anything else.

➤ Your publisher will do some publicity, but a more sustained effort is the author's responsibility.

➤ Publicity techniques can be learned, and persistence is the key.

➤ Radio producers decide which guests will be booked on a show. Your press kits should be targeted to them instead of the host.

➤ It is possible to advertise your availability as a radio and television guest.

➤ The longer you publicize your book, the longer it will sell.

Television and Online Publicity

You've learned all about radio interviews, but how do you get yourself on TV to talk about your book? The short answer is: You don't. You don't get yourself on television to talk about your book; you get yourself on television because you have something to say that is of interest to television viewers.

Bright Lights, Big City

Remember the advice from Joel Roberts, the radio guy in Chapter 21, "Maximum Publicity for Maximum Sales"? He said, "We don't care about authors as authors and books as books." What he meant was that a producer's main concern (both on the radio and on television) is putting together an interesting show that viewers will enjoy. If viewers enjoy the show, more viewers will watch, so the channel can charge more for advertising, and the producer gets to keep his job. Got it?

"So," the interviewer begins, "why did you write this book?" And the viewer reaches for the remote control. An author sitting in a chair being interviewed about his book makes for flat TV. But someone sitting in a chair being interviewed about dramatic current events, or sharing information that viewers could use, or sharing a heartfelt story that will move the audience—that makes for good television. The fact that the person in the chair wrote a book is secondary.

So how do you get yourself booked on television to talk about your book? By convincing the television producer that what you have to say is of interest to her viewers and that it will make a lively show.

Gonna Make You a Star!

The process of getting booked on a television show is basically the same as for a radio show:

➤ Find the show you want

➤ Learn the producer's name

➤ Send information to the producer

➤ Follow up with a phone call to make your pitch

The standards for material for TV are quite a bit higher, however. Your press materials have to be more extensive. Instead of just the pitch letter and sample book that sufficed for a radio producer, your press kit for television should contain these items:

➤ A press release

➤ Suggested interview questions

➤ An author bio sheet

➤ A professional-quality author photo

➤ Suggestions for shows based on your book

➤ A copy of your book

Hot Off the Press

It may not be kosher to send goofy gifts to editors, but you can go ahead and send them to producers! "When we sent out the press kits for the book *Mothers Who Drive Their Daughters Crazy*, we included little packets of tissues and aspirin," says Robin Lockwood, the publicist who ran the campaign for Prima Publishing. Here is your chance to get creative. Is your book about cooking? Send along a potholder. Is your book about mending relationships? Send along a box of adhesive bandages. Find anything to make the producer smile, stop, and read your pitch letter.

Please Ask Me

Send along a list of sample questions in your press kit. This is a great way for you to help the producer see how lively and thought-provoking your segment can be. If the producer ends up using those questions in the interview, you will be totally prepared and sound impressive.

And May I Suggest ...

Also send a list of sample show ideas. This is your chance to help the producer envision just how he could build a show around you. Help make his job easy: Describe as best you can a segment that features you and your book. But remember, your show ideas must be timely, informative, provocative, and/or amusing—not just you sitting around being interviewed about your book.

Perhaps you've written a book about dating. You can suggest to the producer that you will find several single people and counsel them on the air about the perils of being single, and then the cameras can follow them out on an actual date. That's much more interesting to watch than just you and an interviewer.

Pay attention to the news. Can you somehow tie a current event in to your book? Authors of relationship books can comment on celebrity couples, authors of health books can tie in to recent health studies, and authors of parenting books can comment on juvenile crime sprees. You get the idea. From now on, you must watch the news with an eye toward your own publicity.

> **Slush Pile**
>
> Don't go to the trouble of getting booked on television without also taking steps to be prepared once you step in front of the camera. Practice, practice, and then practice again. Write down your key points, and then memorize them. Develop short "sound bites," or talking points, with the information you want viewers to remember.

Show to Show

Sure, you know which local television shows you'd like to be on in your area, but how can you find the regional shows across the country? And is it worth your time to try to get booked on regional shows?

Once again, turn to *Bacon's Media* or the *Gale Directory of Publication and Broadcast Media*. The very same reference books that list radio stations across the nation also list television shows. And don't forget to ask your friends and family across the country what they watch in their area.

Small Can Be Beautiful

Does regional television make a difference? "Regional TV is valuable," says Robin Lockwood, a California-based book publicist. "You reach a smaller market, but if you do enough regional TV, it can really add up. A great example of a strong regional show is *Good Day Atlanta*. They do lots of authors on that show."

Slush Pile

To succeed on TV, you need to have that perky Katie Couric kind of open-eyed facial expression, one that lets the audience know to stay tuned, that you're on the verge of saying something really interesting. Sit up straight and tall; don't slump back. One trainer suggests that you perch at the end of the chair with only one buttock resting on the seat. But please practice this at home before trying it on camera!

Mail Call

When you have targeted the television show—and the producer—that you want to reach, pop your press kit in the mail. Then wait. A good rule of thumb is to give your press kit a one-week head start before you make a follow-up call. Call the show and ask for the producer. Tell him that you are following up on a press kit that you sent—did he receive it? And does he have any questions? Practice your 30-second phone pitch; the producer won't give you much time, so try to hook him quickly.

Satellite Television Tours

As with the satellite radio tours, it is also possible to sit in one place and do television interview after television interview. You are simply the talking head shown on the screen, while the host asks questions (the same questions the last host asked). These satellite television tours must be professionally arranged. Again, the best known firm is Planned Television Arts in New York.

With a satellite television tour, you spend a few hours in a studio doing television interviews across the country, one station at a time. "In 2½ hours, you can do 22 interviews," says Rick Frishman of Planned Television Arts. Most of the shows you're hitting are the local noon-hour broadcasts on affiliate stations for NBC, ABC, CBS, and Fox.

How much is a satellite television tour? To do the whole country costs in the $12,000 to $15,000 range. It's an expensive undertaking, but it can hit many markets all at once. And compared to the cost of actually going on tour ($1,500 to 2,000 per city in travel costs alone), it's reasonable.

Bookmarks

A producer might ask you for a **video clip,** a tape of an appearance you've made on another television show.

Oprah and Friends

These small stations are all well and good, but what author isn't dazzled by the prospect of the big time: a nationally syndicated afternoon talk show. *The Rosie O'Donnell Show, Montel Williams, Gayle King, Leeza, Jenny Jones* … the list goes on. And all authors, regardless of what kind of book they've written, harbor hopes of appearing on *Oprah*.

Am I the Main Attraction?

Does an appearance on *Oprah* guarantee a bestseller? No. Although the show has certainly built many bestsellers, countless other authors have appeared on *Oprah* and have seen little effect on book sales. What makes the difference? On *Oprah*, as on any other television talk show, the theme of the show itself makes a difference.

Pamela Redmond Satran, author of the baby-name book *Beyond Jennifer & Jason*, described in *Working Woman* magazine how her appearance on *Oprah* went: "I was, it appeared, just a minor act in the three-ring circus of Oprah's Biggest Baby Show Ever. Instantly, the question was not whether I was going to get rich, but whether I was even going to get on the air."

Will It Sell Books?

Make sure to ask the producer if you and your book's topic are the sole focus of the show. If so, and if the host holds your book up in the air and says, "This book is incredible, everyone should buy a copy," that could make a dramatic difference in sales.

But if you are on the stage as a part of a *panel* of experts (each with a different viewpoint), there'll probably be little impact on book sales. But what the heck, you got a free trip to New York (or Chicago or Los Angeles). And all the producers from all the shows are watching, so you might get a call from another show. At the very least, you will have a tape of your appearance that you can now send to other television producers as proof of your knowledge and charisma.

Experts Say

Satellite television tours didn't even exist until a few short years ago. "We started doing them in 1989," says Rick Frishman of Planned Television Arts. "To succeed in publicity, you've always got to think of new ways to reach people faster, cheaper, smarter. Think of a satellite television tour as the ultimate armchair publicity tour."

Bookmarks

On television, **featured guests** are those who are central to the show. **Panel** members are those who make up a roster of experts on a topic.

Hands Off (for Now)

With the top national talk shows, let your publisher's publicity staff handle the bookings. If your book has been out for several months and nothing is forthcoming, ask as politely as you can if they mind if you take a crack at it. Remember, be diplomatic. Thank them for all the efforts the publicity department has made on behalf of your book. Then take it from there.

How do you pitch these big talk shows? The same way you pitch your local noon news: with a pitch letter, a press kit, and a follow-up phone call. As publicist Arielle Ford suggests (see Chapter 21), perhaps a prayer will help, too!

Bookmarks

Shows that are aired as they are broadcast are **live**. Shows that are filmed and then shown some time later are **taped**. Barbara Walter's show on ABC, *The View*, is live. *Oprah* is taped.

About That Plaid Jacket You Have ...

Going on television? Hey, great! Now, what are you going to wear? This seems like a silly question, but it really is not.

Here's your chance to watch a great deal of television and call it "work." Turn on the set and watch closely. Study what the news anchors wear, how reporters are dressed in the field, and what the characters on your favorite sitcom are walking around in. Take notes.

Does the woman on the 11 P.M. news wear a bright white sweater? No, she knows that it would create problems with the camera. And her co-anchor, is he wearing a loud plaid jacket and a paisley tie? Nope. He is decked out in a dark navy jacket and a light shirt, with a tie that has a medium-sized print on it.

Dress for (TV) Success

There is a real science to dressing for television. You need to consider not only the way your clothes look on screen—especially the colors and patterns—but also what your clothes say about you. Are you trying to position yourself as an expert on a scientific topic? Better dress like a scientific expert. Are you a romance novelist? Go ahead and let your outfit show it.

One great way to check how your clothes (and you, too) look on camera is to do a practice run with a video camera. Have a friend or family member tape you in a few different outfits, and then look at them all with a critical eye. Choose the outfit that both looks the best and presents you in the proper mode.

Different Looks for Different Books

In a two-week period last fall, co-author Jennifer was featured on several different television shows, for several different books. So, she had several different looks.

She appeared on the national show *American Journal* as a small-business expert with her book *101 Best Extra Income Opportunities for Women*. She wasn't there as a big-business expert in a dark blue suit, but as a small-business expert in a light turtleneck sweater and a camel-hair jacket. The effect was very friendly and approachable.

The next week, she appeared on a local television show for the *Christmas Miracles* book. Same outfit? No. She needed to look like the author of a Christmas book, not a business book. And although she does have an off-white suit embroidered with gold thread and decorated with sequins and bugle beads to wear to bookstore readings, she knew it wouldn't work for a minute on a television screen. So, she appeared on camera in a bright blue, fuzzy sweater. Happy holidays!

Hot Off the Press

Jan Tilmon of KVIE has produced many television shows featuring bestselling authors. Covert Bailey, of the *Fit or Fat* television series, and Leo Buscaglia, are among the successful folks featured on the PBS specials she's produced. From time to time, she's had to give wardrobe advice to her authors: "The first show we did with Covert, we didn't control the wardrobe," Tilmon recalls. "He showed up in an awful gray suit with cuffs. Here was this trim, energetic man wearing a stuffy-looking, poorly fitted suit. We put him in khakis, bright colored shirts, and fun ties that matched his wit and charm. He came to life on camera. It made all the difference in the world."

What Really Works Online?

Ah, the World Wide Web—is it the television of the future? Will we all turn off our sets and get our information from our computer screens someday? Only time will tell. But until then, can you promote and publicize your book online? Yes. Does it actually sell books? Sometimes.

Unlike other types of media such as newspapers, radio, and television, the idea behind Web marketing is to "fish where the fish are." You can find highly specialized user groups that are most interested in your book. These are not mass audiences made up

of people who may or may not be interested in you and your book; they're highly targeted groups of people.

Here are the steps:

➤ To properly promote your book on the Web, you must first get a domain name that features your book's title, such as www.mybooktitle.com. You should be able to get this from your local Internet provider at a cost of around $75.

➤ Register your domain name with all the major search engines, such as Yahoo, Excite, and others. As of this writing, this is a free service. There are also companies such as Exploit that will register you with all the obscure search engines as well. This way, you will be listed in all of them.

➤ Join lists and participate in newsgroups related to your book's topic. Don't overdo it, but try to mention your book where you can. You want to create positive word of mouth about the fact your book exists, not annoy other members by talking endlessly about your book.

Experts Say

Joining newsgroup discussions related to your topic can be a great way to promote your book. But don't be a jerk about it. "The most subtle way is to make sure that your book's title is embedded in your own online signature," says author and agent Bill Adler Jr.

Should I Create a Web Site?

Creating a Web site can also promote—as well as sell—your book. As a matter of fact, Web sites can serve as a sort of 1-800 number for you. When you are promoting your book in an interview, you can tell folks that it is available from your Web site at www.mybooktitle.com. To actually sell books to the people who visit your Web site, both Barnes and Noble online and Amazon.com will partner with you. You can register with them to have them handle the sales from your site. Creating a Web site can be free—many e-mail services let their customers create free Web sites—or quite costly (if you hire an expert to do it for you).

But if your Web site is just a vanity site about your book, don't expect to be flooded with visitors. People who surf the Web visit a new Web site and ask themselves, "What's in it for me?" If there isn't anything in it for them, in the form of excerpts, quizzes, interactive functions, links to related sites, or other jazzy tools, why would they stay? Ask yourself that question as you are planning your site. Try to achieve what Web marketers call "stickiness."

Link Up

In addition to creating a Web site for your book, make every effort to link your Web site to other, similar topics. Contact other Web sites that would complement yours.

With a health title, for instance, ask to be linked with the major Web sites for diseases and afflictions covered in your book. That will make it even easier for folks to find you online, even when they aren't looking for you!

Read All About Me!

Another great aspect of the Web is that more journalists are poking around there. Why? They're looking for story ideas, for experts, and for ways to legitimize trends. Curtis Hougland, director of new media for Middleburg and Associates in New York, shared this success story with us:

> "We had a client, AncientSites.com, who wanted more than anything to be featured in *The Wall Street Journal*. That was their no. 1 goal, and a daunting one at that! Their site was for history buffs, and we concentrated on getting them the best online PR we could. One of the stories we got was on Wired News. And just one week after the Wired News story appeared, a writer from *The Wall Street Journal* called us. She'd seen the story, and in no time at all, there was a two-column story on AncientSites in *The Journal!*"

So keep trying online; you never know who is out there.

Future Shock

Don't be frightened or intimidated by the online world. It can be an affordable way to publicize your book on your own. If you don't have the knowledge or the skills, seek out a Web expert who does. Why ignore a great publicity venue?

The Least You Need to Know

➤ TV publicity can be booked directly with the show's producer by sending a press kit and a pitch letter, and then following up with a phone call.

➤ TV shows aren't looking for authors, per se, but rather for timely, topical, and interesting guests. So, send them a list of great show ideas based on you.

➤ An appearance on *Oprah* does not an automatic bestseller make.

➤ You can hit many TV markets in one day with a satellite television tour. It's an expensive option, but it's cheaper than touring many cities one at a time.

➤ Many publicity opportunities exist online; it can be a powerful way to create word of mouth for your book.

➤ Get a domain name that includes the title of your book, such as www.mybooktitle.com.

Chapter 23

Real-Life Publicity and Marketing Ideas

In This Chapter

➤ Creating media interest in your book

➤ Secrets of the great book promoters

➤ How to make your bookstore event a success

➤ Can you really afford a bestseller?

Radio publicity, television publicity, online promotion—what does this all really mean for you and your book? It seems so unreal. Could you and your book really end up on national television?

Sure. The media need programming 24 hours a day. Hundreds of newspapers are published around the country every single day of the week. Just think of how many stories need to be generated to fill up that space. And they can't all be about Bill Gates and Madonna. Many of those stories could be about you and the book you wrote.

Yes, P.T. Barnum would be proud. No, not because of his famous quote, "There's a sucker born every minute." Barnum was the original publicity hound, creating media events out of thin air to draw attention to his circus. You also need to learn to create events. You need to learn how to get the media to come looking for you!

Creating Media Events

Some of what you read in the newspaper or hear about on radio and television is the result of publicity efforts. It's either a staged media event, a press release, or a story idea suggested by a public relations professional on behalf of a client.

Instead of moaning about the shallowness of this situation, though, why not jump in and learn to make it work for you?

Just What Is a Media Event?

A media event is an artificially created event staged solely for the benefit of the radio microphones, television cameras, and reporters' notepads. Once the media event is over, these members of the press return to the studio or newsroom and write about what just happened.

You can learn to create media events to promote yourself and your book. A successful media event is one that draws a great deal of press attendance. Events that create a draw usually have one (or more) of the following characteristics:

➤ Timeliness

➤ Visually interesting activities or backgrounds

➤ Controversial content

➤ Humorous subjects or backgrounds

Bookmarks

A **media market** is a geographic area covered by a particular station or newspaper. Some markets, such as New York, are large media markets; others, such as Omaha, are small.

The Timely Event

Is there a way to tie your book and its topic into what is happening in the news right this minute? You learned to think about how to do this when crafting a press release in Chapter 21, "Maximum Publicity for Maximum Sales." Let's imagine that you have written a book on sexual addiction and that a major political figure has just been caught in the act. This is a perfect moment for you to create a media event by calling a press conference. Alert the media (via a press release) to the fact that, at the press conference, you will reveal the no. 1 reason that politicians are likely to cheat on their spouses.

Will anyone show up to your press conference? You betcha!

A Visually Interesting Event

We live in a visual world, and the press will come if you can supply a good visual image. You know the type—those large newspaper pictures of a cute child frolicking on the banks of a lake on a sunny day.

Bookmarks

A **press conference** is a meeting to share something newsworthy with members of the media. A **placement** is a story or a mention of the author or the book that has been placed in the media due to the PR efforts.

While managing a bookstore many years ago, co-author Jennifer created a media event on a sunny day by alerting TV stations to the fact that employees would be standing on a street corner blowing giant bubbles with wands. She was promoting a bubble book that came packaged with a plastic bubble wand. She was also promoting the bookstore. Did the television crews come? Yes. Those giant bubbles floating through the air made a wonderful visual image to show on the evening news.

Can you dress in a funny suit to promote your book? Can you ride a bicycle in public with a billboard attached to it? Can you have a large poster or photo on a tripod next to you as you speak? Anything that will make a cute picture stands a chance of drawing media coverage. Keep this in mind when you are creating an event. Always include a visual element to ensure that photos will run.

Bookmarks

Radio shows that play between 6 A.M. and 9 A.M. are **morning drive-time shows.** They're ideal for book promotions. Listenership is high during these hours, and many stations feature live hosts who do interviews.

A Controversial Event

Is the topic of your book controversial? Can you create an event in which hundreds of angry people waving signs appear in front of a courthouse or a state capitol building? Then do it, because controversy sells. So does a surprise announcement or an amazing revelation. But if you plan to stage this kind of event, make sure that you are prepared to verbally defend yourself and your beliefs.

A Humorous Event

Can you create an amusing event around your book? Perhaps design a silly contest or create an attention-getting award that you will bestow on some public figure. These kinds of events are ideal for radio, particularly the kind of silliness that goes on during the morning radio shows. Producers of these shows are always on the lookout for something funny (or someone they can make fun of) and something that's outrageous. Be warned, though: Wear a thick skin because this sort of event could backfire.

Slush Pile

You've heard it before: Practice before you go on the air! Practice before you stand at the podium facing a sea of television cameras. Practice before you call a newspaper reporter on the phone to discuss a story idea. If you don't practice and get it right the first time, there may not be a second time.

What Good Did That Do?

You staged an event, and the media came. But when you turned on the TV that night, you heard the newsman say everything but the name of your book. And the lengthy newspaper article didn't even mention your book. So what good did that do?

Quite a bit. Even if your book did not get any exposure, you did. You now have more experience in dealing with the media. You now have a newspaper article that you can send out, or a video or audio tape of you on the air. Keep trying. You will soon learn how to make sure that your book gets as much coverage as you do.

Let's take a look at two real-life examples from authors just like you. One is an author you've probably never heard of, and one is someone who started small and became prominent. How the heck did they get the media to pay attention to their books?

Secrets of Great Book Promoters

Many years ago, literary agent Bill Adler Jr., wrote a book called *Outwitting Squirrels: 101 Cunning Stratagems to Reduce Dramatically the Egregious Misappropriation of Seed from Your Birdfeeder by Squirrels*. It was rejected by 20 publishers (yep, even agents get rejected). Finally, Chicago Review Press agreed to publish it in 1988. Adler's book has been the focus of countless newspaper, magazine, and television stories and now has more than 150,000 copies in print. How did he do it?

Persistence Pays Off

He never gave up. He sent press releases to every newspaper he could think of—and some of them wrote about *Outwitting Squirrels*. He pitched television stories over and over again—and sometimes *Outwitting Squirrels* was on TV. He sent ideas again and again to the national talk shows, and one day, Rosie called. Well, not exactly; one of her producers called.

Like millions of people who feed birds, Rosie had problems with squirrels. And Adler's book had answers (he suggests that, as a last resort, you can throw the book at them). Rosie liked *Outwitting Squirrels,* but doing a major talk show is more involved than simply showing up the day they want you. To get the most mileage out of his appearance, Adler brought along props: stuffed squirrels and sample birdfeeders, to be exact.

Do the Producer's Work for Him

"I've learned from other talk show appearances that producers love it when their guests can help put a show together," Adler says. "Anything you can do to make it easier for the show will make it easier for you to get on the show. Producers are typically juggling a dozen or more shows at a time, and they appreciate the help."

Was Adler's spot on Rosie successful? The week after the show aired, his book shot up to the no. 1 position on book distributor Ingram's nature bestseller list.

The Christmas Cash Box

In the past few years, one young man has come to dominate the bestseller list at Christmastime: Richard Paul Evans, with his book *The Christmas Box*. With almost 3.5 million copies of *The Christmas Box* and his two follow-up books in print, Evans is a master at publicity and promotion.

Was he always this way? No. Evans's story is now the stuff of publishing legend. He self-published the book and then sold it to Simon & Schuster for $4.2 million. But his background was not in writing and publishing; it was in advertising and campaigns. He took the same skills he'd honed while engineering political campaigns and applied the principles to book publicity. And it worked.

Radio-Free Utah

For the Christmas 1997 season, Evans created an unusual campaign. Drawing on his background, he produced a free two-hour radio program on the story behind *The Christmas Box*. This tape was sent, along with a copy of the book, to 896 radio stations around the country. Many of the stations ran the broadcast around Thanksgiving. In essence, it was a two-hour long commercial for Evans's books, a brilliant publicity campaign.

Could you do something like that for your book? Not right away. Evans's free programming was used because the stations, after several years of bestseller status, were already aware of who he was and what his book was about.

But take heed of what both Adler and Evans did: They made a producer's job easy. Whether it meant showing up with a stuffed squirrel or sending along a free two-hour radio program, both authors succeeded because they smoothed the process, making it easy for producers to create a show around them.

Experts Say

Even *The New York Times* Business section thinks that Richard Paul Evans is good at what he does. In a lengthy article, the paper noted, "Like any savvy pol [politician], he maintains a computer database with the names and addresses of 4,000 fans who have corresponded with him. His address is published in *The Christmas Box*, and postcards are sent to his fans, alerting them to new titles." Good idea—an inexpensive way to stay in touch.

Effective Bookstore Events

Okay, so maybe you're not quite ready for prime time TV. But what about an appearance at your local bookstore? That sounds easy enough. It's simpler than getting on TV, but to have an effective in-store event still takes quite a bit of planning.

Many bookstores—particularly the large national chains—have a staff member whose primary function is to coordinate in-store activities. The book business is quite competitive nowadays, and every bookstore tries hard to become a community center of sorts, the type of place where you head on a Friday night just to see what's happening. Music, poetry readings, author signings, appearances by children's book characters—all kinds of activities go on at bookstores.

Bookmarks

Many bookstores have an **events coordinator** on staff. This person's primary function is to arrange author appearances and other kinds of bookstore events. Sometimes he or she is called a **community relations coordinator**.

There are few experiences in life as disappointing as an author appearance that flops. To sit at a desk surrounded by a stack of books, looking hopefully at people as they walk past without stopping … it's pretty awful. Many authors have been there. Read on to learn how to create a successful bookstore appearance.

An Event Is Better Than a Signing

An author book-signing is a pretty dull event, especially if the author is unknown. So anything you can do to turn a bookstore appearance into an event will help create excitement and a crowd. Steve Allen (or a Steve Allen lookalike) telling jokes and playing the piano before signing books is an event. Giving an informative talk on your topic is an event. Don't sit behind a table and expect strangers to approach you. They won't. Give them a reason to come over and see what's happening for themselves.

Invite Everyone You Know

Really, do invite everyone you know. A crowd builds a crowd. If a bookstore customer sees a crowd of people in a corner, curiosity will draw them over, too. For the author, it is always better to look out and see friendly and familiar faces before you. Just to play it safe, ask everyone you invite to bring a friend.

Don't Rely on the Bookstore for Publicity

Ask the bookstore what its standard procedure is for publicity, and then do more. Don't make the retailer angry, but don't assume that the bookstore will do it all for you. This is a perfect time to approach a reporter for a feature article on you and your book. Bookstore appearances that are preceded by a newspaper story (and that are mentioned in the story) are always more successful than those that haven't received any coverage. Be creative about where you try to get publicity; try to get the message out to whatever group you believe will be interested in your book.

Ask for a Display

Even if your appearance is a disappointment, you might make some gains if your book is on display. Many stores have a special area where they display the books whose authors are coming. Many stores will also make large posters for your book or will display a poster that you make. If your book is on display for a week or two, that is a victory in itself.

Hot Off the Press

Every author has a tale of a disastrous bookstore signing. If no one comes, use this as an opportunity to learn how to do the next one better. While giving in-store readings from her book, *Christmas Miracles*, Jennifer spent several hours one weekend afternoon at two different San Francisco bookstores sitting alone on a chair reading Christmas stories into a microphone. Embarrassing, but true. Even an ex-boyfriend who happened by unexpectedly wouldn't stay and listen! So, if it happens to you, don't feel alone. You are now a bonafide member of a very, very large club.

Bring Food

Yes, a plate of cookies can sometimes make a difference. Anyone who comes by for a bite will feel obligated to stop and listen to you for a moment, anyway.

Can You Really Afford a Bestseller?

After all the information we've shared about publicity and how to get it, why would we ask you if you really can afford a bestseller? It may seem like an odd question, but it's worth thinking about.

Many of the authors that we have mentioned in this book—everyone from the authors of the *Chicken Soup for the Soul* series, to Richard Paul Evans and *The Christmas Box*, from David Chilton of *The Wealthy Barber* and M. Scott Peck of *The Road Less*

Traveled—have one thing in common. They are driven to succeed. Becoming a best-selling author is a job that requires work 24 hours a day, seven day a week.

Do you have that drive? Can you afford it emotionally, physically, or even financially?

➤ Are you willing to spend less time with your family? Many bestselling authors tour constantly, living in hotel rooms across the country and sleeping on overnight flights. More than one marriage has been strained as a result of this lifestyle.

➤ Do you have the stamina to be on the go all day long, from early morning interviews through to late-night talk shows? It can be a physically demanding job.

➤ Some authors pay for constant promotion of their books. Richard Paul Evans runs (and pays for) an elaborate publicity network that employs four people. Jack Canfield and Mark Victor Hansen pay for much of their own publicity. It is a costly undertaking, one that few publishers are willing to fund forever. (Of course, if your book makes it big and makes big bucks, then you'll recoup your investment.)

Before you take the plunge and dedicate yourself to building a bestseller, stop and consider the effect your decision will have on others in your life. This is a major lifestyle change, and once undertaken, it's hard to turn back.

Hot Off the Press

"I heard that Steve Allen was coming to town for a special Valentine's Day piano performance," says Terry Foley, community relations coordinator for a Borders bookstore in northern California. "And I got on the phone and pleaded with his publisher to let him come for a book signing." To make certain there was a crowd, Foley alerted the retirement communities near his store. There was a standing-room-only crowd of 350 rapt fans who listened to Allen's snappy banter and piano playing for several hours. The moral of this story? Think about who your audience is, and then make every effort to let them know about your event.

The Least You Need to Know

➤ There is a constant need on the part of the media for new and interesting stories; learn how to exploit this for your book's benefit.

➤ Creating media events that receive coverage can be a powerful way to spread the word about your book.

➤ To catch the media's eye, your event should be timely, controversial, visual, or humorous.

➤ Anything you can do to make a producer's job easier will increase your chances of getting a good spot on TV.

➤ Bookstore events need much promotion and publicity to really work.

➤ Having a bestselling book can extract a heavy toll emotionally, physically, and financially.

Part 5

My Brilliant Career: Continuing Your Career as an Author

Your book is on the bookstore shelves, but for how long? The more you understand about what happens in the stores and what it means to you, the better you can make decisions about your future.

And is the life of an author really for you? How do you decide if your book is a success? Do you want to do it again? We'll help you make the decision on where to go from here, and we'll give you ideas on other ways you can make money with your writing talents.

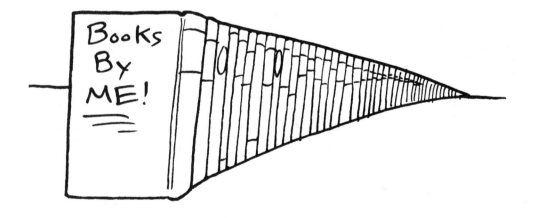

Chapter 24

After the Party Is Over

In This Chapter

➤ The shelf life of a book

➤ Returns to sender

➤ Another chance as a paperback, new edition, or sequel

➤ Evaluating your success

➤ Getting better all the time

➤ Moving on to the next phase

Meanwhile, back at the bookstore .... What is happening with your book? Both you and your publisher are working as hard as you to let the world know that your book exists. What happens to books once the box is unpacked and the book is placed on the shelf?

There was a time when books sat on bookstore shelves for years, growing ever dustier. Once or twice a year, a bespectacled bookseller would comb the shelves for the oldest-looking books and return them to the publisher. The average life span of a published book was long. But today, it is a different story.

You may remember from the beginning of this book that the retail book business is 100 percent returnable. Books that are ordered from the publisher, are placed on the bookstore shelf, and then remain unsold may be returned to the publisher for full credit.

Hot Off the Press

In an attempt to head off large returns, some publishers have taken to remaindering in place. A case in point is Kitty Kelly's book *The Royals*. According to *USA Today*, just four short months after this book was published, Warner Books saw that it wasn't selling well, so it offered retailers a $6.75 credit, allowing the retailer to deeply discount the book and sell it at 50 percent off the cover price. This helps everyone involved skip the expensive process of shipping back unsold books to the publisher, selling overstock to a remaindering company, and having the bookstores buy those very same books back from the remainder company to place on their bargain table—hence the term "remaindering in place."

Sold Once, and Then Again

One of the more peculiar aspects of publishing is that books essentially have to be sold twice. The first time, the sales rep sells it to the bookstore. Then the bookstore has to sell it to the customer. Until that second step occurs, you haven't really sold a single book.

Will a customer be able to find your book once she goes into a bookstore looking for it? If your publicity creates demand, will there be supply to meet that demand?

If someone goes into a bookstore looking for your title, both you and your publisher hope that she can easily find a copy on the shelf. And if she can't find the book (and a bookstore employee can't find it, either), she can order it. Several large book distributors in the country can send special-ordered books in just a matter of days. Now the world also has Amazon.com and Barnes & Noble online. Writers and agents everywhere hold out hope that the online bookstores will help ease the short shelf-life situation that new books now face. Time will tell.

Experts Say

The publishing industry was rocked by massive returns in 1996 and 1997, and many smaller publishers were pushed to the brink by the unexpectedly large returns of unsold books. Much of this had to do with the buying habits of the superstores. With large initial orders, there is always the chance of large returns.

Your Book's Inventory: It's Gotta Move

In this fast-paced world in which we all now dwell, the shelf life of a new book has shortened considerably. Some industry experts believe that the window of opportunity for a new book is as short as six weeks. The clock begins ticking the minute that a book is placed on the store shelf.

With a heavy reliance on computers, many bookstores know exactly when an individual book arrived in its warehouse and when (and where) it was placed on the bookstore shelf. Unless the computer notes that it has sold, that book will someday be hunted down for returns.

Why? As far as the bookstores are concerned, that's money sitting there on the shelf. And money tied up in a book that isn't moving could be freed up and then spent on buying another book—one that might sell quicker!

Extending Shelf Life

What keeps your book on the shelf? Steady sales. Publicity. Customer requests. Bookstore appearances. Even pleading calls from your publisher. It has happened before (and will happen again) that an expensive publicity and marketing campaign has gone for naught because the book had already been returned by bookstores.

Do you, the author, have any control or input in this process? Not really. With bookstores in your area, you might be able to convince them that you are an aggressive marketer who will send an endless stream of customers in looking for your book. But with the rest of the country, you will just have to cross your fingers.

Returns to Sender

Returns not only make your book disappear from the shelf, but they also make dollars disappear from your royalty account. When books are returned to the publisher, that is noted in the publisher's inventory system. When the publisher's royalty department factors in that information, your account could sink slowly into the west.

Bookmarks

Books that are placed on the shelf with the cover facing out catch a customer's eye better than books that are **spine out,** placed sideways on the shelf so that only the slim back end of the book shows.

Experts Say

Small, independent bookstores seldom return unsold books as aggressively as their larger cousins. "It is a dying habit, but we will give a new hardcover book six months or more before pulling it," says Ann Magruder of Beers Books in Sacramento. "We'd much rather sell it than return it."

Remember, if you have received an advance, you are already in the hole. Your book must sell enough to earn back the advance and move into the black before you will make any more money. Books returned unsold can easily drag you back into the red ink, delaying the long-awaited day you earn back your advance and begin to accrue more royalties. That's another reason to cross your fingers and say your prayers (and send out another press release or two).

For many years, publishers have accused bookstores, both large and small, of returning books in lieu of paying bills. That may have been the case. Streamlined ordering practices can lessen that problem, but this has also lessened the size of publisher's print runs.

Coming Out Again?

If your book was published first in hardcover, you might have something else to look forward to: a paperback edition, either in a trade paperback size or as a mass market paperback. The decision to publish in paperback will be based on sales.

The path from hardcover to paperback used to be quite routine but is now reconsidered with every book. Do the sales figures justify bringing it out again? If so, get ready for another round of cover design, copywriting, and publicity. If not, let's consider what else might lie ahead.

A Rose by Any Other Name ...

As Peggy Lee would sing, "Is that all there is?" If your book dies a slow death on the shelf, or even if it succeeds and sells for many years, is that all there is? You worked so hard for many months (and, in some cases, many years) to produce this book! Is it time to move on to the next thing?

Not necessarily. With a novel, yes, you'll have to take what you've learned from this first experience and get busy with another book.

But with nonfiction books, a few other options are left:

➤ A revised and expanded second edition

➤ A renamed and repackaged book

➤ Electronic publishing

➤ Series and sequels

Revised and Expanded!

If your nonfiction book sold in respectable numbers the first time around (in the 7,500 copy or more range), you can certainly discuss with your publisher the opportunity to revise, update, and expand the material for a new edition—provided, of course, that it is a topic that still has an audience. Almost any nonfiction book can go through this phase—health books, travel books, reference books, and even cookbooks can be revised and expanded. If the second edition succeeds, you can look forward to a third, fourth, fifth, or sixth edition, and so on.

It never hurts to go into a book project with an eye on developing long-term income, and an annual edition or frequently revised book is a great way to go.

Renamed and Repackaged

So, your book didn't sell well. The book has gone out of print, and the publisher has reverted the rights to you. Is it over? Again, if the topic is still timely, it doesn't have to be. But unlike a revised second edition, you will need to completely change your book. To dust it off and make it salable to another publisher, your book will need to undergo quite a face lift as well as a name change. Your book could be reborn with a better title, a tighter editorial focus, or a different format.

If you do decide to work to improve your book and resell it, you will need to be up front about it. Tell your agent, and tell any publisher that expresses an interest, that you once published a similar book under a different title. They'll probably find out later, anyway, and that could spell trouble.

Experts Say

Sometimes a publisher will change the name of a book in between the hardcover and paperback editions. This is done to give the paperback book a fresh start and a better, more tightly focused title. A good example is a book on speeches called *Winning Them Over* in hardcover that was changed to *Ten Steps to Better Speeches* in paperback. The second title gives browsers a better idea of what the book is about.

Taking It to the Superhighway

We've discussed electronic publishing in several different parts of this book, and we bring it up yet again because it is something to consider for the future of your book. If the rights to the book have reverted to you, you can take what you have written and do several things with it:

➤ Turn it into an e-book, or break it up into what Fatbrain.com calls "e-matter."

➤ Sign up with one of the print-on-demand services such as xlibris.com so that your book is always available somewhere, somehow.

Although electronic publishing possibilities are thrilling, that still leaves you, the author, with a basic problem: how to create sales for your book. It is up to you to create demand, a critical part of the print-on-demand equation.

Series and Sequels

Are the sales of your book strong enough to warrant more of the same? Has your editor hinted that she would like to see you do another similar book? Welcome to the world of *series* and *sequels,* where, if one book sells, then another just like it should do fine, too!

Deciding whether to pursue either a sequel to a book or to build it into a series is strictly the publisher's call. A revised, expanded second edition can be developed by the author and perhaps sold to another publisher, but an author generally would not approach another publisher unless the publisher of the original book is not interested. If you aren't sure whether your publisher is interested in a series or a sequel, ask your editor. She will be honest about the chance that this might happen.

Bookmarks

A second book that features many of the same characters as the first is a **sequel.** Several books that are related either in theme, purpose, or content comprise a **series.**

Bookmarks

In the long run, how many books were shipped out to bookstores doesn't matter. What matters is the number of books that **sell through.** Books that sell through are books that bookstore customers bought.

Evaluating Your Success

How do you know if your book is a success? How many books sold are enough? Or, worse yet, how many are too few? Evaluating your book's success strictly by the numbers is relatively easy. Evaluating your book's success in other ways is a little harder.

Show Me the Money

How many books need to sell to make it a success? That question needs to be considered in relationship to the size of your book's first print run.

➤ If your book had a modest first printing of 7,500 and sold at least 5,000 copies, you did fine.

➤ If your book had a first printing of 10,000 and sold 5,000, you didn't do as well.

➤ If the publisher printed aggressively (more than 25,000 for a first-time author) and you didn't *sell through* more than 50 percent, you didn't do as well either.

Remember, the size of the print run was determined by the advance orders. The advance orders were determined by how well the bookstores thought your book would sell. So, if a book with a small print run (a book with modest sales expectations) sold well, that is a heck of a victory. But if a book with a large print run (big sales expectations) didn't do well, that is a disappointment. Does that make sense?

Personal Best

But was the book a personal success for you, the author? You wrote a book, you published a book. That sets you apart from most other people on the planet. Instead of just talking about how someday you plan to write a book, you did it.

Let's return to the reasons to write. In Chapter 1, "So, Why Write?" you looked at a list of reasons:

➤ I'm compelled to write.

➤ I want the personal satisfaction of being published.

➤ I hope to advance my cause.

➤ I want to share my knowledge.

➤ I'd like to advance my career.

➤ I'd like to achieve fame.

➤ I'd like to earn a fortune.

➤ All of the above.

Which reason (or reasons) was yours? Did your book help you achieve it? Even a book with modest sales can easily achieve many of the reasons on the list.

Are you compelled to write? You wrote. Did you seek the personal satisfaction of being published? You have it. Did you want to advance your cause or share your knowledge? Everyone who bought a copy of your book, read about you in the newspaper, or heard you talk on the radio is now aware of both your cause and your knowledge.

Hot Off the Press

Many folks on the professional speaking circuit make money with "back of the room" sales. If a roomful of people already has paid to come and hear you speak on a topic, those people are primed to buy what you've got to sell. These people won't look to see which New York publisher is behind it; they just want to take a little of you home with them. A speaking career is a great way to promote and prolong the life of your book. Buy copies in bulk from your publisher; when those run out and the rights have reverted, publish it yourself. This can make a big difference in your bottom line.

Has your career been advanced? You now have the prestige and distinction of being published. And regardless of how well your book has done in bookstores, you have the opportunity to speak around the country and sell books to clients and your professional audience. If you want, you could keep your book in print forever in a self-published edition.

But Really, Show Me the Money!

Did you achieve fame or fortune? Ah, here is the tricky one. As you learned in the first chapter, it *is* possible to achieve fame without fortune, and vice versa.

Fame may still be achieved. If you continue to promote and sell your book on your own long enough, you can achieve a measure of fame.

Slush Pile

When trying to sell another book, don't ever point the finger of failure for your previous book on your publisher—at least, not when talking to an agent or an editor. Your complaints will fall on deaf ears, and your listeners will consider you a whiner.

Bookmarks

A book that's currently available from a publisher is **in print**. A book that's no longer available from a publisher is **out of print**.

Fortune is not always elusive, either. The mere fact that you published a book may someday spawn other opportunities. Other opportunities may have occurred to you during this long, long ride as well. Or, maybe fortune will come with the next book.

But This Book Was Perfect!

"The publisher screwed up." Ask most authors why their books didn't sell, and that is the reason you will hear: The publisher screwed up, not me.

The book didn't get to the stores in time, the cover (or the title) was awful, they didn't do any publicity, they never cared about my book. The staff was incompetent, my editor left, the sales reps didn't sell it, the stores returned it too soon.

Perhaps. But indulging in that sort of thinking will not further your career as a writer. A better way to spend your time post-book is to do some follow-up work:

➤ Continue to work on your writing.

➤ Sharpen your ability to create a book that large numbers of people will buy.

Work on My Writing?

Yes, work on your writing. Continue to take classes, attend conferences, and seek out other writers. Build your own community of writers around you. No book is ever really perfect, and every writer needs to continue to practice and polish his craft.

You have been published. Now take that accolade and build on it. Write more. Get better.

What Book Will Large Numbers of People Buy?

Hopefully, they'll buy your next one. Again, take what you have learned with this first book and build on it. If that is your goal, work on developing novels and non-fiction books that have the potential to affect large numbers of readers.

Chapter 3, "If You Need an Idea, Stalk the Bestseller List," might not have interested you when you began reading this book. After all, you already knew what you wanted to write. Is it time to go back and reread that chapter? This gives you a clear-eyed view of how book professionals try to develop book ideas with big potential. Read this chapter, and try out a few of the exercises. It will help you begin to think like a publisher.

Moving On to the Next Phase

What is your next move, anyway? Will you try to write another book, or will you try to return to your life as it was before you embarked on all of this?

If you are returning to your previous life, be proud of what you have achieved. You now have a lasting symbol of great and unusual accomplishment: a published book.

If you are committed to continuing your career as a writer, the next two chapters will share more information about how to earn a living with your pen—or, more correctly (as you've now learned), how to earn a living with your computer—your creativity, and an endless ability to keep going in the face of possible defeat.

Experts Say

Why go to writers' conferences after you've already been published? Other unpublished writers will look at you with awe. It can be a nice little ego boost. You also will make new contacts with agents and editors, sharpen your skills, and come away reinvigorated.

The Least You Need to Know

➤ The life span of a new book on a bookstore shelf can be short, but steady sales, constant publicity, and customer demand combine to keep a book on the shelves for a long time.

➤ Between special orders placed with distributors and the rise of online book-selling, while your book is in print it is almost always in stock and available somewhere.

➤ If the sales were satisfactory, a hardcover book will come out in paperback, and a paperback might someday come out again as a revised and updated second edition.

➤ Sometimes a book is renamed during the transition from hardcover to paperback to give it a better chance for better sales.

➤ To be considered a sales success, a book must sell through a majority of its print run.

➤ Even if your book has not been a sales success, you might have achieved your reasons for writing.

Writing for Money

You've just written an entire book. So, what else can you write? How can you use your creativity and talent to bring in a little more money?

Writers really are special people. The vast majority of folks are intimidated by a blank page, unable to come up with a simple sentence to get started. So, if you can do it with ease, use it. In this chapter and in Chapter 26, "Working with Book Packagers," you'll learn more about the ways writers can sell words. And if writing for magazines truly intrigues you, check out the book we wrote on the topic, *The Complete Idiot's Guide to Publishing Magazine Articles*.

If Not a Book, How About an Article?

While thinking of your book idea, you came up with several other related ideas. Most of them weren't really books, but only magazine articles. Why not write those magazine articles now? Magazine articles are a great way to further your career as a writer and to keep your name in the public eye. They also can be a powerful way to promote your book.

Why magazines?

There are many great reasons to write for magazines.

It's a Boost to Your Writing Career

Whether you write fiction or nonfiction, if it's your intention to continue writing books, magazine articles increase your chances. This adds to your portfolio and your clips, and it establishes your credentials as an experienced writer.

It's a Good First Step to Becoming an Expert

Writing for magazines often is a first step to becoming an expert on a subject. It gives you a chance to do research, accumulate material, make contacts, and conduct interviews, all of which can be used later while writing a book. It also gives you an inside view on what works; a popular magazine article means that there is interest in a topic. If the article works in a big way, a book might, too.

It Can Be Easier to Get Published in Magazines

It's sometimes easier—and almost always faster—to get a magazine article published than a full-length book. Writing for magazines can be a faster way to make money than devoting all your time to writing books.

It Helps You Polish Your Writing Skills

The short deadlines on magazine articles can help you develop as a writer. And anything that helps your writing also helps your publishing career.

The Big Idea

Of course, just as with book writing, you'll need to start with an idea for a magazine article. What exactly would you like to write about? Even better, what exactly do you think people would like to read about?

Sit down with a piece of paper and write down as many ideas as you can. Is there an expertise you have that you can exploit? Or do you have a hobby that you can teach others about? Just like developing an idea for a book, you will need to devote time and energy to create a salable idea for a magazine article. But it can be done; just keep trying.

The Big Magazine Market

For what magazines would your ideas be suited? There are literally thousands of markets for magazine and newspaper articles, many more than there are book publishers. The odds are actually better in this market!

What Type of Article?

The major types of articles can be broken down into the following categories:

➤ **Op-ed piece**—Usually a 600-word first-person opinionated essay on a topical subject you know about firsthand.

➤ **Personal essay**—A 500- to 1,000-word first-person essay on a personal or topical subject.

➤ **Review**—A 200- to 2,000-word critique of a book, movie, play, or restaurant.

➤ **Service piece**—A 500- to 3,500-word third-person, informative, and educational piece that includes lists, phone numbers, and addresses.

➤ **Q&A**—A 200- to 5,000-word third-person interview that includes your questions and the subject's answers.

➤ **Profile**—A 200- to 5,000-word third-person interview without questions, using mostly narratives and quotes.

➤ **News story**—A 200- to 2,000-word third-person informational piece that gives new, topical information in a serious format.

➤ **Round-up**—A 500- to 3,500-word entertaining, informative piece, usually about where to find something specific.

➤ **Cultural commentary**—A 600- to 6,000-word commentary or overview of a cultural phenomenon with an opinionated slant.

➤ **Humor piece**—A 500- to 1,000-word humorous essay, often on a topical issue that could be personal, political, parody, or farce.

➤ **Feature article**—A 500- to 5,000-word entertaining, third-person piece on a special person, cultural topic, or provocative issue.

Experts Say

"The smartest thing you can do is to take an adult writing class," says Susan Shapiro, a humor writer and writing instructor at New York University and the New School. "I've had 125 students in the last four years who've gotten published. The joke is that, if they sell their first article for more than $1,000, they owe me dinner. I've had seven dinners."

➤ Sidebar—A 50- to 500-word list, often printed in a box, that gives added information for an article.

Of all these different types of articles, what are the easiest pieces to get published? The easiest, we think, are op-ed pieces, service pieces, first-person essays, reviews, and profiles.

Get the Guidelines

Just as in the romance publishing business, magazines have writer's guidelines available. Before you query a magazine with an article idea, call or write and ask for a copy of its guidelines. You will save yourself countless mistakes and disappointments this way.

Steve's Way

Freelance writer Steve Morrill has published more than 1,000 magazine and newspaper articles. How? For every article idea, he has a marketing plan. In the same way that writers can succeed in the book business by being businesslike, freelance article writers can develop successful businesslike habits as well.

Be Scientific About It

First, list five types of magazines for which you'd like to write—not the names of five magazines themselves (not *Time, Redbook, New Woman,* and so on), but five types (such as airline magazines, trade magazines, and women's magazines). When you have an idea for a topic, try to think of as many variations of it as you can, with each variation targeted to a particular type of magazine.

Slush Pile

Do not send multiple queries to magazine editors. Query only one editor at one magazine within a magazine group or category at a time (see the previous section "Steve's Way").

For instance, let's say you want to write an article about herbs. For an airline magazine, you can pitch an article about herbs that help overcome jet lag. For a woman's magazine, you can pitch an article about herbs that help with PMS, or one on herbal baths. For the trade magazine, you can pitch an article about the increasing market for organic herbs.

Now take a directory of magazines, such as *Writer's Market,* and start to research the magazines in each category. Which woman's magazine pays the most? Which airline magazine pays the most? Under each of the five types of magazines, list five actual magazines, ranked in order of pay.

Five Queries at a Time

You now have a list of 25 magazines in five groups, and at least one idea for each group. Start the query process at the head of the line: In each type, start with the magazine that pays the most money. If that magazine says no, go on to the next magazine in that category.

Morrill's idea is brilliant because it gets around the problem of exclusive queries. Magazines do expect each query to be an exclusive, but they can be so slow in responding. With this method, however, query away. The magazines do not overlap in readership, and your ideas are not exactly the same for each magazine type.

A Thick Skin

Another benefit to having a marketing plan like the one Morrill developed is that it helps you withstand rejections. Instead of crying when you spot the thin, white envelope in your mail, you can just shrug and go on to the next magazine on your list. And who knows, you might sell an article to each of the five different magazine types after all!

Magazine Queries

A magazine query letter is pretty much the same as a book query letter. It's a brief, one-page letter in which you state what the idea is and why you are the best person to write the article. Make sure that you've addressed the letter to the right person. If you have been published in magazines and newspapers before, include up to three clips.

Read 'Em First

To write for magazines, you have to read magazines. It's a simple step, but it's one too often overlooked. And you have to read more than one issue. Study each issue, see who writes what, and see who edits what section. Study it as though you were applying for a job—in a way, you are! Memorize the different sections and what types of articles run in each. Don't query an editor until you feel confident that you know what kind of magazine he edits.

Slush Pile

Never send a query letter addressed to "The Editorial Department." It will end up in the janitorial department when the garbage cans are emptied.

Slush Pile

Don't overload an editor with several ideas at once. Until you have a very good working relationship with an editor, query only one article idea per letter.

What Should You Send?

Sometimes sending just a query letter is the right way to go. Sometimes you'll need to send the whole article. How do you know which approach is right?

Think book publishing. With nonfiction books, you could get away with doing just the book proposal first. With fiction, you had to write the whole darn thing before you could even think about selling it.

Research-oriented, nonfiction articles often get sold on the basis of a one-page query letter (and send along your clips, if you have them). In your query, describe how you plan to do your research, how you envision the finished piece, and why you are ideal to write it.

With creative nonfiction, such as humor, op-ed pieces, and personal essays, you will have to write the entire thing first. Then send the piece, along with a letter, to the appropriate editor. Your letter can be fairly short.

Your New Best Friend

Sometimes you can develop a relationship with an editor at a magazine over a period of time. After you've published a piece or two, you might even find that the editor will call you with an idea! Once you've established a relationship, you might be able to skip the pitch letter step and just call the editor with your article ideas.

Don't Give Up Your Day Job

Writing for magazines can be a great way for writers to make money, but it is tough to actually support yourself or your family that way. If that's your dream, you'll need to establish relationships with several different magazines. Cozy as it is to have a close relationship with an editor, don't forget that this person might not always be there. Co-author Jennifer used to write freelance articles for a food magazine, but she lost interest when it went through three different editors in a six-month period! It's hard to befriend an editor over, and over, and over ....

Never depend 100 percent on one magazine. Try to establish yourself with at least three or four different magazines.

Writing for the Web

Yes, online magazines will pay freelance writers for articles in the same way that slick paper magazines will. Your best bet here is to find the online magazines and then read them. It is still a pretty quirky format, and every magazine tries hard to create a distinctive personality. Many of the Web sites have handy little buttons to click that say "Write for Us." And the good thing is, they will e-mail you their guidelines!

If you decide to go after Web writing with gusto, you should know about a few sites:

➤ **www.craigslist.com**—Information on freelance writing jobs changes daily. Many of the jobs listed are for dotcoms in the San Francisco Bay area, but if you read it frequently, you will find work-from-home freelance writing positions listed.

➤ **www.writersmarket.com**—This Web site continues to expand the section that covers online publications, guidelines, and query information.

➤ **www.guru.com**—Guru.com specializes in matching up freelancers of all stripes with the companies that need to hire them. You can advertise your writing skills and hope to find a match.

Building up some clips with Web writing is a great way to help you establish yourself with the print media. In fact, you may find such success with your online writing jobs that you might turn your back on the print media for good!

They Want Me!

When a newspaper or magazine accepts your article, an editor will usually send you a contract. If not, request one. Thankfully, this contract won't be nearly as long or complicated as the book-publishing contract, but it will spell out things such as these:

➤ What you are expected to write, including a description and length

➤ How much you will be paid

➤ When you will be paid

➤ What rights you are licensing to the magazine

➤ How much you will be paid if the piece is not used (a kill fee)

Ideally, you want to limit the publisher to buying one-time North American serial rights. This means that, although the magazine is paying you to run the article in its pages, you will then still own the piece and be free to sell the piece again elsewhere.

Experts Say

What does it take to be a ghost-writer? Anne Basye, ghostwriter and collaborator on a half-dozen business books, says, "You need to be able to put aside your own ego and remember that it is someone else's idea. Your job is to help him express it the clearest possible way."

Experts Say

David Kennedy, author and former president of the American Society of Journalists and Authors, has this advice for fellow writers: "Ninety percent of nonfiction writing is organization—organizing your thoughts and thinking in a logical manner. That's the secret."

Bookmarks

Many magazines buy articles and don't pay for them until the article actually runs in the magazine, which can be months later. This is called payment **on publication.**

Sometimes publishers, not always unreasonably, want to restrict when you can republish your piece. Frequently, they would like to pay you when the piece actually appears, not when you hand it in. This is called paying *on publication*.

The Friendly Ghost

With a book or two under your belt, could you be a ghostwriter for someone else?

The real talent a ghostwriter needs to possess is the talent for organization. Ghostwriting often involves organizing someone else's ideas, thoughts, speeches, and writings into a readable book. Mimicry isn't a bad skill to have, either, as you are literally trying to write in someone else's voice.

How do ghostwriters get jobs? This is largely a word-of-mouth business. When you establish a good relationship with your editor, you might find that she recommends ghosting or rewriting jobs to you. Once you begin to ghost books, your clients will also recommend you to their colleagues.

Ghostwriting can pay well. With large jobs, you will want to negotiate a fee in the range of several thousand dollars, perhaps a portion of the royalties the book earns. For smaller jobs, you can tell your clients that you charge by the hour. A standard hourly charge is between $25 and $50, depending on your expertise.

Publicity and Promotional Writing

You learned how to write press releases to promote your book. Now that you have that skill, can you sell it to anyone else? Yes.

Many small-business people lack the ability to write press releases and other kinds of publicity pieces. Spread the word among small businesses that you are ready and available to help. You might find that they could use your skills helping to create media events as well. What should you charge for a press release? For a one-page press release (and all good press releases are only one page), you should charge at least $75. That's not too shabby for an hour's worth of work.

Look Around

You can write. People need writers—they really do. Businesses need writers to help them connect with customers, to convey a message, or to convince a crowd. Make it your business to look around and find new ways to sell the words you can write. As long as you keep trying, you should be able to generate some income from your writing skills. Good luck!

The Least You Need to Know

➤ Writing for magazines can be a great way to sharpen skills, gain credibility and exposure, and find new ideas for books.

➤ Magazine editors expect exclusive queries, so only one magazine can consider your article at one time.

➤ Magazines will send you their writer's guidelines upon request, and online magazines will e-mail their guidelines if you ask for them.

➤ Op-ed pieces, humorous pieces, or personal essays need to be written before they can be submitted.

➤ It is difficult to earn a living solely from freelance magazine and newspaper writing.

➤ Ghostwriting and promotional writing are two other good ways to make money with words.

Working with Book Packagers

This entire book has been about coming up with good ideas for books and then writing those books. But other than ghostwriting, is there any way for you to write books without having to come up with the idea yourself? Yes.

All Books Come in Packages

There are folks in the publishing world called book packagers. Generally speaking, packagers start with their own ideas, develop them, and are able to deliver to a publisher—or a museum, corporation, or organization—anything from a rough manuscript to an edited manuscript, from books on disk to bound books. Packagers rarely do all the work themselves; they often hire people—including writers—to help them. That's where you come in.

Just What Do Packagers Do?

Before Sheree could buy a single vowel on "Wheel of Fortune," she was forced to sum up her job in a sentence for Pat Sajak. So, she came up with, "I'm a *book packager*. I create and develop books for publishers." And if there had been more time, she would have said, "I think of ideas for books, I find writers to write the books, and I sell the books to publishers."

Hot Off the Press

Co-author Sheree loves to tell the story of how, when she was a book packager many years ago, she was playing racquetball with a stranger. He asked Sheree what she did for a living, and she gave her usual answer: "I'm in publishing." She always said that because no one knew what a packager was, and it was difficult to explain. "And what do you do?" Sheree asked him in turn. The man quickly replied, "I'm a packager." She was stunned. "I'm a book packager, too!" she said. The man blushed, "Well, we don't actually make the boxes ...." So after that, Sheree went back to telling people she was in publishing.

That's it, in a nutshell, but book packaging really is a lot more complicated than that. The idea of a book packager has developed over the years, and there are now many different ways to package books and to work with book packagers.

Let's take a closer look at this business before explaining how you can find a packager and start to work with one.

Bookmarks

Book packager, book producer, book developer—are they all the same? Yes. They create books for publishers, providing them with finished manuscripts to finished books, or anything in between. The professional trade association of packagers uses the term *producers;* they call themselves the American Book Producers Association.

Who Produces the Book?

There is a common misconception that packagers do the production of books. The fact is, that's only part of what some—indeed, most—packagers do. Traditionally, besides bringing the idea to an author or publisher, packagers also bring to projects an array of publishing production skills. That's why most packaged books are heavily designed affairs and sometimes even include nonbook items.

The popular *Bug and Bottle* books that Workman publishes so successfully are actually packaged and produced by a Canadian packager called Somerville House. These eye-catching children's books about bug collecting come encased in a plastic bug-collecting bottle. Somerville House is well known for packaging that sort of book.

Many packagers are designers and book compositors as well, especially those who started their careers in the book production side of publishing rather than the editorial side. In fact, these packagers wouldn't consider delivering just a finished manuscript to a publisher.

These people consider themselves packagers because they bring so much more to the publisher—and earn accordingly. Packagers offer specialized skills. One packager might be an expert on packaging high-quality art books for museums. Another might specialize in cookbooks and provide the ability to test recipes and design mouth-watering layouts.

Experts Say

Book packagers come to packaging from all areas of publishing. Many come from publishing houses: some from sales, some from editorial, and many from the production department. Their skills are abundant and varied. One thing they all have in common is that they are entrepreneurs.

The Stonesong Story

For many years, Sheree worked for The Stonesong Press. Stonesong is well known for producing one of the bestselling packaged books of all time: *The New York Public Library Desk Reference.*

Stonesong delivered just the manuscript to the publisher, Simon & Schuster. The publisher then copy edited the manuscript and designed and produced the book. How, then, can you call this a packaged book?

Ideas Matter

Paul Fargis, the owner of The Stonesong Press, came up with the idea of doing this book. First, he approached the New York Public Library about a licensing agreement, then he wrote the book proposal, and finally he sold the idea to Simon & Schuster. He found and then coordinated with Sheree a huge roster of 27 experts who actually wrote the book and did the fact-checking. One single author could not have written a book like this; it was a huge orchestration that demanded the skills of a company the publisher could trust to pull it off.

One of Stonesong's great strengths is its ability to bring in brand names of huge companies and organizations, from the Stanley Tool Company to the Library of Congress. Putting a book together with a trusted brand name is a powerful selling tool; readers tend to go with names that they already know and trust. (Which book would you buy about ice cream recipes: one from an author you didn't recognize, or one from two guys named Ben and Jerry?)

Other packagers have different strengths. Most tend to specialize; for instance, one makes sports books, another does cookbooks, and still another does only children's books.

In a way, a book packager is a producer in the Hollywood sense. The packager's role is quite similar to a movie producer in that he brings talented people together and then oversees the actual production.

Outsourcing

Why do publishers like to work with packagers? It enables them to publish more books with less hassle. Instead of employing a large staff to oversee these complicated books, the publisher can pay attention to other books and know that on the delivery date, a packager will deliver.

Packagers do the work of editors, authors, agents, publishers, designers, production managers, and more. About the only thing they don't do is sell books to bookstores.

Publishers know that they will get a good product from a book packager. They might also get a better price than what it would cost to do it in-house. A book packager with a small staff doesn't have the overhead that a publisher such as Random House has.

The "Cosmo" Quiz

Writing for a packager is not for everyone. To help you decide whether it is right for you, Sheree has designed a quiz. For every "Yes" answer, give yourself one point.

➤ Are you willing to write something and not feel proprietary about it?

➤ Can you regard writing as "just a job" rather than an expression of your own ideas?

➤ Do you prefer to write from assignments as opposed to from your own ideas?

➤ Would you prefer to let someone else write the book proposal from which you will work?

➤ Are you as good at expressing other people's ideas as your own?

➤ Do you like having your ideas organized for you?

➤ Can you be flexible in your opinions?

➤ Do you enjoy research as much as writing?

➤ Do you enjoy working as part of a team?

➤ Are you comfortable discussing your work-in-progress?

➤ Are you comfortable letting someone else have the final say about editing?

➤ Would you feel comfortable earning less for your writing than the packager, who didn't do any of the writing?

Again, most writers who work for packagers would answer "Yes" to almost all these questions. They can regard their writing talent as a skill that can be used to earn money.

Again, writing for a packager is not for everyone. In some instances, it is more like being an advertising copywriter or a ghostwriter than an actual author, even if the result is an authored book with your name on it. And in some instances, you might be hired to just write part of a book, or just a chapter or two.

So Why Work with a Packager?

Why would an author work for a book packager and let someone else make the lion's share of the money? It hardly seems fair. Actually, there are many good reasons to write for a book packager:

➤ You can still say you wrote a book—or part of one—even if you can't think of any commercial ideas on your own.

➤ It is a good way to get your foot in the door with other publishers.

➤ It is a way to make money between other book contracts.

➤ It may be a way to bring in more steady income.

➤ You may actually enjoy being part of a creative team and learn more about putting together a book.

Bookmarks

Writers who are paid a flat fee for their writing are doing **work for hire.** Under a work-for-hire agreement, the writer does not earn royalties and does not own the copyright to the work he has created or to which he has contributed.

Hot Off the Press

Book packaging is hardly a new idea. At the turn of the century, Edward Stratemyer founded a company he called the Stratemyer Syndicate. He had been writing books for many years under several different pen names and was responsible for the popular *Rover Boys* and *Tom Swift* books. But, as his granddaughter, Camilla Witman, explains, "He had so many ideas, he couldn't write them all himself. He'd write up a comprehensive outline and give it to a writer-for-hire." This method produced many of the most popular American young adult novels: the *Bobbsey Twins,* the *Hardy Boys,* and the *Nancy Drew* series. At its height, the Stratemyer Syndicate produced novels under 20 different pen names.

Even Fiction Comes in Packages

Most packaged books are your basic, how-to, nonfiction books. But novels can be packaged, too. Some of the most successful works of fiction have come from packagers, from what are known as writing syndicates. What would your childhood have been like without the Hardy Boys or Nancy Drew? And for today's kids, without the *Sweet Valley High* or the *The Babysitters Club* series? All these books came from writing syndicates.

Carolyn Keene is the name on the spine of all the *Nancy Drew* books. But there was more than one person writing as Carolyn Keene.

Hot Off the Press

You already read about the New York Public Library series of desk references, but did you know that those common-sense financial bestsellers from The Beardstown Ladies are from a packager? The packager's name is Seth Godin, and he also has a series called *If You're Clueless*. Almost any time you see a book that's connected to a magazine, such as *The Woman's Day Cookbook* or a parenting book from *Parents* magazine, you can bet a packager was involved. Check the copyright; if you see a name other than the author's, it's packaged. A recent newspaper article estimated that one in every five books published nowadays is produced by a book packager.

Approaching a Book Packager

Never approach a book packager with an idea for a book. Remember, they think up their own ideas. Keep your ideas to yourself and try to sell those directly to a publisher.

If it sounds like working with a packager might be for you, here are the steps:

➤ Craft a resumé that lists your writing experience.

➤ Include information on other writing-related skills you might have, such as writing book proposals, proofreading, editing, copy editing, ghostwriting, and so forth.

➤ Detail any interests and hobbies you have, such as gardening, cooking, and woodworking. Many packagers specialize in these kinds of books and need writers who understand the fields.

➤ Research book packagers and learn who specializes in what type of book; use the directory of the ABPA, or look them up in *Literary Marketplace*.

You will really need to sell yourself as an experienced writer, and one who can work independently. Book packagers need writers who can write quickly, meet deadlines, and not make a fuss about things. Book packagers are publishing entrepreneurs who run businesses. If you can establish a relationship with a book packager, you might find yourself learning even more about the book business.

Business as Usual

As you can see, we have once again managed to turn the topic to business. Why?

We think that the book publishing business is fascinating. Both of us enjoy what we do for a living, and we can't imagine doing anything else ever! We firmly believe that the more writers learn and understand the business side of publishing, the better they can prosper as writers.

Of course, creativity is essential. But to thrive and prosper as a writer, you must also develop a businesslike attitude toward it.

We've tried to give you a glimpse into how things work, but we also encourage you to learn more. Learn as much as you can about the bookstore business and about the publishing business. Learn as much as you can about your readers and what they want to read. The more you know, the greater your chances for success.

We do hope that this book has given you a solid understanding of what goes on in the publishing industry and how you can find your spot in it. Whatever you do, don't give up. If you believe in yourself and your writing, you will find a way to see your work in print. Remember, writers write. So, turn on your computer and get busy!

Experts Say

To reach the American Book Producers Association, call 212-645-2368. Its membership directory lists very specific information about packaging companies and individual specialties.

Slush Pile

Book packagers don't want to hear your ideas for books. If you have an idea for a book, develop it yourself and find an agent. Book packagers come up with their own ideas for the books they develop.

The Least You Need to Know

➤ Book packagers come up with ideas for books and then hire writers to write the books.

➤ Do not approach a book packager with an idea for a book; rather, write up your own book proposal and try to get it published.

➤ Packagers need professional writers who can deliver on time, can work as part of a team, and will accept a flat fee instead of royalties for each book sold.

➤ Some packagers produce fiction, most often in young adult series such as *The Babysitters Club* or *Sweet Valley High;* the writer works from a comprehensive outline.

➤ Writing for a book packager can be a good way to make some money, work with a team of creative people, and learn more about how a book is put together.

Great Books for Writers

Appelbaum, Judith. *How to Get Happily Published: A Complete and Candid Guide.* New York: Harper Perennial, 1998.

The Chicago Manual of Style: The Essential Guide for Writers, Editors, and Publishers. Chicago: University of Chicago Press, 1993.

Garvey, Mark. *Writer's Market.* Cincinnati, Ohio: Writer's Digest Books, updated annually.

Gross, Gerald. *Editors on Editing: What Writers Need to Know About What Editors Do.* New York: Grove/Atlantic Monthly Press, 1993.

Herman, Jeff. *Writer's Guide to Book Editors, Publishers, and Literary Agents.* Rocklin, California: Prima Publishing, updated annually.

Kremer, John. *1,001 Ways to Market Your Books.* Fairfield, Iowa: Open Horizons, 1998.

Levine, Mark. *Negotiating a Book Contract: A Guide for Authors, Agents, and Lawyers.* Wakefield, Rhode Island: Moyer Bell, 1988.

Literary Marketplace. New York: R.R. Bowker, updated annually.

Mettee, Stephen Blake. *The Portable Writer's Conference: Your Guide to Getting and Staying Published.* Fresno, California: Quill Driver Books, 1997.

Poynter, Dan. *The Self-Publishing Manual: How to Write, Print, and Sell Your Own Book.* Santa Barbara, California: Para Publishing, 1989.

Snell, Mike, Kim Baker, and Sunny Baker. *From Book Idea to Bestseller.* Rocklin, California: Prima Publishing, 1997.

Strunk, William Jr., and E.B. White. *The Elements of Style.* New York: Macmillan, 1979.

Yudkin, Marcia. *Six Steps to Free Publicity: And Dozens of Other Ways to Win Free Media Attention for You and Your Business.* New York: Plume, 1994.

Zinsser, William. *On Writing Well: The Classic Guide to Writing Nonfiction.* New York: Harper Perennial, 1998.

Zuckerman, Albert J. *Writing the Blockbuster Novel.* Cincinnati, Ohio: Writer's Digest Books, 1993.

More Good Resources

Professional Associations

Agents association:

> P.O. Box 237201, Ansonia Station
> New York, NY 10023
> www.aar-online.org

Book packagers association:

> American Book Producers Association
> 160 Fifth Ave., Suite 604
> New York, NY 10010-7000
> 212-645-2368

Freelance editors association:

> Editorial Freelance Association
> 71 West 23rd St.
> New York, NY 10010
> 212-929-5400
> www.the-efa.org

Self-publishers group:

> Publishers Marketing Association
> 310-372-2732
> www.pma-online.org

Writers organizations:

> American Society of Journalists
> and Authors, Inc.
> 1501 Broadway, Suite 302
> New York, NY 10036
> 212-997-0947
> www.asja.org
> e-mail: staff@asja.org

> Author's Guild
> 330 West 42nd St.
> New York, NY 10036
> 212-563-5904

> National Writer's Union
> 113 University Place, 6th Floor
> New York, NY 10003
> 212-254-0279
> www.nwu.com

> Romance Writers of America
> 13700 Veterans Memorial Dr., #315
> Houston, TX 77014
> 281-440-6885

Sisters in Crime
P.O. Box 442124
Lawrence, KS 66044-8933
785-842-1325
sistersincrime@juno.com

Society of Children's Book Writers and Illustrators
8271 Beverly Blvd.
Los Angeles, CA 90048
323-782-1010
www.scbwi.org

Publicity Agencies

Book publicists:

Planned Television Arts
Rick Frishman
301 East 57th St.
New York, NY 10022
212-593-5820

Book publicity information:

You're On the Air

A 90-minute videotape about how to get on and perform well on television and radio. $69.95 for the video and two books. For information, call 1-800-562-4357.

Media trainer:

Joel Roberts and Associates
310-286-0631

Seminars and Publications

Seminar:

The Secrets of Getting Published
Sheree Bykofsky
The Seminar Center, New York City
212-655-0077
Info@seminarcenter.com

How to Create a Speaking and Writing Empire
Mark Victor Hansen
949-759-9304

Short-run book printer:

Morris Publishing
3212 East Highway30
Kearney, NE 68847
1-800-650-7888

Trade publications:

Publishers Weekly
245 West 17th St.
New York, NY 10011
1-800-278-2991

Web Sites of Note

amazon.com (online bookstore, good for competitive research)

barnesandnoble.com, bn.com, (online bookstore, good for competitive research)

www.bookpublishing.com (filled with useful information for self-publishers, and an online publication, *The Independent Publisher*)

www.bookwire.com (timely publishing news from Bookwire)

www.iUniverse.com (a good way to stay abreast of the ever-changing e-publishing scene)

shereebee.com (information for writers)

www.writersdigest.com (contact information for book publishers, information on conferences, and discussion forums)

Sample Proposals: *Christmas Miracles* and *The Quotable Businesswoman*

Magical Stories of Modern-Day Miracles compiled and edited by

Jamie Miller
Laura Lewis
Jennifer Basye Sander

Fall 1996

Introduction

miracle n. 1. An event that seems impossible to explain by natural laws and so is regarded as supernatural in origin or as an act of God. 2. An event that excites admiration or awe.

Blind to the possibilities of miracles for 11 months of the year, each year at Christmastime even the most jaded hearts are softened by reports of wondrous occurrences, everything from unlikely reunions to dramatic medical recoveries, from newly formed romances to the sudden reappearance of long-lost loves. Why should these things happen just at this time of year, and why do we feel so touched by them?

During the Christmas season, mankind the world over is looking for miracles, opening their hearts to the possibility of a miracle for just a few short weeks. World-weary souls soften and become open windows through which miraculous deeds can fly and happen upon the unwary, those who keep them shut out at other times of the year. Churchgoers sit amidst hundreds of flickering candles at midnight services, remembering an ancient pilgrimage to a stable and a star, awed by the beauty of the sight and ready to see an angel on the way home. Tired shoppers drag home from yet another crowded mall, disgusted by the season's commercialism and ready to see a miracle in the small gesture of a stranger. Miracles big and small happen every day during Christmas if we are open to receive them.

In the pages of *Christmas Miracles,* you will find true stories of miraculous occurrences that happened to folks just like you—small, sweet stories of remarkable events that happened on or near Christmas. You will read of people who are suddenly willing to stoop down and consider the needs and desires of little children; people who remember the weaknesses and loneliness of the elderly; folks who, if only for one short season, stop asking how much their friends love them and instead wonder how much love they can show to their friends.

Albert Einstein said, "There are only two ways to live your life. One is as though nothing is a miracle. The other is as if everything is." The stories in *Christmas Miracles* weave the magic of brotherhood, fill hearts with peace, and cause a frightened world to pause, to remember, and to hope. Keep your eyes open, keep your heart open, and let the miracles begin.

The Market

The market for inspirational true story collections seems to expand and grow from month to month. Sales of *Chicken Soup for the Soul* and its many sequels chug along, *Random Acts of Kindness* continues to sell several years after first appearing, and the just-released book *Family: Everyday Stories About the Miracle of Love* has been awarded The Family Channel Seal of Approval. All these give evidence of the public's continued interest in and appetite for heartwarming tales. The world is a scary place, and readers are turning again and again to the comfort that can be found in a homey tale of triumph and wonder that reassures us that maybe other folks aren't so bad after all. Even the television airwaves display this trend, with shows such as "Dr. Quinn, Medicine Woman" and "Second Noah" delivering genuine, heartwarming entertainment that reaffirms the goodness of man.

According to a recent Gallup poll, 83 percent of Americans believe in miracles. *Christmas Miracles* will strike a deep chord on many levels. It will resonate not just with those who are comforted by the idea that miracles do indeed occur, but also with those who believe in angels, those who believe in life after death, and those who are seeking spiritual fulfillment in their lives.

The extraordinary sales of books such as *Embraced by the Light* reaffirm the market's strong interest in the topic of the supernatural—not the frightening "X-Files" sort of supernatural, but rather the comforting "Touched by an Angel" feeling that someone else is guiding us toward safety and salvation.

Sales of Christmas books have also increased dramatically, with the runaway success of books such as *The Christmas Box* once again affirming the readiness of readers to accept a book whose message concerns the more spiritual aspect of the Christmas season rather than the crass commercialism of gift-giving and Santa Claus. These books shine a spotlight on the better aspects of the human spirit, such as love, sharing, and helping each other. These books help us all believe that miracles can and do still occur.

It is worth noting that two of the successful books mentioned here, *The Christmas Box* and *Embraced by the Light,* received their first big sales in the Mormon market before being purchased by mainstream publishers and launched into the general marketplace. It is our hope that *Christmas Miracles* will also be popular in the Mormon market. Although it is by no means a Mormon book, the book has the following things going for it:

➤ The lead author, Jamie Miller, is a member of a well-known Mormon family, the singing King Family, and will receive a great deal of attention and publicity in Mormon publications.

➤ Word of mouth already is building for *Christmas Miracles* as Mormon wards (congregations) across the country are being asked to contribute to the collection.

The Stories

The stories in *Christmas Miracles* run the gamut from heart-pounding miracles of medical recoveries to sweet little tales of lost dogs returned home. By talking to friends and family, drawing on their own experiences, and combing through old newspapers and magazines, the authors have put together a well-rounded collection that truly reflects the book's subtitle: "Magical Stories of Modern-Day Miracles in the Season of Love."

Among the stories you'll find in *Christmas Miracles* are these:

➤ "Embraced by the Sound." A dying music teacher listens to her students singing *The Messiah.*

➤ "A Christmas Mystery." A young boy's gift is repaid.

➤ "One Cold Canadian Christmas." A family receives unexpected gifts in a snowstorm.

➤ "Through Children's Eyes." A children's Christmas play teaches the true meaning of the holiday.

➤ "Christmas Doesn't Come from a Store." Children give the greatest gifts to those who need them more.

➤ "Brotherly Love." A handicapped boy teaches his own brother about giving.

➤ "A Christmas Awakening." A young girl learns about her mother's love.

➤ "The Homeless Santa." Two privileged girls learn the meaning of giving on Christmas Eve.

➤ "Good Samaritans on the Road." Total strangers come together at the scene of a Christmas Day accident.

➤ "Big Guy Takes a Cab." A beloved dog is lost on Christmas Day.

➤ "The Secret Dolls." Long after a mother's death, an unforgettable Christmas gift appears.

➤ "Snow for Cathleen." A miracle snowfall answers a December birthday wish.

➤ "I'm Dreaming of a 'Right' Christmas." Mr. Right appears at the office Christmas party.

➤ "Christmas Wedding Bells." An annual Christmas party turns into an impromptu wedding.

➤ "The Christmas Coat." A family gives all it has left to those who need it more.

➤ "Miracle Music." An unlikely couple fall in love to the sounds of the song "Miracle."

➤ "The Best Gift of All." A young wife asks God for help.

➤ And many more true stories of miracles big and small, 75 stories total.

Competition

Although there have been several recent Christmas book successes, *Christmas Miracles* is, to the best of our knowledge, the first book to concentrate on miracles.

These titles are among the more successful Christmas books:

➤ *The Christmas Box* (Simon and Schuster). Originally self-published, this book has had phenomenal success in the stores as well as on the television screen, and will leave book buyers looking for more stories of wonder during the holiday season.

➤ *The Cat Who Came for Christmas* (Penguin). Cleveland Amory's tale of a homeless cat underscores the success of heartwarming tales of all kinds built around Christmas themes.

➤ *A Cup of Christmas Tea* (Waldman House). Described by the publisher as "the Christmas story that brings sweet tears," this book has sold 1 million copies.

According to *Publishers Weekly*, the following new books will be on the shelves during the 1996 Christmas season:

➤ *Sally's Christmas Miracle* (Harper Collins). A new Peanuts book for children from Charles Schulz, this is the story of a Christmas tree that appears in answer to a wish.

➤ *A Gift of Sharing: In Celebration of the Holidays* (Dove). This book will feature stories, memories, and recipes from celebrities such as Hugh Downs, George and Barbara Bush, and Andy Griffith. Proceeds will benefit the homeless.

➤ *A Stranger for Christmas* (St. Martin's Press). Long a successful book in the Mormon market, this sweet tale will now be published by St. Martin's Press.

Books that are not directly targeted toward the Christmas market but that display the public's strong interest in miracles and in spiritually uplifting stories are as follows:

➤ *A Book of Angels* (Bantam). This book started the angel phenomenon and has sold in big numbers for the past six years.

➤ *Random Acts of Kindness* (Conari Press). None of the random acts of kindness featured in this bestselling book happened at Christmas!

➤ *Chicken Soup for the Soul* (Health Communications). These inspirational stories cover a variety of topics but do not emphasize miracles or the miraculous. Instead, their focus is on perseverance and hard work.

➤ *Expect a Miracle* (Harper). Subtitled "The Miraculous Things That Happen to Ordinary People," this book is a bit pedantic at times, and many of the stories focus on recovery from drugs and drinking.

➤ *Heaven Hears Each Whisper* (Berkeley Publishing Group). These stories of answered prayers do not distinguish between Christmastime and any other season.

➤ *Touched by Angels* (Warner Books). These are tales of true encounters with angels, close encounters of the celestial kind.

➤ *Embraced by the Light* (Bantam). Betty Eadie's bestselling account of her near-death experience reassures people that there is more to life than meets the eye. The stories in *Christmas Miracles* achieve a similar purpose.

Publicity and Promotion

Christmas Miracles will prove to be an easy book to promote. The media, from radio and television to newspapers and magazines, all look for heartwarming stories to feature during the Christmas season, and what better place to turn than a whole collection of Christmas miracles?

All three authors themselves are skilled promoters. Jamie Miller is a former professional singer with vast amounts of performance ability and an ease in front of crowds. Laura Lewis is a professional book publicist who will devote her full time and attention toward promoting the book. Jennifer Basye Sander is an editor whose best talent is creating book ideas that sell. All three would be available and eager to promote *Christmas Miracles*.

The authors could easily put together a panel of folks to whom these miracles occurred, which would be a very effective format for an afternoon talk show. The topics of miracles, extraordinary occurrences, and coincidences are just as popular on television as they are in the bookstore.

The best targets to either excerpt or feature parts of *Christmas Miracles* would be women's magazines, such as *Ladies Home Journal, Redbook,* and *Good Housekeeping,* that traditionally run these kinds of heartwarming features in their December issues. Of the large circulation mainstream magazines, *Reader's Digest* is also a likely target.

By grouping the stories into categories, special-interest magazines could also be targeted for excerpts, parenting magazines could be approached with the stories that feature children, Christian magazines could be approached with those stories most Christian in tone, and magazines with a younger female audience (such as *Cosmopolitan* or *Glamour*) could be approached with the romance stories.

The stories themselves feature a wide range of topics, from miracles involving pets to miracles involving firefighters. Targeted mailings to magazines, and newsletters that address the appropriate audience could easily be done.

Christmas Miracles could also be used as an ideal holiday giveaway for radio stations to use during their constant on-air promotions. As a way to tap into the holiday spirit, disk jockeys could announce "A free book to the 12th caller."

About the Authors of *Christmas Miracles*

Jamie Miller is a member of the singing King Family and was for many years a featured performer on their nationally televised weekly variety show. The mother of five children and active in her family's church, Jamie has long collected Christmas stories. She is an associate editor at Prima Publishing and is hard at work on her first book, *10-Minute Life Lessons for Kids*.

Laura Lewis was for many years the director of marketing and publicity for Prima Publishing. She has operated her own book publicity business in the Boulder area for three years and is a stay-at-home mom for her own two miracles, Olivia and Evan.

Jennifer Basye Sander is the senior editor at Prima Publishing. The author of one travel book (*The Air Courier's Handbook*, Big City Books) and one business book (*How to Become a Successful Weekend Entrepreneur*, Prima), she is currently working on *101 Best Extra Income Opportunities for Women* (Prima, Spring 1997). The mother of one little bundle of energy, she is open to miracles always.

Sample Stories

"Homeless Santa"

A crummy 1988 was winding down as my roommate Margaret and I set out for an afternoon snack on Christmas Eve. I'd just returned to California after a dark three months of hiding in the Swedish woods in my own private Ingmar Bergman film after the breakup of a long-term romance. My arrival home had been as dramatic as my sudden departure some months before. I was booked on a Pan Am flight from London to San Francisco. Had I missed the flight, I would have taken the next available flight, Pan Am 103. I made my flight with just minutes to spare. The San Francisco flight was checking in at a counter directly across from the New York flight, but I absentmindedly got into the wrong line with the New York-bound folks. When I noticed my mistake, I joked about it to the people in line and made my way across the room.

As my parents drove home from the airport over slow-moving California freeways, they told me about the mid-air explosion of flight 103 over Lockerbie, Scotland. "But I saw those people," I said. "How can they all be dead?" My dreams that night were haunted by the image of the Scottish countryside strewn with carefully packed Christmas gifts, steamed puddings from Harrod's, and little piles of Christmas candy that an airport Santa had handed to everyone waiting in line to go through the security X-ray.

After such a close brush with death, I was feeling a little peculiar on that bright California afternoon, a little tentative and oddly disconnected to what was going on around me. I'd come home after an absence of three months but yet didn't feel like I'd come back in one piece.

Craving the taste of authentic Mexican food, Margaret and I chose to head for a ramshackle burrito house in a dicey part of town. Near the train tracks and several homeless shelters, it was not the part of town you'd expect to find two middle-class girls visiting on Christmas Eve. We ordered our burritos and sat outside in the sun. The streets around us were deserted—office workers and commuters had gone home to get an early start on the holiday.

Margaret nudged my arm. "Oh great," she said. "Looks like we're about to get hit up for money." A disheveled man was making his way toward us through the parking lot of the burrito house, his progress slowed both by his age and the oversized green sack he carried on his back. His hair was long and snowy white, his thick beard spread over the top of his tattered jacket. Margaret and I clucked our tongues and shook our heads and began to search our pockets for loose change in order to dispense with him quickly and get on with our meal.

Slowly and quietly, he made his way across the blacktop until he was standing in front of us. He stopped, and without saying a word he rolled his heavy bag off his shoulder and set it on the ground before us. Untying the top, he reached in and began to rummage through the contents of his bag. Margaret and I watched as he found what he was seeking and removed his hand. He held a shiny red apple. In total silence and with great dignity, he held the apple out to Margaret. She reached out and accepted his gift. He reached into his green duffel bag again and this time pulled out a Snickers bar and offered it to me. "No," I said, "we can't take your food—you need it." Margaret and I both held our new gifts back out to him. "We can't take your food." The man smiled shyly and shook his head. "I can't eat it. My teeth are no good. Merry Christmas."

He would not accept the money we tried to give him that afternoon. He just kept quietly shaking his head and smiling as we tried to press dollar bills into his hand. Finally, he agreed to the purchase of a cup of coffee for him. He took the steaming Styrofoam container and, shouldering his bag once again, continued on his way.

I think about that homeless man whenever I pass down that street. I think about the quiet man with the big white beard and bag of presents who gave two privileged girls part of the only food he had. The spirit of giving is all around us and can come upon us so unexpectedly. We need to be able to give back what we can to those who need it most.

Jennifer Basye Sander, Granite Bay, California

"George Misses a Shift"

My high school boyfriend, George Bingham, was awfully proud of his car. A hand-me-down from his mother his last year in high school, it was a yellow 1968 Chevy Impala—not exactly a hip car for a senior to drive in 1974, but it was a set of wheels. Determined to turn it into a "hot ride," he'd made many changes to it, jacking the back end up with air shocks so that it rode high off the ground, adding glass packs to the exhaust system to give it a throaty rumble, buying fancy wide tires, and saving up to buy the fanciest eight-track stereo system he could find.

The final touch, though, was changing the transmission. When his parents first purchased the car, it was a three-speed on the column, which meant that you had to change gears by shifting a lever on the steering wheel column. George was extremely embarrassed by that feature of his car—it simply wasn't cool. All through the fall he'd explained his plans to me how he would buy a kit from the auto parts store and "drop it to the floor." A stick shift he could reach down and shift—now that would be cool.

He bought the kit at Thanksgiving and spent the extra days off school on the floor of the garage, with the car jacked up and lit from below by flashlights as he worked away. And finally it was ready. He at last had the cool car he'd dreamed of.

Driving became central to our dates after that, long drives in the country where he could run the car up and down through the gears, speeding up and slowing down and showing me how it all worked. He was so proud of the job he'd done, and I was awfully proud of my boyfriend, too.

Christmas was a wonderful time for us, with so many days of vacation from school. George drove me everywhere: back and forth from his house to mine, to work, and to the mall for Christmas shopping. The souped-up yellow Impala flashed through intersections all over town.

Christmas morning, he drove to my parents' house to pick me up. We spent the day at his house with his parents, opening presents, listening to carols, and feasting on roasted goose. Late that night we climbed into the Impala once again for the trip across town.

George pulled up to a busy intersection not far from the freeway onramp and stopped for a red light. The night was almost over, always a bittersweet time for two high school sweethearts. Sitting at the red light, we joked about how well the day had gone. The light turned green. George reached down to shift his car into first gear and pull into the intersection, but the gear shifter would not move. "Oh man!" Flustered, George pushed the clutch in again and tried to shift—nothing. He swore under his breath, embarrassed to seem so feeble in front of his girlfriend. "Come *on!*"

he shouted, trying the process once again. This time the transmission went into gear and he began to pull out into the intersection. Suddenly a car roared through the intersection a few feet in front of the Impala. A drunken holiday reveler had run the red light! Had George been able to shift smoothly and pull into the intersection when our light turned green, we would have been broadsided by a full-sized car traveling at top speed. A few seconds worth of fumbling with a homemade stick shift had saved our lives on Christmas night.

Julia Berenson, Berkeley, California

"Snow for Cathleen"

The winter of 1968 was very cold and windy, with a few intermittent showers. Pretty basic winter weather for Sacramento, California. It was December 17th, and I'd had a fun day at school. It was my birthday, and all my friends were doing special things for me.

When I returned home from school that afternoon, my mother surprised me with my favorite cake, an angel food cake covered with creme de menthe whipped cream frosting and curls of bittersweet chocolate. It was a famous recipe in our family, highly sought after by friends and relatives alike. After my mother and brothers sang "Happy Birthday" to me, I blew out the 10 candles and made my wish. What I wanted more than anything was for snow to fall in Sacramento that Christmas. I knew it couldn't really happen here; the capital city is best known for its 100°-plus summer days, and it had snowed in Sacramento only a few times in recorded history. It was a beautiful fantasy: I wanted to see everything covered in sparkly white snow just like up in the Sierra mountains. My mother spent her childhood in Germany and had told me many a bedtime story about her own snowy white Christmases with freshly cut trees and sleighs and skis.

My big birthday gift was a dinner out at one of the best restaurants in town at that time, a place called The Coral Reef. A favorite restaurant for kids, it had enormous fish aquariums scattered throughout the dining rooms, each one lit from below with dim blue and pink neon lights to give the fancy tropical fish an eerie glow. Seafaring relics such as old nets, ropes, floats, and dried puffer fish hung from the rafters, and exotic palms, plants, and trees made it easy to imagine that you were far away from Northern California on a South Sea island.

Because my mother had told the waiters about my birthday, I was treated like a mini-queen. The best part was that, for the first time in my life, I was allowed to order anything at all on the menu. My choice was, of course, the lobster. It was a huge creature that took up the whole plate and could never have been eaten by one little girl at one sitting. Walking out of the restaurant with an actual "people bag" of leftovers made me feel extremely special.

As I left the tropical warmth of the restaurant with my family into the cold blowing wind, something touched my eyelash, and then something brushed against my cheek. What was that?! Could it be my wish had come true? No! It doesn't snow in

281

Sacramento. But sure enough, as I stood speechless and awestruck in the parking lot of The Coral Reef, beautifully shaped snowflakes were floating down from the sky and melting as they hit the pavement. Their short lives were exquisite little miracles that brought incredible joy and delight to one 10-year-old girl. Magically, my wish had come true.

I have never forgotten that wonderful birthday, and on every December 17th since, there comes a moment in the day when I stop what I am doing for just a moment, look up toward the sky, and wish again.

Cathleen Swanson, Sacramento, California

The Quotable Businesswoman

Compiled by Laura Boswell, USAToday.com

Women's quote books have sold consistently for the last thirty years, a byproduct of the women's movement in the seventies and the desire to celebrate women's thoughts and accomplishments. But the greatest accomplishment of all has been sorely overlooked by those books—the astonishing achievements women have made in the business world. Whereas it was once quite unusual to find women anywhere in the business world, now women are found everywhere—including in the CEO spot.

Business quote books have lately achieved great popularity. Readers now know what happens when *Bill Gates Speaks, Warren Buffett Speaks*, or *Jack Welch Speaks*. But where is the quote collection that celebrates women's business success? *The Quotable Businesswoman* will include snippets of wisdom, advice, humor, and insight on a wide variety of topics. Sure, the world knows what businessmen like Bill Gates, Donald Trump, and Jack Welch think and say; now there is a chance to hear what Carly Fiorina of Hewlett-Packard, Andrea Jung of Avon, Geraldine Laybourne of Oxygen Media, and other high-powered women think about:

Success * Money * Employees * Investing * Men * Failure * Business * Love *
Women * History * Golf * Power * the Internet * Hiring * Firing * Education *
the United States * Partners * Humor * Clothes * Politics and Politicians * Fear *
Family * Children * Stress * Marketing * Taxes *

And many more topics of interest.

In addition to spotlighting women's success in business, *The Quotable Businesswoman* will also help women in the business world develop a body of handy quotes that they can use in meetings, correspondence, speeches, and conversation. So, instead of quoting someone like Al "Chainsaw" Dunlap on his method of laying off employees, the thinking businesswoman will soon be able to cite the beliefs of Gun Denhart, the founder of the multi-million dollar Hanna Anderson mail order catalog: "Do it in a way that people understand why it is happening."

Culled from a variety of published sources, *The Quotable Businesswoman* will feature the words of businesswomen such as ...

Linda Wachner * Pleasant Rowland * Marcia Kilgore * Ellen Gordon * Abby Joseph Cohen * Madonna * Donna Karan * Estee Lauder * Mary Kay Ash * Ann Fudge* Rebecca Matthias * Lillian Vernon * Anita Roddick * Jenny Craig * Kathleen Brown * Oprah Winfrey * Vera Wang * Faith Popcorn * Sandra Lerner * Rose Marie Bravo * Abigail Johnson * Susie Tompkins * Kathleen Graham * Joyce Raley Teel * Caroline Hunt * Tomima Edmark * Geraldine Laybourne * Jill Barad * Darla Moore * Candace Carpenter * Muriel Siebert * Elizabeth Bramwell * Diana Brooks * Carleton "Carly" Fiorina * Meg Whitman * Charlotte Beers * Bobbi Brown * Jane Friedman * Missy "Misdemeanor" Elliott * Nina DiSesa * Heidi Kunz * Karen Fukuma * Patricia Hambrecht * Ruth Fertel * Elisa Salinas * Candace Krugman Beinecke * Kathy Levinson ...

... and as many more high-profile, high-powered businesswomen as we can find!

The quotes will be arranged by topic, with several pages devoted to each individual topic. The speakers will be identified after each quote, and a brief one-line description will identify them for the readers. In addition, the back of the book will include a complete alphabetical listing of all of the women quoted, with a one- or two-paragraph description of their accomplishments. Although the book's emphasis will be on businesswomen whose names are known by the public, many of the highest-powered women in the business world (the heads of major corporations) are not well known. The information in the back of the book will serve as a real eye-opener about women's success in business.

About the editor: Laura Boswell is the Careers and Small Business Editor for USATODAY.com, the number one ranked general news site on the Web. A skilled researcher and writer, she is in frequent contact with businesswomen around the country. A graduate of Centre College in Danville, Kentucky, she has worked for USATODAY.com since 1995. About Big City Books: The packager of the successful "Miracles" series from William Morrow (over 200,000 in print), Big City Books was founded by Jennifer Basye Sander, the former senior editor and in-house packager at Prima Publishing. Book ideas created and developed by Jennifer in the last ten years now have in excess of fifteen million dollars in retail sales.

Sample Topics and Quotes from **The Quotable Businesswoman**

THE INTERNET

"If the Internet hadn't come along, I'd probably be managing money and raising three kids in Greenwich."

—Mary Meeker, Chief Internet Analyst, Morgan Stanley Dean Witter

"The Internet is a natural place for women, because they care so much about relationships and staying connected."

—Geraldine Laybourne, COO of Oxygen Media and former head of cable television for Disney/ABC

WORK/LIFE BALANCE

"I know that in the final analysis, workaholics are not business successes."

—Patti Manuel, President and COO, long-distance division, Sprint Corporation

"It's kind of crazy to have a car and a driver. But you know why I'm a normal person? It's my husband. He's like, 'Get over yourself!'"

—Bobbi Brown, Founder, Bobbi Brown Cosmetics

"I've seen too many women feel guilty about getting help in maintaining their house because they feel it is their moral obligation to vacuum, clean the bathroom, and do all the childcare even when they are starting a business or running a business or working outside the home. They have never learned to value their time."

—Rebecca Matthias, President and Founder, Mothers Work, Inc.

"… not only do I work with my husband, I work with my two sons—there must be a special place in heaven reserved for me."

—JoAnne Shaw, President, The Coffee Beanery, Ltd.

"I'm always thinking about the business. I compare it to the way parents think about their children. No matter where you are, you're always thinking about your children as they are growing up or if you leave your kids with a babysitter, your mind is always still on them. Well, I'm always thinking about my business because this is my baby."

—Sharon Lobel, Founder, Seal-It, Inc.

COMPETITION AND COMPETITORS

"We have to avoid burning bridges. The competitor you burn today you may have to partner with tomorrow."

—Kim Polese, President and CEO, Marimba Inc.

"I like competitors in the marketplace that are good. It makes us sharper and better and makes us work harder."

—JoAnne Shaw, President, The Coffee Beanery, Ltd.

"It's expected that you have competition. The important thing is to know who they are and have a plan to beat them."

—Rebecca Matthias, President and Founder, Mothers Work, Inc.

"I wanted my competitors to think of me as this crazy woman so that they wouldn't mess with me."

—Tomima Edmark, inventor of the Topsy Tail

EMPLOYEES

"As a manager, I try to figure out what people's dreams are. In most cases, the only thing holding them back is themselves."

—Candace Carpenter, CEO, iVillage.com

"I like to ask about their worst failure [when interviewing] ... If it's not big enough, they're not a risk taker. And if you've never been put in a difficult situation, I don't want you there."

—Jill Barad, CEO, Mattel Inc.

"Being called into the boss's office is like being called into the dentist. I try to keep it as soft and soothing as I can."

—Carol Wallace, Managing Editor, *People* magazine

"I find that if you must criticize, it's best to sandwich it between two thick layers of praise."

—Mary Kay Ash, Founder, Mary Kay Cosmetics

"I want my employees to know that they are a large part of this business. I always tell them that I could never have done all this by myself."

—Sharon Lobel, Founder, Seal-It, Inc.

WOMEN'S MANAGEMENT STYLE

"I'm not suggesting men should weep in meetings, but they should embrace what we usually think of as female attributes: teamwork, relationship building, collaboration, and empathy."

—Nina DiSesa, Chairman and Chief Creative Officer, McCann-Erickson

"The truth is that thinking like a woman can be a tremendous advantage."

—Mary Kay Ash, Founder, Mary Kay Cosmetics

"Grit your teeth, because it is a matter of resilience, stamina, and energy. And never try to imitate what the boys do."

—Christine Lagarde, Chairman and Managing Partner, Baker & McKenzie

"I'm very emotionally attached to this business in a way I don't think many men would be attached to a business."

—Doris Christopher, Founder and President, The Pampered Chef, Ltd.

"I believe the human elements in a business are critical in the success of a company. The spirit of an organization is a primary driving force."

—Joy Mangano, Chairman and President, Ingenious Designs, Inc.

REPUTATION

"[at 43] I've still got time to blow my reputation in the business community."

—Darla Moore, head of the Rainwater Corporation, *Fortune* magazine's "toughest babe in business"

"Identity—what other people believe about you—comes down to what *you* believe."

—Marty Rodriguez, top broker worldwide for Century 21

PERSONAL SUCCESS AND ACCOMPLISHMENT

"Nothing great is ever accomplished by one person."

—Sheryl Leach, creator of Barney

"The way I'll measure myself is by how much wealth I helped create ..."

—Mary Meeker, Chief Internet Analyst, Morgan Stanley Dean Witter

"That I've survived [in investment banking] is a great validation. The good guys win."

—Nancy Peretsman, Allen & Company

MARKETING

"You can't open a lemonade stand and just sit there waiting for someone to come. You have to run out into the road and flag people down!"

—Mary Ellen Sheets, Founder and CEO, Two Men and a Truck/International

"If you start a business, stay in the face of your customers to make sure they're happy."

—Dorothy J. White, President, Miracle Services, Inc.

"... I sent out this question to 4,000 people: Are men and women the same? And every person answered the same: No. [So] why are we marketing to them the same way?"

—Faith Popcorn, founder, Brain Reserve

"Children are very, very smart consumers. They know what they want."

—Pleasant Rowland, The Pleasant Company, producers of the American Girls doll collection

"To go into business and not even know if there's a need out there is suicidal."

—Jenny Craig, Founder, Jenny Craig International

INSPIRATION AND MOTIVATION

"I went into TV because I thought it was a disgrace for kids."

—Geraldine Laybourne, Chairman and CEO, Oxygen Media, Inc.

"This is a tough world today, a cynical world, a vulgar world, filled with a lot of tawdry and violent images for kids. We wanted to be something different."

—Pleasant Rowland

"If we go a day without laughing in this building, we will turn off the lights, close the doors, and shut down the place. If we're not going to have fun at this, then we might as well not do it."

—Mary Ellen Sheets, Founder and CEO, Two Men and a Truck/International

"Your best ideas happen when you're playing, laughing, goofing around."

—Geraldine Laybourne, Chairman and CEO, Oxygen Media, Inc.

SEXISM AND DISCRIMINATION

"I hope we are at a point that everyone has figured out that there is not a glass ceiling."

—Carly Fiorina, CEO, Hewlett-Packard

"With pleasure, and could you photocopy these for me?"

—Diana "Dede" Brooks, CEO, Sotheby's, after being asked by a man to fetch a cup of coffee

"And the word [bitch] can be positive ... We gotta stop thinkin' of it as bein' negative, 'cause it's gonna be used regardless. Men call us that when they're intimidated."

—Missy "Misdemeanor" Elliot, Rapper and Founder of Gold Mind, Inc.

"At trade shows, many times when people come to our booth with a technical question, they will ask one of my salesmen, assuming that as a woman I wouldn't know the answer. Such is life ... As long as we get the order, that's okay with me."

—Sharon Lobel, Founder, Seal-It, Inc.

CAREER PATH

"I had no intention of working for a bank. I thought I'd rather take chloroform."

—Patricia Dunn, Chairman and CEO, Barclays Global Investors

"As everyone knows, moving and trucking are mostly men's businesses, but I didn't let it make any difference to me. I went my own way and re-invented the wheel."

—Mary Ellen Sheets, CEO, Two Men and a Truck/International

"When young people come to me now complaining about their horrible bosses, I say, 'Aren't you lucky.' Because the more examples of bad management you see, the more you'll learn. I learned more from my worst boss than I did from my best boss. I was taking notes about how I would not manage."

—Geraldine Laybourne, Chairman and CEO, Oxygen Media, Inc.

POWER

"Once, power was considered a masculine attribute. In fact, power has no sex."

—Katherine Graham, The Washington Post Company

EDUCATION

"If I'd had an MBA I suppose I would have done things a lot differently … and, probably wouldn't have believed I could have done it."

—Pleasant Rowland

"Education will not do it for you—it took me a long time to figure that out. I used to worry and think, 'If only I had a little more education.' It [business success] has nothing to do with education. It is the way you treat people."

—Dorothy J. White, President, Miracle Services, Inc.

MONEY

"Having money is rather like being a blond. It is more fun but not vital."

—Mary Quant, Founder, Mary Quant Cosmetics

MY PARENTS

"When I was in Catholic school I always sold the most Christmas cards. My Dad used to discipline me because I'd come home late—after selling candy to my friends on the way home. Now I tell him that I'm doing the same thing—only now I get paid instead of getting spanked."

—Marty Rodriguez, top broker worldwide for Century 21

"I think the greatest gift parents can give their kids is a feeling of independence and confidence."

—Jenny Craig, Founder, Jenny Craig International

"Daddy always said, 'If you do a good job, someone will notice.'"

—Dorothy J. White, President, Miracle Services, Inc.

" … my father helped me most in teaching me to get over fear [of failure] by making me realize that you *should* be scared. If you're not scared, then you don't realize the risks you're taking."

—Sherrie Myers, General Manager, Lansing Lugnuts

"I never felt any sense of limitation. No one [my parents] ever said to me 'You should do this.'"

—Nancy Peretsman, Allen & Company

"My business sense I got from my father, who was a stockbroker. He … took me to his office every Saturday and taught me how to analyze companies. My opinion almost always turned out to be right, but he rarely took my advice. Who's going to listen to an eight-year-old? Little did either of us know then that listening to eight-year-olds would one day change my life."

—Geraldine Laybourne, Chairman and CEO, Oxygen Media, Inc.

ENTREPRENEURS

"Owning a business is like owning the greatest toy in the world."

—Mary Ellen Sheets, Founder and CEO, Two Men and a Truck/International

"The scary thing about being an entrepreneur is that in those early years you have no idea which piece could put you under if you don't do it right."

—Pleasant Rowland

"It helps to have a broad range of business experiences, so when you hit hard times as an entrepreneur, you'll have a tremendous reserve to fall back on."

—Julie Schoenfeld, CEO, Net Effect

"The transition from doing a task to supervising someone else doing that same task is always a hard one for us entrepreneurs. I had to learn to accomplish things through other people so that I could leverage my own efforts."

—Rebecca Matthias, Founder and President, Mothers Work, Inc.

INVESTING

"I view myself as being bullish on the United States; my enthusiasm for stocks is secondary."

—Abby Joseph Cohen, partner, Goldman Sachs

WORK HABITS

"All of my products are wired to the minds of teenage girls, so organization is something I definitely need."

—Laura Groppe, President and CEO, Girl Games, Inc.

"I eat and work simultaneously and very seldom get the chance to digest my lunch."

—Vera Wang, bridal gown designer

HIRING AND PROMOTING WOMEN

"The smart CEO has to do that. Why would you give up 50 percent of the population when talent's such a scarce resource?"

—Shelly Lazarus, CEO, Ogilvy & Mather Worldwide

Competition for The Quotable Businesswoman

There are a number of women's quote books already on the market, but none of them emphasize businesswomen or business-related quotes in any way. The major titles are ...

The Quotable Woman, Running Press, $12.95 hardcover

The book was published in 1991 and is now in its 12th printing.

Women's Words: The Columbia Book of Quotations by Women, May Briggs, editor, Columbia University Press, $22.95, 1996

The New Quotable Woman: The Definitive Treasury of Notable Words by Women from Eve to the Present, Elaine Partnow, 1993

The Uncommon Wisdom of Oprah Winfrey, edited by Bill Adler, Citadel Press, 1997

There are also a number of business quote books on the market, including two recent releases:

The Wiley Book of Business Quotations: More Than 2,000 Insights, Opinions, and Witticisms About Doing Business Today, Henry Erlich, John Wiley & Sons, $30.00, 1999

The Ultimate Book of Business Quotations, Stuart Crainer, Amacom, 1998, $24.95

And as previously mentioned, there are also quote books based on the words of several well-known individual businessmen and investment gurus:

Bill Gates Speaks, edited by Janet Lowe, John Wiley & Sons, 1998, $16.95

Jack Welch Speaks, edited by Janet Lowe, John Wiley & Sons, 1998, $16.95

Warren Buffett Speaks, edited by Janet Lowe, John Wiley & Sons, 1997, $17.95

Based on the steady sales success of books in both categories, it does seem that combining the ideas of both women's quotes and business quotes would be a winner.

The Quotable Businesswoman: Wise, Witty, and Well-Informed Observations on Business and Life from Women at the Top of American Business

Compiled by Laura Boswell
Careers and Small Business Editor, USATODAY.com
A Big City Books Idea
Represented by Sheree Bykofsky Associates, Inc.

16 W. 36th Street, 13th Floor
New York, New York 10018
212-244-4144

Sample descriptions of the women included in *The Quotable Businesswoman*:

Carleton "Carly" Fiorina is the CEO of Hewlett-Packard. Before being named to this post she ran the Lucent Technology division of ATT. *Fortune* magazine named her the most powerful woman in American business in 1998.

Sheryl Leach is the creator of the licensing juggernaut Barney the purple dinosaur. In addition to the PBS show, 27 Barney books have been bestsellers, Barney Music is the third-largest children's music label, and it is estimated that 90 percent of American children under the age of six have Barney products at home.

Rebecca Matthias is the founder and CEO of Mothers Work, Inc. Starting with her first brainstorm—to create a business suit for pregnant executives—her company now owns 620 maternity stores around the country.

Kim Polese is president and CEO of Marimba Inc., a publicly traded internet software company based in Mountain View, California.

Abby Joseph Cohen is a partner and the chief investment strategist for investment banking firm Goldman Sachs. Famous for her bullish stance on the stock market, her words can calm the market during troubled times.

Jill Barad is the chief executive of Mattel Inc., the world's largest toy maker. She began her rise as the marketing director for Barbie, and grew Barbie into a 1.7 billion-dollar brand.

Sample Author/Agent Agreement

[date]

Dear [name],

This letter confirms the Agreement between [name of agency], (the "Agency") and you (the "Author"). Our Agreement is as follows.

In consideration of services rendered and to be rendered, the Author has appointed the Agency as the Author's sole and exclusive agent and representative with respect to [title], hereafter known as "the Work."

The Author represents and warrants that the author is the author of the Work and that the Author has the right to enter into the Agreement, having obtained the necessary agreements from any other participants. The Agency agrees to counsel and advise the Author with respect to the further development and completion of the Work, and upon receipt of a manuscript or proposal acceptable to the Agent to use the Agency's best efforts to place it for publication with a publisher acceptable to the Author, and to exploit and turn to account such other publication and subsidiary rights in and to the Work as may be appropriate under the circumstances. The Agency shall have the right to use and/or employ subagents and corresponding agents for such purposes.

The Agency shall have the right to receive and/or retain as commission the following listed percentages of all gross proceeds, emoluments, and other things of value at any time received or derived by the Author from the publication of the Work, in whole or in part, in any and all languages, and from the sale, lease, license, disposition, or other exploitation throughout the world of any and all rights in and to the Work:

   a. 15 percent of such gross proceeds from the exploitation of English language publication rights in the United States and Canada, and from the exercise of print and related subsidiary rights in such territories.

   b. 20 percent of such gross proceeds from the exploitation of British and so-called "foreign" publication rights, and from the exercise of any and all subsidiary rights (both print and nonprint) in any territory outside the United States and Canada. However, if British and/or "foreign" publication rights are controlled and sold by the American publisher, the Agency's commission with respect to such proceeds shall be 15 percent thereof in lieu of 20 percent thereof.

c. Fifteen percent of such gross proceeds from the exploitation of motion picture, television, radio, dramatic, and all other nonprint subsidiary rights in the United States and Canada. The Agency and its right to receive commissions hereunder shall be co-extensive with the life of the copyright of the Work and any renewals thereof.

In the event the Agency uses a subagent to sell foreign rights, it is understood that the Agency will keep 10 percent of the Author's income relevant to the sale, and that an additional 10 percent of the Author's income will be paid to the subagent. These terms will also exist in other situations where both the Agency and the Author concur that retaining a subagent would be advantageous.

All publishers of the Work, as well as all purchasers and licensees of subsidiary rights therein, shall be directed and authorized by the Author to remit the Author's payments to the Agency, as the Author's agent. Receipt of such payments by the Agency shall be deemed receipt by the Author.

The Agency shall remit payments to the Author, after deducting the Agency's commission, not later than fourteen (14) days after monies have been received. The Agency will send copies to the Author of all royalty statements, checks, and contracts received from the Publisher concerning the Work.

There will be a clause in the Author-Publisher contract stating these terms and conditions. The Author's heirs will respect and adhere to this Agreement's intentions.

In addition to the aforementioned commissions, the Agency shall be reimbursed for the expenses incurred on behalf of the Work (not to exceed a total of $150 without written permission), including photocopying, messengers, cables, and overseas postage in connection with submissions for sales both foreign and domestic, long-distance telephone calls, copies of the published book when purchased by the Agency for subsidiary rights submissions, and other similar and related charges.

The Agency shall bill the Author periodically for such expenses, or deduct same from funds received by the Agency for the Author's account.

Prior to or upon signing this Agreement, the Author agrees to provide the Agency with a complete written list of editors and publishers, if any, who have seen the Work or a proposal for the Work in its current form or in a prior form or draft.

The Agency or the Author shall have the right to terminate this Agreement in the event that the Work has not been placed for publication with a publisher acceptable to the Author within twelve (12) months from the Author's submission to the Agency of the Author's final completed proposal or manuscript, termination to be effective upon the expiration of 30 days. Notwithstanding the right of termination provided in the preceding sentence, if within four months after the effective date of termination of this Agreement a publisher to whom the Work had been submitted by the Agency prior to the effective date of termination of this Agreement, notifies the Author or the Agency that it wants to publish the Work and a contract results, the Agency is entitled to all rights provided to it under this Agreement, including, but not limited to, its right to receive commissions, and, if requested by the Author, the Agency will negotiate the book contract on behalf of the Author. In the event this agreement is terminated in accordance with the terms of this paragraph, the Agency will have no rights, including the right to receive commissions, in and to the Work and any derivations thereof.

If any controversy, claim, or dispute arising out of, or in connection with, this Agreement, or the breach thereof between the Agency and the Author, cannot be resolved, then the Author and the Agency agree to arbitrate their differences in [agent's state] in accordance with the rules of the American Arbitration Association, and judgment confirming the Arbitrator's award may be entered in any court of competent jurisdiction. The Agency agrees not to sign any contract for the Author or to otherwise make any commitment on the Author's behalf without written or oral authorization from the Author.

Any written notice called for by this Agreement must be sent by registered U.S. mail, return receipt requested to the addresses set forth in this Agreement.

This Agreement represents the complete understanding between the Author and the Agency, supersedes any prior oral understandings, and may not be amended except in writing signed by the Author and the Agency.

If the foregoing is acceptable to you, please so indicate by signing your name below.

Sincerely,

[agent name]

ACCEPTED AND AGREED TO:

Name _____   Social Security or Federal I.D.# _____

Sample Publishing Contract

AGREEMENT MADE this _____ day of March 2000, between [name of publisher] (referred to as the "Publisher") and [name of author] (referred to as the "Author").

WHEREAS the parties wish respectively to publish and have published a book (referred to as the "Work") provisionally titled "[book title]";

NOW, THEREFORE, they mutually agree as follows:

1. Grants of Rights: The Author grants to the Publisher during the term of copyright, including renewals and extensions thereof:

   a) Exclusive right in the English language, throughout the world, to:

      i) Print, publish, and sell the Work as a soft-cover (mass-market and/or trade paperback) book; and

      ii) License publication of a reprint edition(s) by other publishers.

   b) Non-exclusive right in the English language, throughout the world, to print, publish, and sell the Work as a hard-cover book.

   c) Subsidiary Rights and Licenses:

      i) The Publisher shall have the exclusive right, throughout the world, to sell or license the rights in the Work indicated below upon such terms as the Publisher deems advisable. The proceeds received by the Publisher from the sale or license of such rights shall be divided between the Author and the Publisher as set forth in paragraph 11:

         a) book club rights;

         b) textbook rights;

         c) anthology rights;

         d) first serial rights (i.e., publication of condensations, excerpts, digests, serializations, and extracts in newspapers and periodicals before first publication in book form);

e) second serial rights (i.e., publication of condensations, excerpts, digests, serializations, and extracts in newspapers and periodicals after first publication in book form);

f) selection rights, (such as a catalogue that produces its own edition of the work);

g) abridgment/condensation rights;

h) large print rights;

i) mass-market paperback rights;

j) trade (quality) paperback rights;

k) foreign language rights;

l) British Commonwealth rights;

m) merchandising and commercial rights;

n) audio rights (i.e., the right to use or adapt the Work or any portion thereof as a basis for audio through any method of recording or transmission now known or hereafter devised, including, without limitation, copying or recording by phonographic, magnetic, laser, electronic, or any other means and whether on phonograph records, audio cassettes, audio discs, or any other human or machine-readable audio medium and the broadcast or transmission thereof, now known or which may be devised in the future);

o) online database (via time-sharing access equipment or direct downloading);

p) CD-ROM optical discs in all forms now or to be utilized;

q) all other forms, formats, platforms, and standards now in use or which may in the future be in use during the term of this agreement and its option terms; and

r) picture, dramatic, television, radio, and allied rights.

Any subsidiary rights not exploited within 18 months of publication shall become nonexclusive.

d) Exclusive right to license in all foreign languages and all countries, the rights granted in subparagraphs (a) and (b) above;

e) The right of first refusal as to any sequel, revision, or republication of the work. During the period of this agreement, and for five (5) years thereafter, except in the case of termination in accordance with paragraph 17 herein, the Author shall not submit any sequel, revision, or republication of the Work to other publishers, nor seek offers from nor negotiate with others, with respect thereto until first offering said work to the Publisher. After submission of said proposed sequel, revision, or republication, the Publisher shall have thirty (30) days to determine whether to publish the said next work; if so, the parties shall negotiate in good faith the terms of the publishing agreement. If the parties are unable to reach agreement before the thirty (30) days shall expire, then the Author shall be free to offer the said sequel, revision, or republication to others, but only on terms more favorable than those offered by the Publisher. The Author shall notify the Publisher in writing of such offer, and all particulars, within seven (7) days of the receipt of said offer, and the Publisher shall have the right for thirty (30) days to match said offer of any other publisher.

f) To use or license others to use the approved name, likeness, and biography of the Author, the work and the title of the work, in whole or in part, or any adaptation thereof as the basis for trademark or trade name for other products or for any other commercial use in connection with such other products.

2. Delivery of Satisfactory Copy: The Publisher acknowledges receipt of an acceptable manuscript OR the Author agrees to deliver two complete copies (original and clean copy) of the revised manuscript of the work in the English language, together with any necessary permissions and all photographs, illustrations, drawings, and indexes suitable for reproduction and necessary to the completion of the manuscript not later than [date].

If the Author fails to deliver the manuscript within thirty (30) days after the above date, or if any manuscript that is delivered is not, in the Publisher's judgment, satisfactory, the Publisher shall give the Author written notice describing such failure and permit the Author to cure this defect within thirty (30) days of that notice. If the Author fails to do so, the Publisher may have the option to remedy the defect. The Publisher may deduct its reasonable expenses for curing such defect from any proceeds that come due to the Author, and no proceeds will be paid to the Author until said expenses are reimbursed to the Publisher. Alternatively, the Publisher may opt to terminate this agreement by giving written notice, whereupon the Author agrees to repay forthwith all amounts which may have been advanced hereunder.

3. Permission for Copyrighted Material: If the Author incorporates in the work copyrighted material, she shall procure, at her expense, written permission to reprint it.

4. Author's Warranties and Indemnities: The Author warrants that she is the sole author of the work; that she is the sole owner of all the rights granted to the Publisher; that she has not previously assigned, pledged, or otherwise encumbered the same; that she has full power to enter into this agreement; that except for the material obtained pursuant to Paragraph 3, the work is original, has not

299

been published before in the form submitted by the Author, and is not in the public domain; that it does not violate any right of privacy; and that it does not infringe upon any statutory or common-law copyright.

In the event of any claim, action, or proceeding based upon an alleged violation of any of these warranties, (i) the Publisher shall have the right to defend the same through counsel of its own choosing, and (ii) no settlement shall be effected without the prior written consent of the Author, which consent shall not unreasonably be withheld, and (iii) the Author shall hold harmless the Publisher, any seller of the work, and any licensee of a subsidiary right in the work, against any damages finally sustained. If such claim, action, or proceeding is successfully defended or settled, the Author's indemnity hereunder shall be limited to fifty percent (50%) of the expense (including reasonable counsel fees) attributable to such defense or settlement; however, such limitation of liability shall not apply if the claim, action, or proceeding is based on copyright infringement.

If any such claim, action, or proceeding is instituted, the Publisher shall promptly notify the Author, who shall fully cooperate and shall have the right but not the obligation to participate in the defense thereof, and the Publisher may withhold payments of reasonable amounts due her under this or any other agreement between the parties.

Such payments shall be released within one year if there is no action pending. These warranties and indemnities shall survive the termination of this agreement.

5. Conflicting Publication: The Author agrees that until termination of this agreement, she will not, without the written permission of the Publisher, publish or permit to be published any book that is directly competitive with the work. The Author does have the right to publish and distribute training manuals that support her seminar.

6. Date, Style, and Price of Publication: The Publisher shall publish the work at its own expense, in such style and manner, under such imprint and at such price as it deems suitable by [date]. The Publisher shall not be responsible for delays caused by any circumstance beyond its control. In no event shall the Publisher be obligated to publish a work which, in its opinion, violates the common-law or statutory copyright or the right of privacy of any person or contains libelous or obscene matter. The Publisher shall consult with the Author on the design of the book and the cover. The Publisher shall have final approval.

7. Proofreading and Author's Corrections: The Author agrees to read, revise, correct, and return promptly all proofs of the work and to pay in cash or, at the option of the Publisher, to have charged against him the cost of alterations, in type or in plates, required by the Author, other than those due to the printer's

or the Publisher's errors, in excess of ten percent (10%) of the cost of setting type, provided a statement of these charges is sent to the Author within thirty (30) days of the receipt of the printer's bills and the corrected proofs are presented upon request for his inspection.

8. Copyright: The Publisher shall copyright the work in the name of the Author, in the United States, in compliance with the Universal Copyright Convention, and apply for renewals of such copyright. If copyright in any country should be in the name of the Publisher, it shall assign such copyright upon request of the Author.

9. Advance Payments: The Publisher shall pay to the Author as an advance against and on account of all moneys accruing to her under this agreement, the sum of X dollars ($X), payable:

$X upon signing;

$X upon acceptance; and

$X upon publication

10. Royalty Payments: The Publisher shall pay to the Author a royalty on every copy sold by the Publisher and paid for, less actual returns and a reasonable reserve [note: typical reserves can be up to 30 percent of monies owed] for returns (except as set forth below):

    i) Softcover: For the first 10,000 copies sold: seven and one-half percent (7 1/2%) of retail price; From 10,001 to 50,000 copies sold: eight percent (8%) of retail price; From 50,001 copies sold: ten percent (10%) of retail price.

    ii) Hardcover: For the first 5,000 copies sold: ten percent (10%) of retail price; From 5,001 to 10,000 copies sold: twelve and one-half percent (12 1/2%) of retail price; From 10,001 copies sold: fifteen percent (15%) of retail price.

  b) No Royalty Copies: No royalty shall be paid on copies sold below or at cost including expenses incurred, or furnished gratis to the Author, or for review, advertising, sample or like purposes.

  c) Proceeds from revenues derived from the sale of all nonexclusive and subsidiary rights under paragraph 1(b) and (c) shall be divided as follows:

    i) Book club rights [note: typically 50 percent to the Publisher, 50 percent to the Author]

    ii) Hardcover rights [note: typically 50 percent to the Publisher, 50 percent to the Author]

    iii) First serial rights [note: authors can often get 90 percent here]

    iv) All other subsidiary rights

11. Reports and Payments: The Publisher shall render semiannual statements of account to the last day of December and the last day of June, and shall mail such statements during the third month following, together with checks in payment of the amounts due thereon.

    Should the Author receive an overpayment of royalty arising from copies reported sold but subsequently returned, the Publisher may deduct such overpayment from any further sums due the Author.

    Upon written request, the Author may examine or cause to be examined through certified public accountants or other qualified representatives the books of account of the Publisher insofar as they relate to the sale or licensing of the work. If there is a discrepancy of more than eight percent (8%), the cost of the audit will be borne by the Publisher.

12. Payment to Author's Representative: All monies due to the Author under the terms of this agreement shall be paid to the Author's duly assigned representative, [agent's name and address], whose receipt thereof shall be a valid discharge of the Publisher's obligation. The Author shall irrevocably assign to the Agent a sum equal to [agent's percentage] of the income accruing to the Author's account under the terms of this agreement, and the said Agent is empowered by the Author to act on her behalf in all matters arising from and pertaining to this agreement. The term "Author" as used in this paragraph includes but is not limited to all author(s) named elsewhere in this agreement and their successors, assigns, licensees, heirs, legal representatives, administrators and executors, and anyone acting on their behalf or in their place and stead.

13. Copies to Author: On publication, the Publisher shall give X (X) free copies to the Author, and X (X) free copies to her agent, each of whom may purchase further copies for personal use at a discount of [note: typically 50 percent] from the retail price. The Author may order full case quantities at a discount of [note: can be as much as 60 percent].

14. Discontinuance of Publication: If the Publisher fails to keep the work in print and the Author makes written demand to reprint it, the Publisher shall, within sixty (60) days after the receipt of such demand, notify the Author in writing if it intends to comply. Within six (6) months thereafter, the Publisher shall reprint the work unless prevented from doing so by circumstances beyond its control. If the Publisher fails to notify the Author within the sixty (60) days described above that it intends to comply, or, within six (6) months after such notification, the Publisher declines or neglects to reprint the work, then this agreement shall terminate and all rights granted hereunder shall revert to the Author, subject to licenses previously granted, provided the Author is not indebted to the Publisher for any sum owing to it under this agreement. After such reversion, the Publisher shall continue to participate to the extent set forth in this agreement in moneys received from any license previously granted by it.

Upon such termination, the Author shall have the right for sixty (60) days thereafter to purchase the plates, if any, at one fourth of the cost (including typesetting).

If the work is under contract for publication or on sale in any book edition in the United States in quantities sufficient for distribution in the trade, it shall be considered to be in print. A work shall not be deemed in print by reason of a license granted by the Publisher for the reproduction of single copies of the work. If the Publisher should determine that there is not sufficient sale for the work to enable it to continue its publication and sale profitably, the Publisher may dispose of the copies remaining on hand as it deems best, subject to the royalty provisions of paragraph 10. In such event, the Author shall have the right, within two (2) weeks of the forwarding of a written notice from the Publisher, to a single purchase of copies at the "remainder" price.

15. Author's Property: Except for loss or damage due to its own negligence, the Publisher shall not be responsible for loss or damage to any property of the Author.

16. Suits for Infringement of Copyright: If the copyright of the work is infringed, and if the parties proceed jointly, the expenses and recoveries, if any, shall be shared equally; and if they do not proceed jointly, either party shall have the right to prosecute such action, and such party shall bear the expenses thereof, and any recoveries shall belong to such party; and if such party shall not hold the record title of the copyright, the other party hereby consents that the action be brought in his or its name.

17. Bankruptcy and Liquidation: If (a) a petition in bankruptcy is filed by the Publisher, or (b) a petition in bankruptcy is filed against the Publisher and such petition is finally sustained, or (c) a petition for arrangement is filed by the Publisher or a petition for reorganization is filed by or against the Publisher, and an order is entered directly the liquidation of the Publisher as in bankruptcy, or (d) the Publisher makes an assignment for the benefit of creditors, or (e) the Publisher liquidates its business for any cause whatever, the Author may, subject to any orders or rulings from a Court of competent jurisdiction, terminate this agreement by written notice and thereupon all rights granted by him hereunder shall revert to him. Upon such termination, the Author, at his option, may purchase the plates and the remaining copies at one fourth of the manufacturing cost, exclusive of the Publisher's overhead. If he fails to exercise such option within sixty (60) days after the happening of any one of the events referred to above, the Trustee, Receiver, or Assignee may destroy the plates and sell the copies remaining on hand, subject to the royalty provisions of Paragraph 10. Publisher shall notify author within thirty (30) days of the occurrence of any of the events described in this paragraph.

303

18. Sums Due and Owing: Any sums due and owing from the Author to the Publisher, whether or not arising out of this agreement, may be deducted from any sum due or to become due from the Publisher to the Author pursuant to this agreement.

19. Law Applicable: This agreement, including all rights and liability of the parties, shall be governed by the laws of the State of [wherever the publisher is located].

20. Copyright: It is a condition of the rights granted hereby that the Publisher agrees that all copies of the work that are distributed to the public shall bear the copyright notice prescribed by the applicable copyrights laws of the United States of America. The Author hereby appoints the Publisher as his attorney-in-fact in his name and in his stead to execute all documents for recording in the Copyright Office evidencing transfer of ownership in the exclusive rights granted to the Publisher hereunder.

21. Assignment: This agreement shall be binding upon the heirs, executors, administrators, and assigns of the Author, and upon the successors and assigns of the Publisher.

22. Complete Agreement and Modification: This agreement constitutes the complete understanding of the parties. No modification or waiver of any provision shall be valid unless in writing and signed by both parties.

23. Dispute Resolution: Any controversy or claim arising out of or relating to this agreement shall be submitted in [wherever publisher is located], to American Mediation Council, LLC, under its Mediation Rules, before the parties resort to arbitration, litigation, or some other dispute-resolution procedure.

IN WITNESS WHEREOF, the parties have duly executed this agreement:

PUBLISHER

By:_____

Dated:

AUTHOR

By:_____

Dated:

Sample Press Release

[insert date here]

FOR IMMEDIATE RELEASE

Contact: Emeline Malpas [insert telephone number here]

A Woman's Firsthand Account of World War II: Before, During, and After

Emeline Malpas was there. And for the past 50 years, she has watched in disbelief as the good work of 35,000 WACs, Red Cross, and Army nurses who volunteered for duty in Europe has been ignored and lost in the mists of time.

Run Away to War is Emeline Malpas' evocative account of life as a Red Cross volunteer. As an overseas Red Cross Hospital Recreation Worker in 1944, she cared for soldiers wounded in the Battle of the Bulge at a Paris girl's school converted to a 1,000-bed hospital. From her send-off from Eleanor Roosevelt, through dramatic descriptions of wartime events, and ending with Paris on V-E Day and her return home to the States, Emeline Malpas gives readers a front-row account of life in Europe during World War II.

Not just a dry description of treating wounded soldiers, Malpas gives a swift-moving account that presents the war in a way that contemporary readers will enjoy. Novelist Elizabeth Talent praised Malpas as "... droll, indomitable, clever, virtuous, and staunchly optimistic ... (the book is) a rare and irreplaceable creation."

Available in bookstores throughout the country (or directly from the author), *Run Away to War* is a remarkable nonfiction account that should not be missed.

Run Away to War, ISBN 1-884570-72-0, $12.95, Research Triangle Press

For review copies, or to request an interview with the author, call [insert telephone number here].

Sample Collaboration Agreement

From the American Society of Journalists and Authors

When two (or more) people plan to collaborate on a book, it is a very good idea to have a written agreement that spells out precisely how the responsibilities—and the potential rewards—are going to be divided.

Such an agreement is a very good idea even if the collaborators are long-time acquaintances; even if they have previously worked together; even if (perhaps especially if) they are fast friends. It assures that each of the parties has the same understanding of each party's obligations; in the absence of a written agreement, unwarranted assumptions can easily be made and misunderstandings can easily occur.

The agreement should be drawn up as soon as the parties decide that they will collaborate, and before any work is actually done. If a literary agent is involved in the initial discussion, the agreement should include the agent as well, and the sample agreement that follows assumes such involvement. (If the potential co-authors are, instead, planning to draw up a proposal and then seek an agent, the agreement should so specify.)

A collaboration agreement can be as long or as short, as simple or as complex, as the parties wish, so long as it leaves no doubt as to (1) who is to be responsible for the various tasks necessary to produce the manuscript, (2) how expenses are to be divided, and (3) how income is to be divided. It should also deal with any other concerns the individuals may have. These may, of course, vary considerably and may include such considerations as potential conflicts with other works or contemplated works by any party; commitments to travel if the parties are geographically distant from each other; a designated successor should one party become incapacitated or otherwise unavailable before completion of the project; et al.

Sample Agreement

THIS AGREEMENT is made on the _____ day of _____, 19___, by, between, and among: John M. Yatros, M.D. of New York, New York (hereinafter referred to as Yatros); Wanda Wordsmith of New York, New York (hereinafter referred to as Wordsmith); and the Lunch Associates Literary Agency of New York, New York (hereinafter referred to as Lunch). These parties agree as follows:

1. Subject to the terms and conditions herein, Yatros and Wordsmith agree to collaborate exclusively with each other in the preparation of a book-length manuscript dealing with the subject of _____.

2. It is understood and agreed that Wordsmith shall prepare a proposal and outline for the work, and that Yatros shall cooperate with, and assist, Wordsmith in that preparation by meeting with Wordsmith and furnishing all necessary information regarding the content of the work.[1] Yatros shall pay Wordsmith a total of _____ dollars ($_____) to prepare this material, payable half on signing of this agreement and half on approval of the proposal and outline by Yatros, which approval shall not be unreasonably withheld. Yatros agrees to approve the draft, or correct inaccuracies and suggest reasonable revisions, within ten (10) days of receipt of the draft.[2] Wordsmith agrees to correct any inaccuracies, and to make necessary revisions, promptly.

3. Upon approval of the proposal and outline by Yatros and payment by Yatros to Wordsmith of the full amount stated above, Wordsmith shall deliver to Lunch one (1) original copy of the proposal and outline.

4. Lunch shall offer the proposed work to publishers and diligently endeavor to obtain the best possible terms for publication of the work. No contract or other agreement for disposition of rights in the work shall be executed by Lunch without the approval of Yatros and Wordsmith; such approval shall not be arbitrarily or unreasonably withheld. It is understood that Yatros and Wordsmith are obligated to sign a contract to publish the work if Lunch obtains a contract calling for a minimum advance of _____ thousand dollars ($_____) and standard book royalties and licensing splits between authors and publisher, and providing neither of the authors puts forth any other substantive objection to the publisher or contract terms.[3]

5. When a contract has been signed by Yatros and Wordsmith, it is understood and agreed that the actual writing of the manuscript shall be the responsibility of Wordsmith. Yatros agrees to furnish Wordsmith with all materials and information necessary for preparation of the manuscript, sufficiently in advance to permit Wordsmith to meet the manuscript delivery date stipulated in the agreement with the publisher. Wordsmith agrees to deliver the text of the work to Yatros for Yatros's approval, and Yatros shall promptly approve said text or detail reasonable revisions, if any, in writing. Wordsmith agrees to revise the text, if necessary, according to Yatros's reasonable recommendations.[4]

6. Yatros and Wordsmith agree to revise the text according to the publisher's reasonable requests, if any.

7. The title of the work in all and any English-language publications throughout the world shall be subject to the approval of Yatros and Wordsmith.

8. The names of both Yatros and Wordsmith shall appear on the work, in all forms and languages throughout the world, separated by the word "and" or the word "with" as the authors may decide between them is appropriate.[5] The name of Yatros shall precede the name of Wordsmith, but both names shall be identical in size and type style.[6]

9. Copyright in the work, in all forms and languages throughout the world, shall be held in the names of Yatros and Wordsmith.

10. Yatros agrees to indemnify Wordsmith and hold her harmless against any claim, demand, suit, action, proceeding, or expense of any kind arising from or based upon language, information, advice, citations, anecdotal matter, resource materials, or other content of the work that was provided by Yatros.

11. Costs of typing, photocopying, and other ordinary expenses in connection with preparation of the work shall be borne equally by Yatros and Wordsmith.[7]

12. Yatros and Wordsmith hereby retain Lunch to represent them in connection with the work on an exclusive basis, and Lunch shall retain for services rendered _____ percent (__%) of all monies received for disposition of any rights in the work, except that Lunch shall retain _____ percent (__%) of monies received for disposition of any rights in foreign countries; any commission payable to sub-agents with respect to the disposition of foreign rights shall be paid by Lunch.[8]

13. Upon receipt of statements from publishers, Lunch shall promptly dispatch copies to Yatros and Wordsmith. Upon receipt of any monies from publishers or others for any rights in the work, Lunch shall promptly disburse such monies, less only agency commissions, to Yatros and Wordsmith in the proportions hereinafter specified.

14. Yatros and Wordsmith, jointly or separately, or their authorized representative(s), shall have the right to examine the records of Lunch pertaining to the work, upon request during normal business hours.

15. All proceeds and revenues received from the sale, lease, license, or other disposition of any rights in the work, throughout the world, shall be divided between Yatros and Wordsmith as follows:[9]

 (a) Of the first installment of the advance stipulated in the original publishing contract, Wordsmith shall receive eighty percent (80%), less only agency commission, and Yatros shall receive twenty percent (20%), less only agency commission, except that _____ dollars ($_____) shall be subtracted from Wordsmith's share and added to Yatros's share.[10]

(b) Of the remainder of the advance stipulated in the original publishing contract, Wordsmith shall receive eighty percent (80%), less only agency commission, and Yatros shall receive twenty percent (20%), less only agency commission.

(c) Thereafter, Yatros and Wordsmith shall each receive fifty percent (50%), less only agency commission, of all revenues, from any source, received in connection with the work.

16. The term of this agreement shall be co-extensive with the life of the copyright in the work.

17. This agreement sets forth the entire understanding of the parties hereto and may not be changed except by written consent of all the parties.

18. It is expressly understood and agreed that this agreement shall be automatically considered a part of any and all contracts and agreements made by the authors with respect to rights in the work.

19. The terms and conditions of this agreement shall be binding upon, and the benefits thereof shall inure to, the respective heirs, executors, administrators, successors, and assigns of the parties hereto.

20. All parties to this agreement warrant that they have no other contractual commitment which will or might conflict with this agreement or interfere with the performance of any obligations hereunder.

21. This agreement shall be construed in accordance with the laws of the State of New York.

22. Should any controversy, claim, or dispute arise out of or in connection with this agreement, such controversy, claim, or dispute shall be submitted to arbitration before the American Arbitration Association in accordance with its rules, and judgment confirming the arbitrator's award may be entered in any court of competent jurisdiction.

IN WITNESS WHEREOF, the parties hereto have set their hands on the date first above specified.

Rev 4/97

Notes

1. The physician does not, of course, always provide all the information; it may, for example, be agreed that the physician will furnish clinical data while the writer will be responsible for statistical research.

2. The parties should be certain that any time periods stated are in fact feasible in the context of their own commitments and schedules.

3. Author-Publisher contracts are not limited to monetary terms, and either co-author may wish to specify additional conditions, if there are any of particular concern.

4. The parties may wish to specify time limits, either for the physician's consideration of the manuscript, the writer's revision, or both. It may also be desirable, especially in the case of a work of some length, to handle it in parts or sections and to specify interim deadlines—e.g., to agree that half the work be delivered to the physician, discussed, and revised by a date midway between contract signing and the manuscript due date.

5. If the work treats of the physician's theories or opinions or refers to specific experiences not shared by the writer-author—i.e., if the first person is to be used ("I have found," "among my patients")—the connective should be "with."

6. Different terms may, of course, be specified—that the writer's name be, for example, no less than two thirds (or some other proportion) the size of the physician's. Or, if the matter is of no concern to the writer, reference to type size and style may be omitted entirely.

7. The division need not be equal; one party may agree to assume more than half of such expenses, or clerical services may under some circumstances be available without charge. If additional expenses—travel, database searches, research assistants, or other outlays—are contemplated, how they are to be divided should also be spelled out.

8. The usual commission is 10 or 15 percent, with a higher percentage payable in connection with disposition of foreign rights; the latter sum enables the agent, in turn, to pay a commission to an agent, based in the foreign country, who handles arrangements there. A higher percentage may also be applicable in connection with disposition of other rights—e.g., film—involving co-agenting.

9. The proportions used here are chosen arbitrarily. In practice, the writer's share of the advance may range from 50 percent (rare) to 100 percent (also rare). Special arrangements may also be made: The writer may, for example, agree to a lower percentage if a higher advance is obtained; or, it may be agreed that the writer will receive the full first half of the advance, with the second half to be divided between the co-authors.

10. This is the sum previously paid for creation of the proposal/outline.

Writer's Conference

Selected Writers' Conferences

The following were generously provided by and selected from The Guide to Writers Conferences & Workshops at www.shawguides.com, which provides more than 600 detailed listings, including upcoming dates, faculty, and programs.

Antioch Writers' Workshop. www.antiochwritersworkshop.com. Contact: Antioch Writers' Workshop, P.O. Box 494, Yellow Springs, OH 45387. Phone 937-767-9409, e-mail Info@AntiochWriters Workshop.com.

Ashland Writers' Conference. Contact: Ashland Writers' Conference, 295 E. Main, Suite 4, Ashland, OR 97520. Phone 541-482-2783, fax 541-482-4923, e-mail awcore@aol.com.

ASJA Annual Writers' Conference. www.asja.org. Contact: ASJA 29th Annual Writers' Conference, 1501 Broadway, Suite 302, New York, NY 10036. Phone 212-997-0947, fax 212-768-7414, e-mail staff@asja.org.

Aspen Summer Words. Contact: Aspen Writers' Foundation, P.O. Box 7726, Aspen, CO 81612. Phone 1-800-925-2526 or 970-925-3122, fax 970-920-5700, e-mail Aspenwrite@aol.com.

Booming Ground Writers' Community. www.arts.ubc.ca/bg. Contact: Booming Ground Writers' Community, Buch E-462, 1866 Main Mall, University of British Columbia, Vancouver, BC V6T 1Z1. Phone 604-822-2469, fax 604-822-3616, e-mail bg@arts.ubc.ca.

Bread Loaf Writers' Conference. www.middlebury.edu/~blwc. Contact: Bread Loaf Writers' Conference, Middlebury College, Middlebury, VT 05753. Phone 802-443-5286, fax 802-443-2087, e-mail blwc@mail.middlebury.edu.

Cape Cod Writers' Conference. www.capecod.net/writers. Contact: Cape Cod Writers' Conference, Cape Cod Writers' Center, P.O. Box 186, Barnstable, MA 02630. Phone 508-375-0516, e-mail ccwc@capecod.net.

Catskill Poetry Workshop. www.hartwick.edu/library/catskill/poetry.htm. Contact: Catskill Poetry Workshop, c/o Special Programs Office, Hartwick College, Oneonta, NY 13820. Phone 607-431-4415.

Clarion West Science Fiction and Fantasy Writers' Workshop. www.sff.net/clarionwest. Contact: Clarion West, 340 15th Ave. E, #350, Seattle, WA 98112-5156. Phone 206-322-9083.

Clarion Writers' Workshop. www.msu.edu/~lbs/clarion/select.html. Contact: Clarion Workshop, Michigan State University, E-193 Holmes Hall, E. Lansing, MI 48825-1107. Phone 517-355-9598, fax 517-353-4765, e-mail sherida3@pilot.msu.edu.

Colgate University Chenango Valley Writers' Conference. Contact: Chenango Valley Writers' Conference, Colgate University, Hamilton, NY 13346. Phone 315-228-7770, 315-228-7771, fax 315-228-7975, e-mail MLeone@mail.colgate.edu.

Erma Bombeck Conference on Popular American Humor. www.activedayton.com/entertainment/erma. Contact: Erma Bombeck Conference on Popular American Humor, 300 College Park, Dayton, OH 45469-1679. Phone 937-229-3241, e-mail erma@udayton.edu.

Flight of the Mind Summer Writing Workshop for Women. Contact: Flight of the Mind Summer Writing Workshop, 622 SE 29th Ave., Portland, OR 97214. Phone 503-233-3936, fax 503-233-0774.

Florida First Coast Writers' Festival. www.fccj.org/wf. Contact: Florida First Coast Writers' Festival, Florida Community College at Jacksonville, Jacksonville, FL 32202. Phone 904-633-8327, fax 904-633-8435, e-mail kclower@fccj.org.

Florida Suncoast Writers' Conference. Contact: Florida Center for Writers, University of South Florida Department of English, CPR 107, Tampa, FL 33620. Phone 813-974-1711, fax 813-974-2270.

Foothill Writers' Conference. Contact: Foothill College, 12345 El Monte Road, Los Altos Hills, CA 94022-4599. Phone 650-949-7316, e-mail ksw4102@mercury.fhda.edu.

Frost Place Annual Festival of Poetry. Contact: The Frost Place, Ridge Road, Franconia, NH 03580. Phone 603-823-5510, fax 603-646-2159, e-mail donald. sheehan@dartmouth.edu.

Great River Arts Institute. www.greatriverarts.org. Contact: Great River Arts Institute, P.O. Box 639, Walpole, NH 03608. Phone 603-756-3638, fax 603-756-4308, e-mail grai@sover.net.

Green River Writers Novels-In-Progress Workshop and Writers' Retreat. Contact: Green River Writers, Inc., 11906 Locust Road, Middletown, KY 40243. Phone 502-245-4902 or 502-244-0857.

Haystack Mountain School of Crafts. www.haystack-mtn.org. Contact: Haystack Mountain School of Crafts, P.O. Box 518, Deer Isle, ME 04627. Phone 207-348-2306, fax 207-348-2307, e-mail haystack@haystack-mtn.org.

Haystack Writing Program at Portland State University. www.haystack.pdx.edu. Contact: Haystack Writing Program, Portland State University, School of Extended Studies, P.O. Box 1491, Portland, OR 97207-1491. Phone 1-800-547-8887 or 503-725-4027, fax 503-725-4840.

Indiana University Writers' Conference. php.indiana.edu/~iuwc/. Contact: Indiana University Writers' Conference, 464 Ballantine Hall, Bloomington, IN 47405. Phone 812-855-1877, fax 812-855-9535, e-mail stanton@indiana.edu.

International Film Writers' Workshops.www.meworkshops.com. Contact: The Maine Photographic Workshops, P.O. Box 200, 2 Central St., Rockport, ME 04856. Phone 207-236-8581, fax 207-236-2558, e-mail info@meworkshops.com.

International Women's Writing Guild. www.iwwg.com. Contact: International Women's Writing Guild, P.O. Box 810, Gracie Station, New York, NY 10028. Phone 212-737-7536, fax 212-737-9469, e-mail iwwg@iwwg.com.

Iowa Summer Writing Festival. www.uiowa.edu/~iswfest. Contact: Iowa Summer Writing Festival, 100 Oakdale Campus W310, Iowa City, IA 52242. Phone 319-335-4160, fax 319-335-4039, e-mail amy-margolis@uiowa.edu.

Jackson Hole Writers' Conference. ses.uwyo.edu/conferences/98jackson.html. Contact: University of Wyoming, Box 3972, Laramie, WY 82071-3972. Phone 1-800-448-7801, ext. 2, or 307-766-2124; fax 307-766-3914; e-mail bbarnes@uwyo.edu.

Kenyon Review Writers' Workshops. www.kenyonreview.org/. Contact: The Kenyon Review, Kenyon College, Gambier, OH 43022. Phone 740-427-5207, fax 740-427-5417, e-mail kenyonreview@kenyon.edu.

Key West Literary Seminar. www.KeyWestLiterarySeminar.org/. Contact: Key West Literary Seminar, Inc., 4 Portside Lane, Searsport, ME 04974. Phone 888-293-9291 or 508-463-9279, fax 1-888-293-9291 or 508-463-9279, e-mail keywest@mint.net.

Key West Writers' Workshop. Contact: Key West Writers' Workshop, Florida Keys Community College, 5901 College Road, Key West, FL 33040. Phone 305-296-9081, ext. 302; fax 305-292-5155.

Life in the Spotlight Workshop. www.boydsmillspress.com/currentevents/spotlight. html. Contact: Life in the Spotlight Workshop, Highlights Foundation, 814 Court St., Honesdale, PA 18431. Phone 570-253-1192, fax 570-253-0179, e-mail andrea@highlightsfoundation.org.

Livingston Writers' Workshop. library.ycsi.net/new/writers. Contact: Livingston Writers' Workshop, 106 S. Main St., Livingston, MT 59047. Phone 406-222-7766, e-mail mcuminins@ycsi.net.

Lost State Writers' Conference. loststatewriters.xtn.net. Contact: The Lost State Writers' Conference, P.O. Box 1442, Greeneville, TN 37744. Phone 423-636-6738, e-mail tamarac@xtn.net.

Maine Photographic Workshops. www.meworkshops.com. Contact: Maine Photographic Workshops, P.O. Box 200, 2 Central St., Rockport, ME 04856. Phone 877-577-7700 or 207-236-8581, fax 207-236-2558, e-mail info@meworkshops. com.

Manhattanville Summer Writers' Week. www.manhattanville.edu. Contact: Manhattanville Summer Writers' Week, 2900 Purchase St., Purchase, NY 10577. Phone 914-694-3425, fax 914-694-3488, e-mail rdowd@mville.edu.

Maritime Writers' Workshop. Contact: Maritime Writers' Workshop, University of New Brunswick, Extension and Summer Session, Box 4400, Fredericton, NB, E3B 5A3. Phone 506-474-1144, fax 506-474-1144, e-mail K4JC@unb.ca.

Marymount Manhattan College Writers' Conference and Workshop. marymount. mmm.edu/home.htm. Contact: Marymount Manhattan College Writers' Conference, The Writing Center, 221 East 71st St., New York, NY 10021. Phone 212-734-3073 or 212-734-4419, fax 212-734-3140, e-mail lorimartin@hotmail.com.

Maui Writers' Conference and Writers' Retreat. www.mauiwriters.com. Contact: Maui Writers' Conference, P.O. Box 1118, Kihei, HI 96753. Phone 808-879-0061, fax 808-879-6233, e-mail writers@maui.net.

Mendocino Coast Writers' Conference. www.redwoods.cc.ca.us/. Contact: Mendocino Coast Writers' Conference, College of the Redwoods, 1211 Del Mar Dr., Fort Bragg, CA 95437. Phone 707-961-6248, fax 707-961-0943, e-mail mcwc@jps.net.

Mid-Atlantic Creative Nonfiction Writers' Conference. www.goucher.edu/sitemap/ sitemap_index.html. Contact: Mid-Atlantic Creative Nonfiction Writers' Conference, Goucher College, 1021 Dulaney Valley Road, Baltimore, MD 21204. Phone 410-337-6200 or 1-800-697-4646, fax 410-337-6085, e-mail center@goucher.edu.

Midland Writers' Conference. Contact: Grace A. Dow Memorial Library, 1710 W. St. Andrews, Midland, MI 48640. Phone 517-837-3442, fax 517-837-3468, e-mail kred@vlc.lib.mi.us.

Midwest Writers' Conference. www.stark.kent.edu/occs/mwwc. Contact: Midwest Writers' Conference, Kent State University, Stark Campus, 6000 Frank Ave. N.W., Canton, OH 44720-7599. Phone 330-499-9600, ext. 280; e-mail wshoemaker@stark. kent.edu.

Mississippi River Creative Writing Workshop in Poetry and Fiction. Contact: Mississippi River Creative Writers' Workshop, English Office, St. Cloud State University, St. Cloud, MN 56301-4498. Phone 612-255-3061.

Napa Valley Writers' Conference. www.napacommunityed.org/writersconf. Contact: Napa Valley Writers' Conference, Napa Valley College, 1088 College Ave., St. Helena, CA 94558. Phone 707-967-2900, ext. 1611; fax 707-967-2909, e-mail writecon@ campus.nvc.cc.ca.us.

Nashville Screenwriters' Conference. www.nashscreen.com. Contact: Nashville Screenwriters' Conference, 8380 Melrose Ave., Suite 105, Los Angeles, CA 90069. Phone 323-852-1043, e-mail w3pr@yahoo.com.

National Writers' Association Summer Conference. www.nationalwriters.com. Contact: National Writers' Association, 3140 S. Peoria, #295, Aurora, CO 80014. Phone 303-841-0246, fax 303-751-8593, e-mail Conference@nationalwriters.com.

National Writers' Workshop. www.orlandosentinel.com/write98. Contact: Orlando Sentinel/Poynter Institute for Media Studies, 633 N. Orange Ave., Orlando, FL 32801. Phone 407-420-5582, e-mail OSORayos@aol.com.

New York State Summer Writers' Institute. www.skidmore.summer. Contact: Skidmore College, Office of the Dean of Special Programs, 815 North Broadway, Saratoga Springs, NY 12866-1632. Phone 518-580-5590, fax 518-584-5548, e-mail pkennedy@skidmore.edu.

North Carolina Writers' Network Conferences. www.ncwriters.org. Contact: North Carolina Writers' Network, P.O. Box 954, Carrboro, NC 27510. Phone 919-967-9540, fax 919-929-0535, e-mail mail@ncwriters.org.

Northland College Summer Writing Workshops—Wordscapes, Carol Bly, Adventure Journals. www.northland.edu. Contact: Northland College Summer Programs, 1411 Ellis Ave., Ashland, WI 54806. Phone 715-682-1341, fax 715-682-1691, e-mail mrehwald@wheeler.northland.edu.

Pacific Northwest Writers' Conference. www.pnwa.org. Contact: Pacific Northwest Writers' Association Conference, 2608 Third Ave., Suite B, Seattle, WA 98121. Phone 206-443-3807, fax 206-728-7109, e-mail pnwa@pnwa.org.

Philadelphia Writers' Conference. pwcgold.com. Contact: Philadelphia Writers' Conference, 107 Newington Dr., Hatboro, PA 19040-4508. Phone 215-744-1417, fax 215-442-1987, e-mail pwc@pwcgold.com.

Pikes Peak Writers' Conference. www.ppwc.net. Contact: Pikes Peak Writers' Conference, 5550 N. Union Blvd., Colorado Springs, CO 80918. E-mail ppwc@poboxes.com.

Pima Writers' Workshop. www.geocities.com/SoHo/Bistro/2420/. Contact: Pima Writers' Workshop, Pima Community College, 2202 W. Anklam Road, Tucson, AZ 85709-0295. Phone 520-206-6974, e-mail mfiles@pimacc.pima.edu.

Port Townsend Writers' Conference. www.centrum.org/Writers'.html. Contact: Port Townsend Writers' Conference, Ft. Worden State Park, Box 1158, Port Townsend, WA 98368. Phone 360-385-3102, fax 360-385-2470, e-mail lizzy@centrum.org.

Rappahannock Fiction Writers' Workshop. members.aol.com/ficwriters. Contact: The Fiction Workshop, P.O. Box 633, Carlisle, PA 17013. Phone 717-243-3205, fax 717-243-3205, e-mail FicWriters@aol.com.

Recursos de Santa Fe Literary Center. Contact: Recursos de Santa Fe, 826 Camino del Monte Rey, Santa Fe, NM 87505. Phone 505-982-0807 or 1-800-732-6881, fax 505-989-8608, e-mail recursos@aol.com.

Robert McKee's Story Structure. www.mckeestory.com. Contact: Two Arts, Inc., P.O. Box 452930, Los Angeles, CA 90045. Phone 888-676-2533, fax 310-348-9095, e-mail contact@McKeeStory.com.

Romance Writers of America Annual National Conference. www.rwanational.com. Contact: Romance Writers' of America Annual National Conference, 3707 FM 1960 W., #555, Houston, TX 77068. Phone 281-440-6885, fax 281-440-7510, e-mail info@rwanational.com.

RopeWalk Writers' Retreat. www.usi.edu/extserv/ropewalk. Contact: RopeWalk Writers' Retreat, Extended Services, USI, 8600 University Blvd., Evansville, IN 47712. Phone 1-800-467-8600 or 812-464-1989, fax 812-465-7061, e-mail lcleek@usi.edu.

Sage Hill Writing Experience. www.lights.com/sagehill. Contact: Sage Hill Writing Experience, Box 1731, Saskatoon, SK, S7K 3S1. Phone 306-652-7395, e-mail sage.hill@sk.sympatico.ca.

San Diego State University Writers' Conference. www.ces.sdsu.edu. Contact: San Diego State University Writers' Conference, SDSU College of Extended Studies, 5250 Campanile Dr., San Diego, CA 92182-1920. Phone 619-594-5152 or 619-594-2517, e-mail SDSUWriters'Conf@aol.com.

Sandhills Writers' Conference. www.aug.edu/langlitcom/sand_hills_conference. Contact: Sandhills Writers' Conference, Augusta State University, Department of Languages, Literature and Communication, 2500 Walton Way, Augusta, GA 30904-2200. Phone 706-737-1500, fax 706-667-4770, e-mail lkellman@aug.edu.

Sandy Cove Christian Writers' Conference. Contact: Sandy Cove Christian Writers' Conference. Phone 1-800-234-COVE.

Santa Barbara Writers' Conference. Contact: SBWC, Box 304, Carpinteria, CA 93014. Phone 805-684-2250.

Santa Cruz Writers' Retreat. www.santacruzwriters.org. Contact: Santa Cruz Writers' Retreat, P.O. Box 3633, Santa Cruz, CA 95063. Phone 831-469-3764, fax 831-464-7678, e-mail liapell@aol.com.

School of the Arts at Rhinelander. www.dcs.wisc.edu/art/soa.htm. Contact: School of the Arts at Rhinelander University of Wisconsin, #713, Lowell Hall, 610 Langdon St., Madison, WI 53703. Phone 608-263-3494, fax 608-265-2475, e-mail kathy.berigan@ccmail.adp.wisc.edu.

Sewanee Writers' Conferences. www.sewanee.edu/Writers_Conference/home.html. Contact: Sewanee Writers' Conferences, University of the South, 310G St. Luke's Hall, 735 University Ave., Sewanee, TN 37383-1000. Phone 931-598-1141/1541, fax 931-598-1145, e-mail cpeters@sewanee.edu.

Sitka Center for Art and Ecology. www.sitkacenter.org. Contact: Sitka Center for Art and Ecology, P.O. Box 65, Otis, OR 97368. Phone 541-994-5485, fax 541-994-8024, e-mail info@sitkacenter.org.

Sitka Symposium. www.ptialaska.net/~island/index.html. Contact: The Island Institute, P.O. Box 2420, Sitka, AK 99835. Phone 907-747-3794, fax 907-747-6554, e-mail island@ptialaska.net.

Society of Children's Book Writers' and Illustrators Annual Conference. www.scbwi.org. Contact: Society of Children's Book Writers' and Illustrators, 8271 Beverly Blvd., Los Angeles, CA 90048. Phone 323-782-1010, fax 323-782-1892, e-mail scbwi@juno.com.

South Florida Writers' Conference. www.writers.SFL.com. Contact: South Florida Writers' Conference, 3109 Grand Ave., PM #175, Miami, FL 33133. Phone 305-285-0283, fax 305-285-0283, e-mail mipress@aol.com.

Southampton College of Long Island University. www.southampton.liunet.edu. Contact: Southampton College, 239 Montauk Hwy., Southampton, NY 11968. Phone 516-287-8175, flash 8349; fax 516-287-8118; e-mail summer@southampton.liunet.edu.

Southern California Writers' Conference—San Diego. www.writersconference.com. Contact: Southern California Writers' Conference—San Diego, 4555 Rhode Island St., San Diego, CA 92116. Phone 619-291-6805, e-mail caucusdb@incom.net.

Southern Women Writers' Conference. www.berry.edu/main.html. Contact: Southern Women Writers' Conference, Berry College, Department of English, Box 495010, Mount Berry, GA 30149. Phone 706-233-4081, e-mail ewright@berry.edu.

Southwest Florida Writers' Conference. www.gulfwriters.org. Contact: GCCNWA and Edison Community College, 723 Sand Dollar Dr., Sanibel, FL 33957. Phone 941-472-1393, fax 941-395-0619, e-mail gcsmithjr@sprintmail.com.

Southwest Writers' Workshop. www.southwestwriters.org. Contact: Southwest Writers' Workshop, 8200 Mountain Road N.E., Suite 106, Albuquerque, NM 87110. Phone 505-265-9485, fax 505-265-9483, e-mail Swriters@aol.com.

Space Coast Writers' Guild, Inc. Writers' Conference. members.tripod.com/~SCWG/. Contact: Space Coast Writers' Guild, Inc., P.O. Box 362143, Melbourne, FL 32936-2143. Phone 407-254-1263, e-mail scwgvlgb@aol.com.

Split Rock Arts Program—University of Minnesota. www.cce.umn.edu/splitrockarts/. Contact: Split Rock Arts Program, University of Minnesota, 335 Nolte Center, 315 Pillsbury Dr. S.E., Minneapolis, MN 55455-0139. Phone 612-624-6800, fax 612-624-5891, e-mail srap@cce.umn.edu.

Spoleto Writers' Workshops. www.spoletoarts.com. Contact: Spoleto Arts, 760 West End Ave., #3-A, New York, NY 10025. Phone 212-663-4440, e-mail CLINTONEVE@ aol.com.

Squaw Valley Community of Writers. www.oro.net/~svcw. Contact: Squaw Valley Community of Writers, 10626 Banner Lava Cap Road, Nevada City, CA 95959. Phone 530-274-8551, e-mail svcw@oro.net.

Stonecoast Writers' Conference. www.usm.maine.edu/summer. Contact: Stonecoast Writers' Conference, University of Southern Maine, 37 College Ave., Gorham, ME 04038. Phone 207-780-5422, fax 207-780-5517, e-mail jglabrie@usm.maine.edu.

Sun Valley Writers' Conference and Workshop. Contact: Sun Valley Writers' Conference, P.O. Box 957, Ketchum, ID 83340. Phone 208-726-6670, fax 208-788-0106, e-mail svwc@sunval.com.

Symposium for Professional Food Writers. Contact: Symposium for Professional Food Writers, The Greenbrier, 300 West Main St., White Sulphur Springs, WV 24986. Phone 1-800-624-6070, ext. 7857; fax 304-536-7893; e-mail lynn_swann@greenbrier.com.

Taos Poetry Circus Poetics and Performance Camp. Contact: World Poetry Bout Association, 5275 NDCBU, Taos, NM 87571. Phone 505-758-1800, e-mail wpba@laplaza.org.

Taos Summer Writers' Conference. www.unm.edu/~taosconf. Contact: Taos Summer Writers' Conference, University of New Mexico, Humanities Building, Room 255, Albuquerque, NM 87131. Phone 505-277-6347, fax 505-277-5573, e-mail taosconf@unm.edu.

Tennessee Mountain Writers' Conference. Contact: Tennessee Mountain Writers, P.O. Box 4895, Oak Ridge, TN 37831-4895. Phone 423-482-6567.

Vintage Hudson Valley Travel Writers' Conference. www.vintagehudsonvalley.com. Contact: Vintage Hudson Valley, P.O. Box 288, Irvington, NY 10533. Phone 914-591-4503, fax 914-591-4510, e-mail info@vintagehudsonvalley.com.

Wesleyan Writers' Conference. www.wesleyan.edu/writing/conferen.html. Contact: Wesleyan Writers' Conference, Wesleyan University, Middletown, CT 06459. Phone 860-685-3604, fax 860-347-3996, e-mail agreene@wesleyan.edu.

Whidbey Island Writers' Conference. www.whidbey.com/writers. Contact: Whidbey Island Writers' Conference, 5456 Pleasant View Lane, Freeland, WA 98249. Phone 360-331-6714, e-mail writers@whidbey.com.

White River Writers' Workshop. Contact: Lyon College, Campus Box 2317, Batesville, AR 72503-2317. Phone 501-793-1766, fax 501-698-4622.

Wildacres Writers' Workshop. www.wildacres.com. Contact: Wildacres Writers' Workshop, 233 South Elm St., Greensboro, NC 27401. Phone 1-800-635-2049, fax 910-273-4044, e-mail judihill@aol.com.

Wildbranch Workshop. Contact: Wildbranch Workshop, Sterling College, Craftsbury Common, VT 05827. Phone 1-800-648-3591 or 802-586-7711, fax 802-586-2596, e-mail wldbrnch@sterlingcollege.edu.

Write on the Sound Writers' Conference. Contact: Write on the Sound Writers' Conference, 700 Main St., Edmonds, WA 98020. Phone 425-771-0228, fax 425-771-0253, e-mail wots@ci.edmonds.wa.us.

Writers @ Work. www.ihi-env.com/watw.html. Contact: Writers@Work, P.O. Box 540370, North Salt Lake, UT 84054. Phone 801-292-9285, fax 801-294-5417, e-mail w_at_w@hotmail.com.

Writers' Center at Chautauqua. www.Chautauqua-inst.org. Contact: The Writers' Center at Chautauqua, Box 408, Chautauqua, NY 14722. E-mail Writer888@mindspring.com.

Writers' Retreat Workshop (WRW). www.channel1.com/wisi. Contact: Writers Retreat Workshop, Write It/Sell It, P.O. Box 139, South Lancaster, MA 01561. Phone 1-800-642-2494, e-mail WRWWISI@aol.com.

Writers' Workshop in Science Fiction. falcon.cc.ukans.edu/~sfcenter/. Contact: Center for the Study of Science Fiction, University of Kansas/English Department, Lawrence, KS 66045-2115. Phone 973-864-3380, fax 973-864-4298, e-mail jgunn@falcon.cc.ukans.edu.

Yellow Bay Writers' Workshop. www.umt.edu/ccesp/yellowbay. Contact: Yellow Bay Writers' Workshop, University of Montana, Continuing Education, Missoula, MT 59812. Phone 406-243-2094, fax 406-243-2047, e-mail hhi@selway.umt.edu.

Zoetrope Short Story Writers' Workshop. www.zoetrope-stories.com/workshop/html. Contact: Zoetrope: All-Story, 260 Fifth Ave., Suite 1200, New York, NY 10001. Phone 212-696-5720, e-mail 219-3004@mcimail.com.

Glossary

acquisitions editor   An editor responsible for bringing in new books to publish.

advance   The money that a publisher pays to an author to write a book. Usually one half is paid upon signing a contract, and the remainder is paid upon delivery of an acceptable manuscript. This is an advance against future royalties earned, and the book must sell enough to earn the advance back before more royalty money will be paid out.

assistants   The young, unsung folks who answer the phones, sort the mail, and otherwise keep publishing offices going.

auction   A sale, usually conducted by an agent, that gives several publishers the opportunity to bid on the rights to publish a book. The book goes to the highest bidder.

audience   That part of the population that will be interested in buying a specific book.

author   The writer of a book or books; the term usually implies a published writer.

author queries   A part of the editing process in which the editor and/or copy editor ask the author to further explain meaning, answer questions about accuracy or intent, or rewrite small sections.

backlist   Any book that has been in the bookstore for 90 days or more.

bestseller   A term used quite loosely in the publishing world. Strictly speaking, the term refers to a book that has appeared on a bestseller list somewhere. In reality, publishers and their publicity staffs attach the word to almost any book that they haven't lost money on.

bluelines   The cheap test proof, usually in blue ink, that the printer sends to the publisher for approval before printing the entire job.

boilerplate contract   A publisher's standard contract, before the author or agent requests modifications.

book doctor   See *proposal doctor.*

Book Expo   The annual publishing industry trade show. It used to be called the ABA, but now it is the BEA, short for Book Expo America.

book packager   Packagers (also called producers) create books for publishers, providing them with finished manuscripts to finished books—or anything in between.

book proposal   A packet of information about the writer's book idea. A proposal typically contains a solid description of the book's content, the potential market for the book, competition, and the author's credentials. It also contains a table of contents, an extensive book outline, and at least one sample chapter.

buzz   The word-of-mouth excitement created in the publishing community before a book is released.

camera-ready art   The finished artwork that is ready to be photographed, without alteration, for reproduction.

chapter book   A category of children's books that have longer stories and are written for the intermediate reader.

clip art   Artwork specifically designed to be used by anyone without obtaining permission.

commission   The percentage of the advance and subsequent royalties that an agent receives as his fee after selling your work to a publisher. This can run anywhere from 10 to 25 percent (the larger percentages are for subrights).

community coordinator   See *events coordinator*.

compositor   A person who designs and typesets manuscripts and then prepares formatted disks that are sent to the printer.

counter display   Several copies of a book in a cardboard holder for display in the bookstore. It is also called a counter pack.

deadline   The due date for the completed manuscript as specified in the publishing contract.

demographics   Population statistics, age groups, buying habits, personal income levels, and other categories that can be used to estimate a book's potential success.

dump   Publishing industry slang for a counter display. Dumps are usually the larger cardboard displays that stand on the floor.

easy readers   A category of children's books, with short, simple sentences designed for beginning readers.

editorial board   The group of people who collectively make the decision to publish. Acquisitions editors present book proposals to the editorial board for its approval. This is also sometimes called a pub board.

electronic publishing   Paperless publishing.

electronic rights   Refers to a variety of digital rights.

endcap   The shelves at the end of an aisle in the bookstore. Publishers can some-times pay booksellers for the chance to display their books on the endcap.

English cozy   A type of mystery book that is set in England and that often features a quaint English atmosphere.

e-Rocket® book   One of many handheld devices used to read books that have been downloaded electronically.

events coordinator   A bookstore employee who is responsible for arranging author signings, author appearances, and in-store events. This position may also be called a community coordinator.

exclusive submission   When only one agent or editor is considering your proposal, it is an exclusive submission.

F&Gs   Sheets of paper that have been "folded and gathered" in preparation for printing. This is another test step that the publisher can review and approve before seeing finished, bound books.

face out   Books that are placed on the shelf with the cover facing out toward the customer.

featured guest   A guest who is central to a television show's segment. If a number of experts are used on the same show, the guest is a panel member rather than the focus of the show.

fiction   Works of the imagination.

first printing   The number of books printed in the initial print run.

first serial   An excerpt that appears in a newspaper or magazine before the book's publication and actual release.

floor   The minimum bid in an auction.

formatting   The set of instructions that determines the way that the printed words appear on the page, including things such as margins, indentations, type size, and type font.

front matter   The first several pages of a book that typically contain the half-title page, the title page, copyright information, the dedication, acknowledgments, and the table of contents. Front matter pages are numbered i, ii, iii, iv, and so forth.

frontlist   Books that have just been published.

genre fiction   A term applied to Westerns, romance, sci-fi, horror, thrillers, and fantasy novels.

ghostwriter   A professional writer who writes a book under another person's name.

Ghostwriters are most often hired by high-profile celebrities or businesspeople who don't have the time or the talent to actually write the book.

head   The title introducing a chapter or subdivision of the text.

illustrated books   A category of children's books with lots of pictures and few words.

in print   Books that are currently available from the publisher. If a publisher decides to discontinue publishing a title, the book goes out of print and is no longer available.

independent booksellers   Locally owned and operated bookstores, not affiliated with a large chain such as Borders or Barnes & Noble.

instant book   A book that appears on bookstore shelves just weeks after the event that is the focus of the book.

intellectual property   According to *Random House Legal Dictionary,* this consists of "copyrights, patents, and other rights in creations of the mind; also, the creations themselves, such as a literary work, painting, or computer program."

ISBN   International Standard Book Number; each book has a unique number that identifies it.

list   A publisher's list of forthcoming titles, the books it plans to publish in the coming season or year.

live show   A television or radio show that is broadcast at the same moment it is happening.

manuscript guidelines   A publisher's rules regarding the proper way to prepare the manuscript for submission.

mass market paperback   A 4-by-7-inch softcover book often found in book racks in airports, drugstores, and supermarkets as well as in bookstores. It is sometimes called a pocket book.

mechanicals   Finished pages ready to be sent to the printer.

media market   A geographic area covered by a particular radio station, TV channel, or newspaper. Some markets, such as New York, are large media markets; others are small.

memoir   An account of the events in the author's own life.

midlist   Books that are acquired for modest advances, that are given modest print runs, and that have a relatively short shelf life.

morning drive-time shows   Radio shows that broadcast between the hours of 6 A.M. and 9 A.M., while commuters are headed to work.

multiple queries   When more than one agent or editor is approached at once about a book idea, it is a multiple, rather than exclusive, query.

nonfiction   Works that contain true information or observations.

option clause   A clause typically found in publishing contracts that requires the author to give the publisher the first chance to buy his next book. Also called a next work clause.

out of print   See *in print.*

overview   A Hollywood term now leaking into the book world. The overview is a one-sentence description of a book and its audience.

P and L   A profit and loss statement prepared by an editor in advance of acquiring a book.

page count   The number of book pages. Sometimes the minimum (or maximum) number of pages in a completed manuscript is stipulated in the book contract.

panel member   See *featured guest.*

parody   A comic imitation of a well-known literary work.

payment on publication   A term meaning that the writer is not paid until the work actually appears in print. This is the policy of many magazine publishers and some book publishers.

pdf file   An electronic file that contains camera images of book pages that cannot be manipulated.

permission   The legal right to use someone else's material in a book. The writer must get a permission form signed by the copyright holder.

placements   Stories or mentions of the author or book in the media, resulting from the efforts of publicity.

platform   The author's proven ability to promote and sell her book through public speaking, a television or radio show, or a newspaper column.

prepack   Several copies of a book offered at a special discount and together in a cardboard display.

press conference   A meeting to which members of the press are invited to hear something newsworthy.

print on demand (p-o-d)   Short-run printing from an electronic file.

print run   The number of books printed each time a book goes to press.

promotion   Free publicity methods and/or paid advertising for a book or its author to create public awareness and stimulate sales.

proposal doctor   Experienced editors and writers who are available for hire to help others whip their proposals into shape.

public domain   Creative works, such as writings and artwork, that are no longer protected by copyright law. Works in the public domain may be used by anyone without asking permission or paying royalties or fees.

publicity   Attention directed to a book or its author. Publicity is usually free and includes book reviews, feature articles, television and radio appearances or interviews, and online mentions.

query letter   The initial contact between a writer and an agent or editor. This short letter is meant to spark interest in the writer's project.

readers   The method by which university presses evaluate projects. Readers, or "referees," who are experts in that field are paid to read and pass judgment on the scholarship of a proposed work.

reading fees   A fee requested by an agent to pay for the time he spends reading a writer's project to decide whether it is worth representing.

rejection letter   A formal "no, thanks" letter from an agent or an editor, passing on a project.

remaindered   Books that have been sold by the publisher to a discounter for a fraction of their worth. These books end up on the bargain tables at bookstores.

review copies   Free copies of a book sent out to media people in the hopes that they will review the book or mention it in an article.

royalty   The percentage that the publisher pays the author for each book sold.

SASE   Shorthand for a self-addressed, stamped envelope.

seasons   Publishers put together their lists of books and their catalogs according to two or three seasons: fall, winter, and spring.

second serial   Excerpts from a book that are published after the book is published and available.

self-published   A book that the author has paid to have produced and printed.

sell-through   Books that have actually been purchased at the bookstore level and are not going to be returned unsold to the publisher.

sequel   A second book that features many of the same characters as the first book.

series   Books linked by a brand-name identity or linked in theme, purpose, or content.

sidebar   Text that is set apart in a box, margin, or shaded area, or set in smaller type to distinguish it from the rest of the text on the page.

slush pile   The to-be-read stack of unsolicited manuscripts. They're usually read by an assistant instead of an editor.

small publisher   A general term that is applied to publishing houses with revenues of less than $10 million a year. It is also sometimes called a small press.

spine out   A book that is placed on a bookstore shelf with only the spine showing.

submission   The process by which a writer or agent submits a book proposal or manuscript to a publisher. If the author is not using an agent, it is called an un-agented submission.

syndicated   Broadcast on more than one radio or television station, or published in more than one newspaper.

synopsis   A 10-page summary of a novel, written in third-person present tense. It spells out the plot of the novel in an effective and readable way.

taped show   A television or radio show that is not broadcast immediately but at a later date.

text   Words on a page are called text. This distinguishes them from artwork.

trade paperback   Any paperback book of any size other than the 4-by-7-inch mass market size books.

video clip   A tape of an author's television appearance.

word count   The number of words on a page or in a book. This is often used in a book contract to stipulate the minimum or maximum number of words that a manuscript should contain.

work for hire   An arrangement in which a writer is paid one time for her work. Under a work-for-hire agreement, the writer does not own the copyright and receives no royalties.

Index

N

O

Y-Z

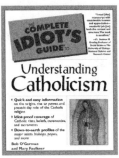

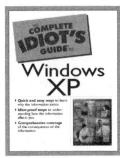